W9-AAT-116

Bully BUSTERS

A Teacher's Manual
for Helping Bullies, Victims, and Bystanders

Grades K–5

Arthur M. Horne

Christi L. Bartolomucci

Dawn Newman-Carlson

Research Press • 2612 North Mattis Avenue • Champaign, Illinois 61822 • (800) 519-2707 • www.researchpress.com

Copyright © 2003 by Arthur M. Horne, Christi L. Bartolomucci, and Dawn Newman-Carlson

All rights reserved.

Printed in the United States of America.

5   4   3   2   1   03   04   05   06   07

In this volume, the following materials may be reproduced for noncommercial use by the original purchaser only, not to extend to reproduction by other parties:

Teacher activity materials (pages 31–38)

Content Reviews and Personal Goals Forms (from modules 1–8)

Handouts accompanying classroom activities for students (from modules 1–8)

My Stressors worksheet (page 325)

Classroom Interaction and Awareness Chart and CIAC Weekly Summary (Appendix A)

Teacher Inventory of Skills and Knowledge–Elementary (Appendix B)

Bully-Victim Measure (Appendix C)

Excerpts may be printed in connection with published reviews in periodicals without express permission. No other part of this book may be reproduced by any means without the written permission of the publisher.

Composition by Jeff Helgesen
Cover design by Linda Brown, Positive I.D. Graphic Design, Inc.
Artwork by Tim Stiles, Stiles Graphic Design
Printed by Von Hoffman Graphics, Inc.

ISBN 0–87822–443–2
Library of Congress Control Number 2002111196

To Gayle
—A. M. H.

To G. J. P.
—C. L. B.

To Erik: The one I laugh with, dream with, live for, love
—D. N. C.

Contents

MODULE 8   Relaxation and Coping Skills   317

Appendix A   Classroom Interaction and Awareness Chart   345

Appendix B   Teacher Inventory of Skills and Knowledge–Elementary   349

Appendix C   Bully-Victim Measure   355

Figures and Tables

FIGURES

TABLES

Preface

The Bully Busters program began at the University of Georgia in 1994 and has been evolving since that time. The focus of our initial published work, *Bully Busters: A Teacher's Manual for Helping Bullies, Victims, and Bystanders* (Newman, Horne, & Bartolomucci, 2000) was on middle schools—the students, teachers, and other school personnel who were faced with problems of bullying in students at the stage of early adolescence. Since publication of that manual, the Bully Busters program has found its way into schools in many states and has even been adapted into educational programs in several countries outside the United States.

In our continued contact and consultation with schools, we discovered that staff at a number of elementary schools had been adapting the information and activities from the first Bully Busters program for younger students. In response to their requests, we offer the present program for the elementary school. With publication of this new manual, we expand and refine the material presented in the original and provide information and activities specifically developed for grades K–5. In creating this manual, we conducted an extensive review of model programs for reducing aggression in schools and, from that review, have updated the information and integrated the best approaches to preventing and intervening in bullying situations.

We recognize the need to apply interventions to address the bullying problem in the elementary grades because we have a strong commitment to prevention. Throughout our original program and the one described in this manual, we stress that it is better to prevent problems from developing than it is to treat them after they have emerged. If children learn more adaptive social and problem-solving skills early on, they will need less support and training in those areas later.

On the basis of our research for the first Bully Busters program, we decided that, although individual and group counseling interventions were powerful, they were insufficient to bring about major changes in the school (Turpeau, 1998). Therefore, in this program we retain our emphasis on working with members of the school community to address the bullying problem at the systemic level of the classroom and school. Our experience of more than 9 years conducting the Bully Busters program with elementary and middle schools has confirmed the power of classroom intervention to reduce the total level of bullying and victimization in schools (Howard, Horne, & Jolliff, 2002; Newman, 1999; Newman & Horne, 2003).

As for the first manual, our approach is solution-focused. Taking a solution-focused approach means not only determining the cause of problems, but also making a commitment to intervene to solve those problems. The solution-focused approach strengthens efforts to prevent and intervene in bullying situations and helps to create a more positive and effective environment for learning, thus benefiting all students.

In our work with schools, we have found the Bully Busters Support Team to be a core element of program success. It occupies the same place in the present program. We continue to encourage collaboration among teachers within the support team, and we include instructions for forming these teams. Teacher activities and "think blocks" promote the development of problem-solving skills and cohesion among team members.

New in the Bully Busters program for the elementary school are the topics of emotional intelligence (Bodine & Crawford, 1999; Goleman, 1995) and aspects of the developmental assets program developed by the Search Institute (Benson, 1999). We include these ideas because they help teachers develop and nourish their students' personal strengths and, consequently, have a positive effect on their interactions with others. Abilities in these areas not only help prevent students from becoming bullies and victims, they are essential to students' success throughout their school years and into adulthood.

Finally, although our original program for the middle school and this elementary school program are similarly structured, the elementary school program truly encompasses a strength-based approach to bully prevention. This means that it includes age-appropriate activities to support your students' development of healthy social skills, abilities to understand and use their emotions wisely, personal ownership and social responsibility within the school environment, and new and positive ways of interacting with one another.

Acknowledgments

A project like the Bully Busters program represents the contributions—both direct and indirect—of many people, and it is difficult to adequately credit all who have provided input, leadership, and constructive contributions to the project. The project has evolved through the efforts of teachers, counselors, and administrators locally as well as nationally and internationally. The contributions of other bullying and aggression reduction programs, and the developers of those programs, have exerted tremendous influence on us in our endeavors to make the Bully Busters program represent not only our best thinking, but also that of other scholars, researchers, and program developers. We have attempted to cite and give credit for all the work others have done, but, obviously, with so much influence from so many directions, sometimes we may fail to give full credit. If so, we do want to acknowledge here all those who have been so committed to helping make the lives of our children and adolescents more productive, peaceful, powerful, and fulfilling.

A number of excellent programs are available to address the problems of bullies and victims. We have been involved with many of these program developers by serving as reviewers for manuscripts, sharing the podium at conventions and conferences, working together at workshops and training opportunities, and sharing our work with one another. Of special note in this regard has been the work of Dorothy Espelage, Susan Swearer, Susan Limber, Gary Melton, Dorothy Ross, Richard Hazler, Mark Kiselica, Tom Dishion, Tony Pelligrini, and Dan Olweus. Thanks to each of you.

Closer to home, three counselors and graduate students who have made significant contributions to the present manual by helping to develop and evaluate activities, ideas, and revisions include Jenny L. Van Overbeke, Laurie Fleckenstein, and Natasha Howard. They have been co-collaborators and trainers at conference presentations and inservice programs for schools as well as "think-tank" friends who helped generate many of the included ideas. In addition, elementary counselors and school psychologists have reviewed the manuscript and activities and have added excellent suggestions, recommendations for revisions, and contributions of activities and examples. These reviewers include Debbie Staniszewski, George McMahon, Gayle Horne, and John Petrocelli.

The Bully Busters program has not evolved in a vacuum. Simultaneously with the development of the program, two other programs have evolved and have exerted enormous influence on the outcome of the Bully Busters project. The first of these is ACT Early, a program funded by the Department of Education, Institute of At-Risk Youth, since 1996 (**www.coe.uga.edu/dev/actearly**). Colleagues on this project who have contributed to the thinking and conceptualization of interventions to address bullying include Jean Baker, Randy Kamphaus, and Anne Winsor; they have been a great team and dear friends for the past years.

The second project is the GREAT Schools and Families Project, a multisite violence prevention program. This program, funded by the Centers for Disease Control and Prevention Program of Injury Prevention and Control, is being conducted at the University of Georgia, Duke University, Virginia Commonwealth University, and the University of Illinois at Chicago. The University of Georgia's GREAT team members include Pamela Orpinas, Tracy Elder, Kristin McMahon, William Quinn, Lori Durham Reaves, Hilary Merlin, Roy Martin, Kate Lindsey, Jamie Marable, and Carl Huberty. The specific focus of the GREAT Schools and Families Project is violence reduction in middle schools; however, reduction of bullying is part of the program, and team members continue to generate creative and important interventions and prevention programs. They are valued collaborators and colleagues as well as good friends. We express our appreciation to both the University of Georgia staff and the staff at the collaborating universities and the Centers for Disease Control and Prevention.

Recently, two elementary schools in Athens–Clarke County, Georgia, have been participating in the Bully Busters program and have provided excellent opportunities for evaluating what works and what doesn't with this age group. Much gratitude is due the Whit Davis Elementary School teachers for their exceptional work on reducing bullying in schools. Our thanks go the school counselor, Debbie Staniszewski; the principal, Terresa Hobson; and teachers Vicki Keenan and Cathleen Tereshinski, as well as to the entire faculty, who have been so supportive of our efforts. Appreciation is due also to the Fourth Street Elementary School counselor, Jan Bell; principal, Bonnie Jackson; and teacher Verne Varnum—as well as to the entire faculty involved in evaluating the Bully Busters program.

The College of Education at the University of Georgia has also supported the Bully Busters Project; we thank former dean Russell Yeany, and our current dean, Louis Castenell, for their encouragement and provision of resources over the years. My former department head, Richard Hayes, and the current department head, John Dagley, have provided wonderful support to the students and the program, as have the faculty of the Department of Counseling and Human Development Services, toward whom appreciation is expressed. Jacquee Rosumny and Art Sturgill both contributed to the preparation of the materials. In addition, David Jolliff, a friend and collaborator in Fort Wayne, Indiana, has conducted training workshops and inservice institutes, in both the United States and Germany, for the Bully Busters program.

Ann Wendel, Russell Pence, Dennis Wiziecki, Gail Salyards, and Karen Steiner, of Research Press, have always been supportive and good friends. Their ongoing enthusiasm for the various projects and activities we have done related to violence reduction, spanning a period of more than 20 years, has provided encouragement and a lot of fun, so thanks to them for all they have done to help children and youth live better lives.

Introduction

School for many is no longer the safe learning environment it was intended to be (Batsche & Knoff, 1994). The harsh reality of bullying is experienced by thousands of children every day (Espelage & Holt, 2001; Hoover, Oliver, & Hazler, 1992; Swearer & Song, 2001), and students are becoming increasingly anxious about witnessing bullying, fearing that they will become the next victims if they have not already been targeted (Olweus, 1978; Ross, 1996). Bullying in schools has reached an alarming rate, causing fear and concern on the part of parents, their children, and the educators responsible for the safety of these children (Geffner & Loring, 2001; Hazler, 1994; Horne & Orpinas, 2003; Horne & Socherman, 1996; National Center for Injury Prevention and Control, 2001).

Children are in school for a large part of their waking lives. They are in constant contact with teachers, and this places teachers in a prime position to address bullying in schools. Unfortunately, many teachers tell us that prevention and intervention skills to address bullying were not a part of their teacher training and that they feel helpless and ill-equipped to address this problem. Some teachers fear that intervening in bullying situations will only add fuel to the fire, causing bullies to escalate their actions against their victims. Others believe that the bully-victim experience is a "rite of passage" or a normal developmental process that all children must experience to develop skills to manage on their own. Because teachers sometimes overlook bullying, students may conclude that their teachers are unaware of these problems or that they choose not to intervene. *If there is one thing that is clearly supported by our research and the research by others on bullying in schools, it is that intervention by teachers is required to reduce bullying and prevent its negative impact on today's youth* (Briggs, 1996; Hazler, 1994; Newman & Horne, in press; Swearer & Doll, 2001; Swearer & Song, 2001; Teglas & Rothman, 2001).

The Bully Busters program for the elementary school gives teachers and other school staff the opportunity to acquire knowledge about bullying and victimization and provides them with the skills and instructional materials they need to prevent and intervene in bullying situations. The program emphasizes teachers' efforts toward both the control and the prevention of bullying behavior. The aim of *control* is to reduce occurrences of bullying, if not to prevent them entirely; the aim of *prevention* is to create conditions in which bullying is less likely to occur in the future.

THE ESSENTIAL ROLE OF TEACHERS

Teachers are in a powerful position to make change. To be most successful, they need to take a proactive, preventive approach. Specifically, they must increase their awareness of and knowledge about bullying; promote an environment in which minimal opportunities for bullying occur; and offer students support, training, and education aimed at attacking the root causes of bullying behavior (Pollack & Sundermann, 2001; Small & Tetrick, 2001).

Addressing bullying in your school and with your students can go a long way toward letting students know that their concerns truly matter and that you value the goal of making the school a safe and productive learning environment for everyone. As an educator at the elementary level, you serve as a primary guide and role model for your students. You are in an excellent position to help students acquire new skills, develop more effective personal resources, and learn positive alternatives to problem behaviors.

Toward these ends, this manual serves as an educational tool and classroom curriculum resource, providing information for teachers and describing classroom activities to increase students' awareness and encourage them to become a part of the change process.

PROGRAM CONTENT

The program is organized as two components. Chapters 1 and 2 focus on concepts helpful in establishing a foundation for the program. The rest of the information is presented as learning modules for teachers and students, with each module devoted to a different aspect of the bully-victim experience.

Program Foundations

Chapter 1, "Setting Up for Success," provides an overview of factors involved in establishing a positive atmosphere and a preventive approach to managing aggression and behavior problems in the classroom. This chapter includes a number of teacher activities designed to be conducted with your Bully Busters Support Team, which is described further on in this introduction. If time is short, many of these activities can be completed alone.

Chapter 2, "Emotional Intelligence and Developmental Assets," describes the relationship between these two recently developed models and the prevention and reduction of bullying and other aggressive behaviors. As conceptualized by Daniel Goleman (1995), emotional intelligence expands the idea of intelligence beyond "book smarts" to include a broader range of capabilities. The 40 developmental assets identified by the Search Institute (Benson, 1997) are a framework of variables identified as "protective factors" for children and adolescents. These assets guard against high-risk behaviors, foster positive development, and increase hardiness or resiliency.

We strongly urge you to review these two chapters before going on to the modules to explore specific aspects of the Bully Busters program. If you decide to skip over them, we encourage you to return to them after your review of the learning modules and before you conduct classroom activities. An understanding of the ideas presented in these chapters will truly inform your work in implementing the Bully Busters program.

Learning Modules

The program offers the following learning modules for students:

Module 1 Increasing Awareness of Bullying

Module 2 Preventing Bullying in Your Classroom

Module 3 Building Personal Power

Module 4 Recognizing the Bully

Module 5 Recognizing the Victim

Module 6 Recommendations and Interventions for Bullying Behavior

Module 7 Recommendations and Interventions for Helping Victims

Module 8 Relaxation and Coping Skills

Teacher Information Component

Each learning module begins with a discussion focused on a particular topic related to the management of bullying. These discussions are designed to offer a solid foundation of knowledge and to suggest issues that are important in relation to your students. As you acquire additional prevention and intervention skills, you and your students will benefit from an improved (i.e., safer and more productive) learning environment. As teachers who have implemented the Bully Busters program in their classrooms have found, as you display these skills, students become more confident in seeking help for problems related to bullying.

The modules include Bully Busters Support Team Think Blocks, including questions and suggestions intended to provoke thought and action on the part of team members. The Think Blocks help teachers master the content of each module and keep them actively involved in working together as a team.

Classroom Activities

Each module includes a number of hands-on classroom activities. These activities relate to the theme of each module and are grouped according to their appropriateness for children in grades K–2, grades K–5, and grades 3–5. These activities are designed to increase student awareness of bullying and to encourage students to participate in preventing and reducing it. The assigned grade levels are recommendations, not prescriptions: We invite you to adapt the activities to suit the level and needs of your class and to integrate the activities into your daily lesson plans.

An important part of conducting the activities is reviewing them afterward with your students. Following each activity, spend time discussing students' experience related to their participation. Typical discussion questions included at the end of each activity concern what the students may have learned from participating in the activity, how they could use what they have learned in their daily lives, and what they have discovered about themselves. It is tempting to focus on the content of the activities, but the process is also important, as are students' feelings about the content. The activities will evoke a range of responses. Most responses will be positive, but less positive outcomes are also possible. Sensitivity is required to deal with guilt, remorse, fear, or other difficult emotions.

PROGRAM IMPLEMENTATION

The Bully Busters program lends itself to implementation in three main ways. First, an individual teacher may use the materials in his or her own classroom. Although a single committed individual can accomplish much, the next two options are more likely to succeed. The second option involves forming a Bully Busters Support Team, a group of school faculty who elect to run the program. Such a group includes teachers, school counseling or social work staff, other support staff, and administrators. A broad base of support reaches more students and is more likely to result in change, both in active participants and in students and staff who, even though not directly involved, experience the effects of the program indirectly. The third option is even more broadly based: In this alternative, the program becomes part of the school curriculum and receives schoolwide support.

Option 1: The Individual Approach

If you are a teacher using the program independently, in your own classroom, we recommend that you review chapters 1 and 2 and all of the modules, then select and engage students in the activities best suited for your classroom. Even if you are unable to create a formal support team, we encourage you to seek the aid of supportive colleagues.

Option 2: The Team Approach

Change is difficult, and support groups help to make change happen. Just as it is helpful to have a support group for losing weight, stopping smoking, or establishing a healthy workout regimen, it is helpful to have a supportive group of colleagues and peers to help address bullying. In this second option, a group of school personnel elect to work together to implement the program.

The Bully Busters Support Team includes from four to eight teachers and other school staff who meet on a regular basis to master program content and offer mutual sharing and support. Members remind one another to continue addressing the problem of bullying, discuss problems in the classroom or with specific students, review what works and what doesn't, and problem solve ways to make the program more effective. Not incidentally, in this context of mutual support and understanding, there is an opportunity for creativity and fun.

It is best to create the Bully Busters Support Team at the start of the school year. This will allow ample opportunity for you to implement the program with the support of your fellow team members. However, we believe that a late start is better than no start at all. The steps required for a group to form a Bully Busters Support Team and to master program content are as follows.

Step 1: Select Team Members

Your support team should consist of teachers and other school staff who meet on a regular basis. Chances are that you already have some kind of support group in place. Think of those teachers you turn to when you are unsure of how to handle a situation or those who seek you out to request your assistance. Take some time to solicit participation from at least four, but no more than eight, of your fellow teachers. (We have found that a group of four to eight teachers is the most successful.) It is important to keep the group small to allow everyone time to participate. Because a mixed group allows teachers to share experiences along a developmental continuum, one option for selection is to encourage teachers from different grades to participate. We have also found that grade-level teacher support groups work exceptionally well.

Step 2: Set Times for the Support Team to Meet

Initially, the team should meet once a week for 3 consecutive weeks, for 2 hours each time. This time can be devoted to reviewing and discussing the content of the first two chapters and the modules, establishing a format to carry out the program, and recommending how to integrate the activities into the classroom curriculum. After the first three meetings, the team should meet at least twice per month, for an hour each time. These follow-up meetings provide the opportunity for support and encouragement, problem solving, skill practice, and review of the conceptual background presented in chapters 1 and 2.

We encourage you to engage your fellow team members outside of your formal meetings to discuss activities and to develop solutions. If you need support or wish to share an experience with another team member, do not wait for your next meeting. It is best to address any problems that arise sooner rather than later.

Step 3: Establish a Meeting Format

Establish a group format for the team meetings. It is important for the team to meet in a quiet, comfortable environment. (If you wish, take turns bringing refreshments.) During the first three meetings, the group will likely discuss ways to become more familiar and comfortable with the Bully Busters program. Team members are encouraged to suggest ways to introduce the activities into their classrooms and to share their stories of success or failure.

During the first meeting, we recommend that the team focus on the conceptual background for the program detailed in chapters 1 and 2, as well as the content of Modules 1, 2, and 3. This will allow discussions related to program foundations, as well as to awareness of bullying, adopting a prevention-oriented approach, and building personal power.

During the second meeting, the focus is on Modules 4, 5, and 6, recognizing and identifying different kinds of bullies and victims, and understanding interventions to prevent and reduce bullying behaviors. The third meeting centers on Module 7, interventions for victims, and Module 8, coping strategies and skills to reduce stress for both teachers and students. If your team is unable to cover the modules in the allotted time, you may decide to extend meeting times, or you may need to host additional meetings to ensure adequate coverage.

Subsequent meetings are likely to differ in format from these first few meetings. We have found the following procedures helpful:

1. At the start of a session, each member should be encouraged to share briefly how the program is working and say whether he or she needs some of the group's time to discuss bullying dilemmas, generate solutions, share a story of success or failure, or introduce an idea for a new classroom activity. One activity useful to repeat at the start of each meeting is "Glads and Sads" (see page 29). Each teacher takes just a minute to write down two or three events that she or he has been glad about since the last team meeting (e.g., an activity that went well, a student whose behavior improved). Each teacher then writes down two or three events he or she is sad about because they did not go as desired or expected (e.g., a fight in the classroom, lack of success with an activity in a particular class). Then the group discusses the glads and sads, gives congratulations and feedback for the glads, and begins using the sads as a starting point for solution-focused problem solving.

2. Once everyone has checked in, the floor is opened for discussion. Everyone who has expressed a need for a portion of the group's time is encouraged to share, starting with the first volunteer. When a member is sharing, the other members give feedback, provide suggestions, and describe their own experiences. (This give and take is likely to come very naturally to team members.)

3. When about 10 minutes are left in the meeting, the group takes the remaining time to summarize the issues discussed. It may be helpful to keep a list of the key concepts (e.g., What were the most helpful points addressed today? In what areas are people making progress? What are some areas of concern? Which activities have worked and not worked?).

Step 4: Provide Ongoing Support

It is important that your Bully Busters Support Team meet consistently throughout the entire school year and beyond. We also encourage you to determine team membership for the following year.

Option 3: The Schoolwide Approach

In this option, the entire school elects to implement the program by integrating Bully Busters into the school curriculum. Implementing the Bully Busters program in a schoolwide format involves many of the same steps as Option 2. When working with the entire school, we recommend using a workshop format that provides continuing education credit for participants. The workshop is an efficient way to disseminate information, encourage participant interaction, and develop Bully Busters Support Teams.

In conducting these workshops, we have found the following procedures useful:

1. Make certain that everyone has a copy of this manual and has reviewed it prior to the first workshop.

2. Convene workshop/training sessions once a week, over the course of 4 weeks, for 2 hours per meeting.

3. During the first workshop, cover the basics of chapters 1 and 2, as well as the material in Modules 1, 2, and 3. During the second workshop, devote attention to Modules 4 and 5. During the third, teach Modules 6 and 7. Devote the last workshop to discussing Module 8, reviewing the entire Bully Busters curriculum, answering questions, and determining membership of Bully Busters Support Teams.

   Each workshop should follow the same instructional format, combining both didactic and experiential approaches. The didactic part includes presenting and discussing the content of the modules. The experiential component involves discussing how participants may use the material; practicing skills, techniques, and activities; and providing feedback so participants may improve their skills.

4. Finalize membership of Bully Busters Support Teams. Divide teachers into separate teams, each including between four and eight team members. Again, groups that are heterogeneous bring more diversity, allowing broader problem solving and creativity. Members selected across grades can help one another identify and practice interventions for differing forms of bullying occurring at different grade levels. The most important factor is group members' willingness to collaborate to solve problems. Initially, teams should meet once a week for 3 consecutive weeks, for 2 hours each time. After the first three meetings, teams should meet at least twice a month, for an hour each time.

After completing the workshop, teachers often question the necessity of forming and maintaining a support team. Our own experience and the research of Shapiro and colleagues (Shapiro, DuPaul, Bradley, & Bailey, 1996) suggest that the workshops are necessary to increase teachers' knowledge and intervention skills and to reduce students' bullying behaviors. However, workshops are insufficient in and of themselves. In fact, teachers who participate in follow-up groups supporting the use of the workshop skills use the skills more often and more effectively in their classrooms. The degree to which teachers' efforts are effective stems largely from their motivation to continue meeting and working as a team.

EVALUATING YOUR PROGRESS

Evaluation of progress is an essential component of the Bully Busters program. At the end of the teacher training component of each module, we recommend that you ask yourself several questions as a means of informally evaluating your readiness to proceed with the classroom activities:

1. Have I reviewed all of the material in this module, and do I understand the concepts well enough to begin implementing them in my classroom?

2. Have I met with my Bully Busters Support Team to discuss the main points of the module and practiced my presentation so I am comfortable introducing this subject to my class?

3. Have I selected and reviewed activities appropriate for my classroom, understood the main concepts and discussion questions, and obtained the materials needed?

After completing a classroom activity, be sure to evaluate how effective the activity was in reaching your students: Did the students understand the material? Were they supporting the plan to prevent and reduce bullying? It is important for you to begin gauging your students' responsiveness to the program material from the very beginning of the program.

If you are not achieving the goals you set forth to accomplish with your students, take time to problem solve and identify ways to improve the process. Consult with your team. In evaluating your students' responses, it is important to remember that many of these concepts are new. Your students' lack of understanding or response may be the result of their unfamiliarity with the topics. At the same time, some changes in students' attitudes and motivation to discuss the topic of bullying should be evident.

Information regarding change can improve your administration of the program, help students identify improvements in themselves and their interactions with peers, document changes in the school environment, and provide school personnel and parents with information about program effectiveness. In this regard, the following evaluation tools have proven to be helpful: the Personal Goals Form, the Classroom Interaction and Awareness Chart (CIAC), the Teacher Inventory of Skills and Knowledge–Elementary (TISK–E), and the Bully-Victim Measure.

Personal Goals Form

A Personal Goals Form is included at the end of every learning module. The form serves as a place for you to record your plans for integrating the information and activities from each module into your classroom. It lists the module goals and gives you the opportunity to identify which activities you will conduct with your students, how you will give them feedback, and how you will cover the topics you and your team members plan. We recommend that you photocopy the Personal Goals Form for each module, then, as you read the teacher information component of each module, keep the form close by so you can record your thoughts. It is also good to photocopy your completed form to share with other members of your team.

Classroom Interaction and Awareness Chart

The Classroom Interaction and Awareness Chart (CIAC) allows you to keep a running log of the bullying incidents you observe on a daily basis. Some teachers choose to record only the incidents they witness directly; others also record events students report. The information you gather can give you an idea of the frequency of bullying incidents and a general sense of the direction of change, as well as insight into which students are involved and what situations may be supporting bullying behaviors.

Complete the form for at least a week before you begin the Bully Busters program, then weekly after the program is begun. The chart is helpful in several ways:

- It pinpoints where bullying is happening in your classroom and in the school.

- It identifies who commits bullying acts and who is the recipient of the aggression.

- It provides you with information about how frequently you address problems related to aggression.

- It provides information for other evaluation purposes—specifically, it is useful in informing students, support team members, administrators, parents, and others about the success of the program.

- If the program is not working effectively, it provides a signal that problem solving is necessary.

Teachers we have worked with have found that the CIAC is very useful and takes little time to complete. A blank copy of the CIAC, along with a page for recording a weekly summary, is given in Appendix A. Please feel free to adapt this form for your own situation and needs.

Teacher Inventory of Skills and Knowledge–Elementary

The Teacher Inventory of Skills and Knowledge–Elementary (TISK–E) assesses your knowledge and use of skills in the areas covered by this manual. To evaluate your mastery of program content, we ask that you complete the TISK–E before beginning Module 1, then return to it after you have completed all of the modules. The inventory and a scoring menu and summary are given in Appendix B.

If you wish, you may complete the TISK–E periodically, as you study and discuss program content. Periodic evaluation will allow you to see whether "slippage," or a gradual drift away from using the skills, has occurred.

Bully-Victim Measure

Given in Appendix C, the Bully-Victim Measure will allow you to estimate the amount of bullying going on in your classroom. Students should complete this measure three times during the year. Have students complete the measure before beginning the Bully Busters program to establish the baseline rate of bullying. After you have initiated the program, have students complete the measure again to gauge program impact. Often bullying actually appears to increase at this point because students have become aware of what constitutes bullying and begin to report it more often. Finally, have students fill out the measure at the end of the school year.

Before Beginning . . .

Before reading further in this manual or participating in Bully Busters training, we encourage you to photocopy and complete the following items:

1. The Classroom Interaction and Awareness Chart (CIAC; Appendix A). The CIAC has been developed to help you evaluate the extent and nature of bullying in your classroom. Please record information for at least a week.

2. The Teacher Inventory of Skills and Knowledge–Elementary (TISK–E; Appendix B). The TISK–E gives an overview of the information presented in this manual and will help you identify specific areas to focus on in the learning process. Once you have completed the TISK–E, score it by using the Scoring Menu and Scoring Summary.

3. The Bully-Victim Measure (Appendix C). Students' responses on this measure give you an estimate of how often the children in your classroom are bullied or themselves engage in bullying behavior.

These items are also helpful as the program progresses. We wish you the best in your efforts to make your school more peaceful and positive and to help your students achieve their potential. Good luck!

CHAPTER

1 Setting Up for Success

In our work with schools, we have found that teachers sometimes encounter situations in which they appear to be "stacking the deck" against themselves. They seem to be putting forth enormous amounts of energy on things that do not appear to be working. Sometimes they take on—or are given—tasks too big and must address problems that cannot be remedied in the school setting. We have also found that some teachers attempt to do their work the way they always have, even when that way does not work any more. Other times they may be required to tackle problems for which they have minimal training or experience. All of these cases are prescriptions for failure, with frustration as the result.

This chapter describes the steps you can take and the skills you will need to "set yourself up for success"—in other words, to work in a way that will increase the likelihood that you will see positive effects in your efforts to prevent and reduce bullying. The concept of setting up for success implies that we can and should actively plan ahead to be successful and consciously follow a plan to accomplish the goal of creating a bully-free school.

Throughout this chapter, we suggest a number of activities to help you apply the information to yourself, and some forms you can photocopy are included at the end of the chapter. Although you can do these activities alone, we strongly suggest that you involve the other members of your Bully Busters Support Team. Sharing your experiences with these activities is one way to gain other viewpoints and begin the process of collaboration.

COMPONENTS OF SUCCESS

We can improve our ability to reach our goals by examining our beliefs and practices in the areas of learning and change, then by making necessary changes.

Understanding the ABCs of Behavior

As emphasized throughout this program, it is always better to prevent a problem than it is to treat a problem after it has arisen. In order to prevent bullying, we need to understand bullying—why and how it occurs—as well as possess the skills to create a bully-free school environment. By analyzing the bullying problems that occur, we can often predict what types of situations will lead to aggression and violence. In behavioral terms, setting up for success involves knowing the ABCs:

A = The antecedent (the situation that leads to bullying)

B = The behavior (the bullying action)

C = Consequence (the result of the bullying action)

For example, suppose students are told to line up to go to lunch and are left on their own to form the line (antecedent). A bully may take this opportunity to become aggressive toward others, pushing and shoving his or her way to the front (behavior). As a result, some children may get hurt or begin to push back, thus escalating the aggressive potential in the situation (consequence). If, instead, the teacher has the class line up by seating or some other preestablished grouping (antecedent), students are much more likely to line up in an orderly fashion (behavior) and find their way to the cafeteria without incident (consequence).

Knowing what antecedents or situations lead to bullying behavior in the classroom and school, then altering those situations, can keep bullying from occurring in the first place. When teachers can pinpoint the antecedents of a bullying problem, they have the ability to change both the subsequent behaviors and the consequences.

TEACHER ACTIVITY: RECOGNIZING THE ABCs

Work through the ABCs of some recurring bullying situations, using the form for identifying classroom problem areas given on page 31; see the sample in Figure 1.

1. If you observe carefully, can you begin to identify what the circumstances are before bullying situations occur? Are there predictable patterns? Can you take steps to change these situations—the antecedents—before aggression is realized?

2. Are there particular areas of your classroom where more problems develop than others? Is this a function of the physical layout of the classroom or the students who occupy that part of the room? Are there other reasons to explain why some areas are problematic?

3. Do certain antecedents lead up to certain problems? Can you identify what precipitates problems in the trouble zones so that you may take steps to prevent these problems?

4. If you passed out the Recognizing the ABCs form to students, would they identify the same problem areas you do? What recommendations would students have for addressing the problems?

Knowing What You Can Influence or Change

We often collaborate with school faculty on the development of programs to address specific bullying problems. As a first step, faculty identify these problems. Once the problems are identified, we list causes of or influences on the problems. For example, if bullying is a

FIGURE 1 Recognizing the ABCs

Antecedent	Behavior	Consequence	Corrective steps
In the first few minutes of class, there is always time when students have no assigned tasks.	Several children move toward the back of the room and begin engaging in teasing and horseplay.	The behavior is distracting and at times escalates to pushing or scuffling.	Develop overhead materials instructing students what to do as they enter the class, practice having students go directly to desks and begin assignments.
Roberto finishes desk work more quickly than other students.	Roberto begins talking to those around him.	Roberto's talking distracts others from their work and causes some to not finish their assignments.	Have Roberto bring a book to read or develop alternative activities for him to do until others finish.

problem, we might identify the following factors as causal or influential: poor anger control on the part of students, parents' spending too little time with children, and violence on television and in movies. We then ask teachers to rank these factors, from highest to lowest, to clarify which are most important and which are least important.

Let's examine how we may come to better understand our sphere of influence. Figure 2 lists some examples of circumstances or situations that may influence bullying.

After teachers identify influential circumstances or situations, we ask them to determine whether they do or do not have control over them. As the figure shows, a plus sign indicates a situation over which you have influence, and a minus indicates those topics over which you have no influence. For example, if a student arrives at school tired and irritable, you likely have no influence to change chaotic circumstances in that student's home. Therefore, "lack of structure at home" would receive a minus sign. If you have a student who whispers to others in class instead of focusing on work, you do have influence. This one— "whispering in class"—would receive a plus.

A third question we raise is "How important is the cause of the problem?" For example, if you wrote "Seats too close together" as a possible cause of bullying behavior, you would indicate how important you felt that factor was, on a scale of 1 to 5 (1 = low; 5 = high), in the third column of Figure 2.

After teachers identify situations or circumstances they believe influence bullying and decide how much influence they have over those causes, we recommend that they use a matrix like the one shown in Figure 3. As shown, the matrix has an x axis (How important is the issue?) and a y axis (How much influence do you have?).

FIGURE 2 Sphere of Influence Chart		
Circumstance or situation that may influence bullying	*Teacher influence (+/–)*	*Importance (1 = low; 5 = high)*
1. Lack of structure at home	–	5
2. Whispering in class	+	1
3. Seats too close together	+	4

After identifying those circumstances/behaviors over which teachers have little or no influence, we ask the group how much time and energy they think they should spend addressing these problems. That is, if we are attempting to set ourselves up for success, how much effort should we expend on situations or circumstances over which we have absolutely no, or very little, influence (e.g., violence in the movies)? Obviously, the answer is not much. We then refocus our energies on those areas over which we have considerable influence—those in the school and classroom. We also examine factors that may be somewhat amenable to our influence (e.g., parent involvement). Teachers notice very quickly that spending lots of energy on and making an emotional commitment to areas over which they have no influence is not setting themselves up for success.

TEACHER ACTIVITY: DEFINING INFLUENCE AND IMPORTANCE

Where have you been spending your time and energy? Is this the best use of your resources, considering the amount of effort it takes and the amount of influence you have in creating change? Take some time to fill out a Sphere of Influence Chart and Influence/Importance Matrix for your own situation (see the forms on pages 32 and 33). Doing so will help you identify areas in which change is desirable and possible.

Rearranging the Environment

Our physical surroundings have a great impact on how we behave. Take a moment to examine your classroom environment. Are there ways to rearrange the room so that it is set up for success—in other words, less conducive to bullying problems? If you know, for example, that certain students are likely to engage in bullying behavior and other students are likely to be targeted, you might consider changing the seating to separate these students.

Does the time before beginning assignments or shifting from activity to activity promote aggressive acts such as pushing or teasing?

FIGURE 3   Influence/Importance Matrix

	Not very important to change	Very important to change
Considerable influence to change	Whispering in class Writing notes in class	Fighting in class Not doing schoolwork Name-calling in the hallway Not paying attention in class
Little influence to change	Watching too much television Not reading for leisure	Neighborhood violence Poor nutrition Lack of family support for education

Generally, one of the most difficult times for managing classroom behavior is during transitions from one location to another or from one activity to the next. Changing from reading to spelling, for example, may require putting away books, getting out materials, and so forth. Can you manage these transitions differently so that these problems are less likely to develop? One of our teachers brought wind chimes to her class, and, as each transition began, she brushed her hand across the chimes and told students they had until the chimes were quiet to be ready for the next activity. The students lowered their voices as they listened to the chimes, becoming quieter and quieter in the process.

TEACHER ACTIVITY: TRANSITIONS

Using the Transitions Worksheet (on page 34), list the regular transitions that occur in your classroom, then indicate the extent to which they go smoothly. (Figure 4 shows a sample entry.) Using a 10-point scale, indicate your level of satisfaction with the transition (10 = very satisfied; 1 = very dissatisfied). After completing this activity, ask yourself the following questions:

1. Are there particular transitions in which more problems develop? Is this a function of the event, the time of day, or the level of direction provided for transitioning, or are there other reasons to explain why some transitions are more problematic?

2. Are there antecedents that lead up to the problem of transitioning? That is, knowing the outcome (consequence) and what happens (the behaviors), can you identify what precipitated problems in the transition process so you may take steps to prevent it?

3. If you gave students a copy of the Transitions Worksheet, would they identify the same problems you do? What recommendations do you think students would have for addressing the problems?

FIGURE 4 Transitions Worksheet		
Transition activity	*Effectiveness* (1 = very dissatisfied; 10 = very satisfied)	*Corrective steps*
Returning to class from lunch	3—Too much activity, talking	Talk to other teachers for ideas. Identify students who are causing trouble.

Establishing Clear Classroom Rules

Generally, teachers do not like to have a long list of "do's and don'ts" in their classrooms because the atmosphere that tends to develop is one of distrust, challenge, and confrontation. Unfortunately, we sometimes end up spending more time and energy on what not to do than on what we would like our students to do. It is important to establish guidelines and expectations for classroom decorum early in the school year. Although each teacher may elect a different level of rule setting at the beginning of the year, a universal expectation is that all members of the school community treat one another with respect and dignity. Whereas some teachers will have "100 Rules for Our Classroom," others will keep rules to a minimum, perhaps to a variant of the Golden Rule: "Do unto others as you would have them do unto you." The guideline of interpersonal respect is important to establish early on. Later, as incidents arise, it is then possible to return to this theme with comments like the following: "You recall that in our classroom we show respect for one another. Name-calling and teasing are not respectful. What can you do that will show respect?"

TEACHER ACTIVITY: CLASSROOM RULES

Brainstorm a list of classroom rules. Then ask your students to do the same. Are there differences between the teacher-generated and student-generated rules? If so, how should these be resolved? Do students have an understanding of the rules that have been established? Discuss the rules with students, and use the experience to develop consistency between teacher and student expectations about classroom behavior and rules.

More discussion of rules appears in Module 2, "Preventing Bullying in Your Classroom."

Being Consistent

One of the themes that arises when we work with students—bullies, victims, and observers—is the importance of justice and fairness. We often hear students complain, "It just isn't fair." One way teachers can avoid being pulled into the quagmire of what is fair and unfair is by treating children consistently. To allow one child to misbehave, then reprimand another for the same behavior, is seen as unfair and unjust. If the rule fits, it should fit all.

At the same time, it is necessary to be sensitive and respond to students with special needs. Our experience is that when teachers are open and direct in explaining why the treatment of students with special needs is different, other students are understanding and accepting. It is when teachers say they will treat all students the same, then provide differential treatment without acknowledging that there are exceptions to the guidelines, that problems develop.

In their efforts to reduce misbehavior in the classroom, teachers must consistently model the characteristics they want from their students and consistently demonstrate the importance of treating others with respect and dignity.

Using Clear, Polite, Specific Language

We encourage teachers to "Say what you mean, and mean what you say." As is the case for consistency and fairness, our experience is that when teachers establish rules for student behavior, they must follow through with the stated consequences for misbehavior. If a teacher does not require students to behave as requested, students learn that the teacher does not mean what he or she says. They then begin to test the limits to see how far they can push the teacher before being "reined in." The language teachers use to enforce consequences must be polite and respectful. If we expect students to demonstrate respect for one another, we must model this respect ourselves.

It is also important that language used with students be clear and specific, not sarcastic, critical, or punitive. A general statement such as "I want all students to behave in my classroom" does not communicate what specifically is expected. The statement "I expect you all to sit at your desks quietly and finish the assignment" states the expectation clearly. Be sure to say what you want, when you want it, and how you want it carried out. Often, when you are working with an aggressive child, it is necessary to establish eye contact, move closer to the student, address the student by name, and wait for acknowledgment that you have been heard.

When working with an aggressive student, it is usually a good idea to "own" your part of the discussion rather than attribute your expectations to the student. By owning we mean that what you are requesting is *your* goal, not necessarily the goal of the student. You could say, for example, "I need you to take a seat now" rather than "Don't you want to take a seat now?" The question provides the opportunity for the student to answer, "No, I don't want to." Expressing what you expect helps to avoid escalating the conflict.

Being Respectful of Students

Think of a time you were patronized or disrespected. How did you feel? How did you respond? How did your response differ from the response you would have given if you had been treated with respect? How would you have liked to respond differently?

Students are very sensitive about being treated respectfully. Many young people have indeed been treated in a respectful manner, and it shows in their actions. However, many other students have not been treated respectfully; in fact, they may have been degraded, emotionally or physically harmed, or ignored. When kids are disrespected, it is unlikely that they will learn and demonstrate respect for others without nurturance and appropriate respectful interactions. Students treated with respect are more likely to develop self-worth, feel valuable, and learn positive ways of treating others.

Showing That You Value Students

As an educator, influencing the lives of children is one of your primary missions. You are obviously invested in children and want to increase their opportunities for success. Yet many students report that they do not have valuable roles within their schools or communities. Feeling valued is inextricably linked with having social responsibility. Allowing students a voice in your classroom to express concerns helps them develop a sense of responsibility; it leads to a feeling of ownership of the classroom and to the confidence that the classroom is a place where students can be heard.

A key way to show students that you value their uniqueness is by showing interest in them as individuals. We recognize that teachers do value students and want to interact with all of them but that schedules and classroom demands often make individual attention difficult. Yet, in our interviews, students report that one of the most important things a teacher can do is to acknowledge students and speak to them directly.

We often find there is a difference between the perceptions of teachers and students with regard to communication. Most teachers think they speak to individual students each day, but many times students don't agree. It is good to know if students think they are not being recognized individually each day, for being connected to the teacher is one of the primary ways students feel unique, valued, and part of the class. A feeling of being valued is also important to teachers, for without it the chance of burnout increases. The more teachers value student uniqueness, the more likely they are to be valued by their students. The following activity can help you determine the extent of your communication with students and their perceptions of your contact with them.

TEACHER ACTIVITY: CLASSROOM INTERACTIONS

Use the Teacher-Student Interaction Form (on page 35) to record the interactions you have with your students over a period of a week. Afterwards, ask yourself the following questions:

1. Do you interact with some students more than others? Is this a function of how the students behave, their learning patterns, or other characteristics?

2. Did you observe any patterns in how you interact with particular students? Are some mostly positive interactions? Are some mostly negative interactions?

3. What changes could you make to improve classroom behavior by interacting with some students differently or more or less often?

Give each student a copy of the Teacher Talk Chart (on page 36), and ask students to record times they think you are talking to them individually. Collect the charts after a week, and compare students' responses with your own observations. Ask yourself the following questions:

1. Are your records of how frequently you talk to students consistent with how often they think you speak to them?

2. Are there students with whom you need to have more contact?

3. Is there a connection between the amount of interaction you have with individual students and the behavior problems you experience with them?

Note: This last activity works best with students in grades 3–5.

Every year, you are likely to get a heads-up about the kids coming to your class: the bright kids, the less motivated kids, the creative kids, the talkers, and, of course, the "bad" kids. You know the "bad" kids; you may already have had their brothers or sisters in your class, or you have heard about them from other teachers. It is very difficult for kids to forge new reputations when stories of their misbehavior precede them. Ask yourself, Why do they act this way? What are they trying to achieve? Do they want attention and a sense of belonging, or are they seeking power or status? Attempt to step outside the constraints of reputations and labels. Challenge yourself to find each child's strengths. They are there, although sometimes we need to dig deep to find them!

When children live out their reputations, they are acting out a self-fulfilling prophecy. In other words, when children are expected to misbehave, they have a tendency to live up to that expectation. Children (and adults as well) resent being "thinged"—labeled or categorized with the assumption that they, and not their behavior, are at fault. At one school we visited, a teacher dragged two students who had been fighting into the office, looked at us, and said, "Project kids, you know how they are . . ." The students were furious about being labeled "project kids," and rightly so.

Avoiding Public Confrontations

We often become aware of bullying behavior in public settings such as the classroom, playground, lunchroom, or hallway. It is important to stop the bullying behavior at once. At the same time, it is best to move toward remediation and change in a more private setting. Attempting to change bullying behavior in the public forum puts the student on the defensive. The student may respond negatively to avoid losing face or being "dissed" in front of peers.

Public confrontations can lead to an escalation of emotions and aggression, neither of which is conducive to positive change. To stop an altercation and establish a later time for remediation, a teacher might say, for example, "Jeremy, stop that now. The rule is that we do not call people names or tease them. I'll talk with you when we return to the classroom about how we are going to handle this. Now continue with your lunch."

Another caution associated with this topic is to avoid power struggles. It is never a good idea to get into a public power struggle with a bully. Engaging in a power struggle is likely to escalate the conflict, and the student may refuse to back down or even resort to increased aggression. Teachers can help the student find a graceful way out of a conflict situation by avoiding public confrontations.

Teaching New Skills

Part of setting up for success is accepting the fact that many of our students lack the skills to engage in the kinds of peer relationships we would like to see. If students do not have the skills, or if their skills are inappropriate, then it becomes our responsibility to incorporate the appropriate skill development instruction into our teaching plans.

As teachers and researchers, we truly believe that students need to develop emotional intelligence and acquire certain assets to lead an effective life (see the discussion of these topics in chapter 2). An effective life involves being able to live and work harmoniously with others. Effective people skills, problem-solving skills, and personal responsibility are as important as the academic subject matter we teach our students.

To help students develop their social and problem-solving skills, we need to evaluate what skills students have, what their current ability levels are for particular skills, and what additional skills they need. Then we need to provide the opportunity for students to learn such skills. Although not all of our academic subjects (e.g., reading and math) lend themselves to the teaching of prosocial skills, we generally can afford a few minutes a day to provide opportunities for social skills learning. Social skills are an important part of living and learning, and it is best for effective role models—the teachers who spend time with students—to offer such training as early as possible.

A SOLUTION-FOCUSED APPROACH TO PROBLEM SOLVING

Terrence would often have emotional outbursts in class. He would be in his seat, appearing to work on assignments, but if someone said something to him that he

*thought was mean, he would scream, often running
across the room to the child who had made the comment.
Other times, Terrence would be behaving well, walking
down the hallway toward lunch or recess, but if another
student touched him or looked at him the "wrong way,"
he would begin yelling and pushing the student. The
teacher requested a psychological evaluation for Terrence
to identify the root causes of his behavior. A school social
worker identified a number of possible influences on
Terrence's behavior, including parents who had divorced
under very unpleasant circumstances; his living with
grandparents while his mother was out of town seeking
work; and residence in a housing project that had been
marked by violence, aggression, and substance abuse. In
addition, a school psychologist identified attention-deficit
concerns and found that Terrence had learning problems. The teacher now had some explanations for
Terrence's behavior but few concrete suggestions on what
to do with this very volatile student.*

Terrence's situation reflects a problem-focused approach. A problem-focused approach to children's behavioral difficulties leads us to focus on the background that has led to the current situation and the reasons for the behavior. Although it is helpful to understand why a problem exists, this understanding does not always lead to answers about what to do to solve the problem. A solution-focused model aims to find solutions for a problem when one is encountered.

Although there are drawbacks to the problem-focused approach, much of our school culture is "problem-focused," with the spotlight on the difficulties teachers encounter. We have spent considerable time in schools and heard extensive discussions of problems and the diagnosis of problems, but the discussions often end there, without effective strategies that lead to solutions. The problem focus puts the emphasis on what is wrong, on what students *can't* do as opposed to what they *can* do, and generally leads to a sense of frustration and exasperation on the part of all those concerned. Teachers may feel hopeless and want to give up. Being solution-focused, on the other hand, leads us to become more proactive than reactive.

A problem-focused approach is often adopted with both bullies and victims. This focus may actually disempower students and teachers. For example, to explain that a student is aggressive because he comes from a family with a history of violence, lives in a housing project, and watches a lot of violence on television may be accurate, but this expla-nation may lead teachers to feel that these burdens cannot be overcome and to become discouraged.

*Ms. Tuttle was furious with four boys in her classroom.
They were ganging up and picking on other kids, teasing
and name-calling, and being aggressive in the cafeteria
and on the playground. Other students were scared of*

the boys and stayed away from them as much as possible. Ms. Tuttle explained to the counselor: "They are awful. They are just uncivilized little monsters. They are always shuffling in late, never have their work done, act belligerent in class, and are constantly taunting other students, who are wimps who won't ever stand up for themselves."

In this example, the bullies are identified for their negative, antagonistic, and aggressive behaviors. Likewise, the victims are blamed for their weak or unskilled responses. Both bullies and victims are described in terms of their negative characteristics. This problem-focused approach has resulted in the discouragement of all involved. An understanding of the problem exists, but there is not much optimism for change.

The solution-focused approach challenges the labels given to both bullies and victims. We do this by providing opportunities for teachers and students to see bullies and victims differently: Are bullies always bullying? Not typically. Are victims victimized all the time? Not usually. Both groups of students have numerous other characteristics that may be overshadowed by their roles as bullies or victims. Using a solution-focused approach helps to create change because it allows teachers and students to see beyond the problem. We are chronically optimistic about the potential for positive change.

The ACT NICE Process

A solution-focused model for teachers to use in the classroom is "ACT NICE." Jean Baker and the ACT Early team at the University of Georgia (Addressing Core Techniques for Early Interventions with At-Risk Students) developed the ACT NICE model to help teachers move from a problem-focused emphasis with children toward a solution-focused approach. The goal is to help teachers focus on strengths and generate positive, proactive solutions.

Core Assumptions

The ACT NICE approach is based on several core assumptions, next described.

Bullying and victimization derive from a mismatch between the competencies of the student and the demands of the classroom and school environment

Having effective social skills represents a high level of cognitive and behavioral development for students, a level that many students have yet to achieve. Some students come from situations in which there are inadequate models for prosocial behavior and few opportunities to observe appropriate peer and adult interactions. Often, in our families today, there is failure to establish effective bonding or attachment to significant adults, resulting in an inability on the part of some students to be empathic or to take others' perspectives. If a student has not learned to understand how others feel, then he or she will be unable to care about whether others are hurt or offended. Focusing on the "whys" of a lack of empathy, a problem-focused approach, does not help us bring about desirable behaviors in the school situation. By becoming solution-focused, we are able to look for ways to teach the skills we desire in our students.

Teachers are experts

Teachers are experts with regard to their students as well as their subject matter. They work with hundreds of students and understand child development, curriculum planning, individual learning styles, and classroom management. Teachers are the "front line" of educating and caring for students. They are the ones who have taken on the responsibility for helping students move through tumultuous periods of their lives as they attempt to master not only academic skills but also the relationship skills that will so powerfully influence their lives in the years to come.

Multiple barriers obstruct teachers' ability to work creatively toward solutions to their students' problems

The world of the teacher today is one of too little time for individualized instruction, a shortage of resources, increasing class sizes, and diminished parental support. In addition, school boards or administrators often look over teachers' shoulders, expecting ever higher levels of productivity.

Today's teachers need support and encouragement to handle the expectations placed upon them. Some of the problems teachers experience can be managed by involving other resources, such as special education classes for children with emotional or behavioral disorders or special learning needs, counseling for those with emotional needs that cannot be met within the classroom, and alternative schools for those for whom the public school environment truly does not fit. Nonetheless, the main responsibility for education and implementing change rests with classroom teachers.

Solution-Focused Components of ACT NICE

The solution-focused components of ACT NICE are N = Notice, I = Increase, C = Create, and E = Encourage.

N = Notice

The ABCs (antecedents, behaviors, consequences), described earlier in this chapter, apply to positive behavior as well as to bullying and victimization. We need to be aware of the antecedents of appropriate behavior. Bullies do not always act aggressively, and victims are not always victimized. At times, bullies and victims interact appropriately. Our job is to notice when, where, with whom, and under what conditions problems are not occurring and bullies and victims are, in fact, behaving appropriately. The process requires that we focus on what we want students to be doing instead of the problematic behavior (the solution, rather than the problem), then *notice* what is happening when students present the appropriate behavior. An expression that typifies this process is "Catch the child being good." One small step we encourage teachers to take when carrying out this component of ACT NICE is to notice at least two good behaviors a student engages in for every negative behavior. This is vital if we want to encourage positive change.

I = Increase

Once we have figured out what As (antecedents) result in the Bs (behaviors) we desire in bullies and victims—not bullying and not being victimized, respectively—we need to increase the circumstances in which these events or behaviors occur. In other words, we need to do more of what already works. When a bully engages in prosocial behavior rather than bullying, bullying is decreased or eliminated. In other words, increasing prosocial behavior automatically decreases bullying, for students cannot simultaneously be prosocial and antisocial. Prosocial behavior also permits positive interactions, which can become reinforcing and result in a subsequent decrease in bullying.

C = Create

Creative thinking on the part of teachers can lead to opportunities for bullies and victims to experience positive interactions at the same time they are reducing aggression and violence, which generally have been our focus. Engaging students in positive discussions, encouraging them to share in supportive tasks, and helping them find alternative ways of being and behaving all call for creative solutions. When teachers work together, share their ideas, and support one another, they establish the environment for creative solutions.

E = Encourage

It is important to distinguish between praise and encouragement, for they are often confused. Praise generally describes something someone has done. For example:

> "Justin, you did a great job of putting away the papers."

> "Michael, that was a great catch on the ball field."

Praise is powerful, but it has drawbacks. It is external in orientation; that is, it comes from someone else, such as a teacher, who defines what is good or bad. Praise works in the immediate situation in which it is given. Once the praise is withdrawn, the child loses the motivation to respond in that way. Praise also diminishes in power if given too easily.

Encouragement, on the other hand, provides feedback in a way that promotes internal motivation. We recommend that teachers encourage and celebrate successes—even small ones—and that they use descriptive statements rather than evaluative praise to let students know what they are doing right. For example:

> "Nathan, you and Alex looked like you were having a difficult time sharing, but you seemed to settle it quickly and in a friendly way. Thanks."

"Mary, I noticed you were including Hope in the group activity. Thanks for being so considerate."

It is also important to remember to use problem-solving, solution-oriented statements that encourage students to think about solutions, rather than problem-finding language. For instance:

"Does name-calling support our class rule about showing respect for others?" (Rather than "Stop name-calling.")

"What do you think we need to do to resolve this problem?" (Rather than "Let me tell you what you need to do.")

The ACT NICE process is a step toward thinking differently about problems and working toward solutions to recurring problems rather than avoiding them or attempting to refer students to someone else. By implementing this approach in your classroom, you are setting your students up for success while simultaneously gaining a greater sense of control over the interactions that occur there.

The Big Questions

The "Big Questions" are part of a solution-focused technique that can help you become an efficient and effective problem solver. Using the Big Questions facilitates your evaluation of whether what you are doing is working and, if necessary, provides an opportunity to consider new and creative alternatives. Table 1 lists the Big Questions and gives a brief explanation of each.

Using the Big Questions with Yourself

The Big Questions are a useful tool for approaching many situations. The following brief example illustrates how a teacher who is encountering difficulty implementing an activity with her students might apply these questions.

- *Question 1:* What is my goal?

    My goal is to help teach my students conflict resolution skills.

- *Question 2:* What am I doing?

    I am standing in front of the class, but I don't have the attention of the students. Jared and Jeff are being disruptive again, calling each other names. I am feeling upset, tired, and frustrated. I feel like quitting for the day.

- *Question 3:* Is what I am doing helping me to achieve my goal?

    No, I am getting upset and frustrated. I am not teaching the conflict resolution skills effectively.

TABLE 1 The Big Questions

Question 1: What is my goal?
Identify what you are attempting to achieve.

Question 2: What am I doing?
Identify the problem.

Question 3: Is what I am doing helping me achieve my goal?
Evaluate the effectiveness of the solutions.

Question 4: *(If not)* **What can I do differently?**
Generate new or alternative solutions.

- *Question 4:* What can I do differently?

> *I am going to take a minute and think about what is happening in my classroom. What usually gets the students' attention and allows them to have a good time while learning something new? Sometimes it is better if we sit on the floor together in a circle or if I ask for several volunteers to help teach. Let me think of what other ideas I can come up with and try one out.*

The next step is for the teacher to try out the chosen idea. If that idea solves the problem, great. If not, the teacher returns to the fourth question, "What can I do differently?" and generates more solutions, repeating this process until success is attained.

Using the Big Questions with Your Students

Your students can also benefit by using the Big Questions to evaluate their behaviors and interactions and to create new or alternative ways to handle challenging situations. We incorporate the Big Questions for you and your students throughout the learning modules in this program, and we encourage you to practice the Big Questions so they will become a regular part of your problem-solving routine.

When using the Big Questions, we are attempting to be solution-focused in a creative way. The first question is designed to help students cease doing what they have been doing and reexamine their goals. Common goals include developing friendships, getting along with others, being respected, and showing respect for others. Often students cannot answer the question "What is your goal?" so we may need to answer this question for them. In fact, sometimes we skip over this question and provide the answer as we move to the second question, "What are you doing?" Consider two different ways in which a teacher might interact with a student who is bothering another student:

> "Katrice, we have a goal of learning to work well with our neighbors in the classroom, but what are you doing?"

With this question, the teacher tells what the goal was and moves on to the behavior. An alternative for students who have not developed the ability to follow the questioning process is to provide answers for the first two questions:

> "Katrice, we have a goal of learning to work well with our neighbors in the classroom *(What is my goal?),* but you are talking to Maureen while she tries to do her work *(What am I doing?),* so that doesn't help you behave like a good neighbor. *(Is what I am doing helping me achieve my goal?)* What could you do instead? *(What can I do differently?).*"

We use the Big Questions extensively with our students and among ourselves. We often give students their own copy of the Big Questions, in the form of cards the students can carry in their pockets. When in a difficult situation, students are encouraged to pull out these cards and work through the Big Questions to find a good solution. (We keep lots of extra copies because the cards tend go through the washing machine!) We have had parents call and request copies for all family members and have even had parents report that the cards have been useful to them at work in solving problems. When students need prompts or reminders, the questions are readily available.

TEACHER ACTIVITY: THE BIG QUESTIONS

Photocopy page 37 on card stock, cut the lists of questions apart, and laminate them. Give each student a card. You may also wish to make photocopies of page 38 and post them in the classroom and in other locations where students will find them useful (cafeteria, library, hallways, etc.).

WORKING TOWARD SUCCESS WITH YOUR BULLY BUSTERS SUPPORT TEAM

One of your team's major goals is to decide what is successful and what isn't in your own particular setting and with your own students. The "Glads and Sads" activity offers a structure for discussing specific bullying events and the techniques you use to respond to them.

TEACHER ACTIVITY: GLADS AND SADS

We all have events in our work we think we handled well and that went the way we wanted, for which we are glad. There are also events we wish had gone differently and had handled better, for which we are sad. Identify "Glads" and "Sads" to share with your Bully Busters Support Team. On a separate sheet of paper, describe these events and your responses to them, then discuss with your team.

If you repeat this activity with your team periodically, over the course of a school year, you will likely see patterns in the types of problems in your school and in the degree of success in your responses and in the responses of other team members.

We have had a number of teachers indicate that they feel burned out on teaching. These feelings are often presented as a function of the types of students they have in their classrooms. Our experience is that teachers don't burn out from too much teaching; burnout occurs when teachers do not feel successful in their work. We all know people who put in very long hours—distance runners who run marathon after marathon, musicians who practice and play endless hours, teachers who remain energized year after year.

People burn out when they no longer feel good about their efforts. It happens when needs—professional, personal, emotional—are no longer being met by an activity. Teachers enter the profession because of their love of teaching and working with young people. When energy is pulled away to address aggression and bullying, there is less energy for teaching. And when teachers feel ill-prepared to deal with bullying, they become even more frustrated.

We believe mastering the skills and activities found in this manual will help empower you to devote more time and energy to your teaching and to feel more accomplished in your management of bullies and victims. As your sense of accomplishment and success as a teacher increases, the feeling of burnout should decrease. Both you and your students will benefit from your increased confidence.

It is important for teachers to stay healthy and experience a sense of well-being. Teachers are people and professionals, and both personal and professional growth must be included among any efforts at setting up for success. Module 8, "Relaxation and Coping Skills," includes stress-relieving and energy-restoring activities helpful to both students and teachers.

As you increase your awareness of bullying problems, it may feel as though bullying is increasing rather than decreasing or that bullying is inevitable and beyond your control. You may find that the techniques described in this manual meet resistance from bullies. However, as your students begin to recognize bullying and its consequences, they are likely to understand the new limits you have implemented and become more accommodating to the interventions. *Hang in there!* It is important for you to stay encouraged. If you have decided to use this program, you have taken an important step toward change.

Recognizing the ABCs

Antecedent	Behavior	Consequence	Corrective steps

Bully Busters: A Teacher's Manual for Helping Bullies, Victims, and Bystanders (Grades K–5)
© 2003 by Arthur M. Horne, Christi L. Bartolomucci, and Dawn Newman-Carlson.
Champaign, IL: Research Press. (800) 519–2707.

Sphere of Influence Chart

Circumstance or situation that may influence bullying	Teacher influence (+/–)	Importance (1 = low; 5 = high)

Bully Busters: A Teacher's Manual for Helping Bullies, Victims, and Bystanders (Grades K–5)
© 2003 by Arthur M. Horne, Christi L. Bartolomucci, and Dawn Newman-Carlson.
Champaign, IL: Research Press. (800) 519–2707.

Influence/Importance Matrix

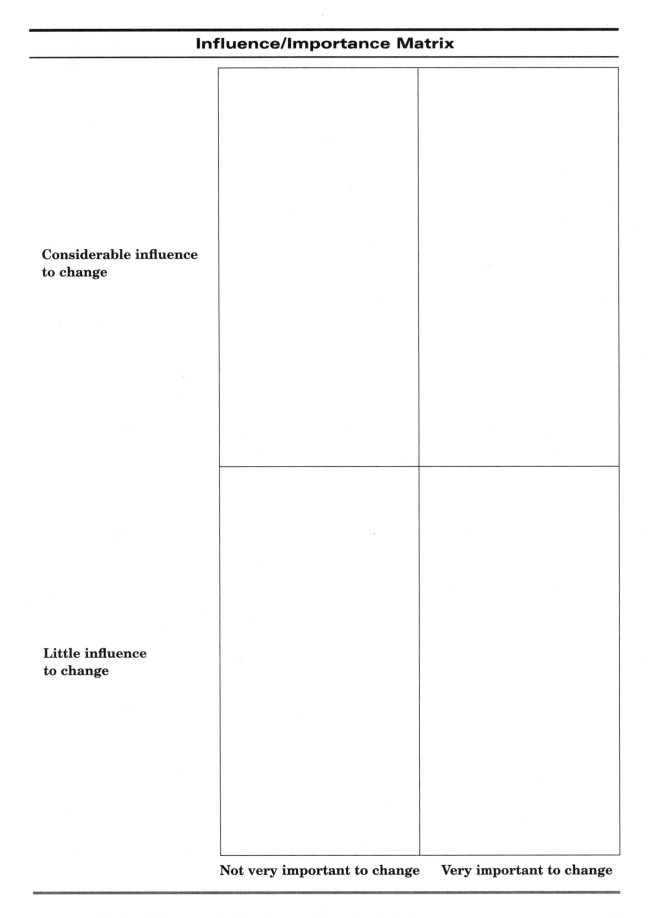

**Considerable influence
to change**

**Little influence
to change**

Not very important to change   Very important to change

© 2003 by Arthur M. Horne, Christi L. Bartolomucci, and Dawn Newman-Carlson.
Champaign, IL: Research Press. (800) 519–2707.

Transitions Worksheet

Transition activity	Effectiveness (1 = very dissatisfied; 10 = very satisfied)	Corrective steps

Bully Busters: A Teacher's Manual for Helping Bullies, Victims, and Bystanders (Grades K–5)
© 2003 by Arthur M. Horne, Christi L. Bartolomucci, and Dawn Newman-Carlson.
Champaign, IL: Research Press. (800) 519–2707.

Teacher-Student Interaction Form

On the left-hand side of the grid, list your students' names. On the right-hand side, record times you spoke to each child individually by putting check marks in the daily column.

Week of _____

Student	Monday	Tuesday	Wednesday	Thursday	Friday

Bully Busters: A Teacher's Manual for Helping Bullies, Victims, and Bystanders (Grades K–5)
© 2003 by Arthur M. Horne, Christi L. Bartolomucci, and Dawn Newman-Carlson.
Champaign, IL: Research Press. (800) 519–2707.

Teacher Talk Chart

Name _____   Week of _____

Please use this chart to record times I talk to you alone this week. Talking to you alone could mean that I say hello to you and ask how you are doing today. It can also include asking what you have been doing or spending special time going over a lesson. It would not include when I talk to the whole class, like when giving directions. If I did spend time and talk to you alone, put a plus (+) mark for the day. If I did not spend any time talking to you alone, put a minus (−) mark.

	Monday	Tuesday	Wednesday	Thursday	Friday
Spoke to me by myself (+)					
Did not speak to me by myself (−)					

Bully Busters: A Teacher's Manual for Helping Bullies, Victims, and Bystanders (Grades K–5)
© 2003 by Arthur M. Horne, Christi L. Bartolomucci, and Dawn Newman-Carlson.
Champaign, IL: Research Press. (800) 519–2707.

THE BIG QUESTIONS

1. What is my goal?
2. What am I doing?
3. Is what I am doing helping me achieve my goal?
4. *(If not)* What can I do differently?

THE BIG QUESTIONS

1. What is my goal?
2. What am I doing?
3. Is what I am doing helping me achieve my goal?
4. *(If not)* What can I do differently?

THE BIG QUESTIONS

1. What is my goal?
2. What am I doing?
3. Is what I am doing helping me achieve my goal?
4. *(If not)* What can I do differently?

THE BIG QUESTIONS

1. What is my goal?
2. What am I doing?
3. Is what I am doing helping me achieve my goal?
4. *(If not)* What can I do differently?

THE BIG QUESTIONS

1. What is my goal?
2. What am I doing?
3. Is what I am doing helping me achieve my goal?
4. *(If not)* What can I do differently?

THE BIG QUESTIONS

1. What is my goal?
2. What am I doing?
3. Is what I am doing helping me achieve my goal?
4. *(If not)* What can I do differently?

THE BIG QUESTIONS

1. What is my goal?
2. What am I doing?
3. Is what I am doing helping me achieve my goal?
4. *(If not)* What can I do differently?

THE BIG QUESTIONS

1. What is my goal?
2. What am I doing?
3. Is what I am doing helping me achieve my goal?
4. *(If not)* What can I do differently?

THE BIG QUESTIONS

1. What is my goal?
2. What am I doing?
3. Is what I am doing helping me achieve my goal?
4. *(If not)* What can I do differently?

THE BIG QUESTIONS

1. What is my goal?
2. What am I doing?
3. Is what I am doing helping me achieve my goal?
4. *(If not)* What can I do differently?

1. What is my goal?

2. What am I doing?

3. Is what I am doing helping me achieve my goal?

4. *(If not)* What can I do differently?

Bully Busters: A Teacher's Manual for Helping Bullies, Victims, and Bystanders (Grades K–5)
© 2003 by Arthur M. Horne, Christi L. Bartolomucci, and Dawn Newman-Carlson.
Champaign, IL: Research Press. (800) 519–2707.

CHAPTER

2 Emotional Intelligence and Developmental Assets

This chapter offers a description of two recently developed models that have implications for reducing and preventing bullying: emotional intelligence and developmental assets. The first, emotional intelligence, expands the concept of intelligence to include a person's ability to use his or her emotions to guide thinking and behavior (Goleman, 1995). As defined by the Search Institute, developmental assets are conditions or qualities that serve as protective factors against high-risk behaviors, foster positive development, and increase resiliency in children and adolescents.

EMOTIONAL INTELLIGENCE

When educators and the general public think of intelligence, the picture that comes to mind is how "book smart" a student is and how well the student performs in school. Daniel Goleman's (1995) identification of emotional intelligence has sparked a whole new approach to assessing the abilities of both children and adults. Goleman recognizes that, in addition to intellectual ability, an individual's emotional abilities and well-being greatly influence that person's likelihood of interpersonal success. His research in this area suggests an exciting approach to improving students' safety within the school environment, one that could be expected to have a profound effect on the problems of bullying and other forms of aggression in the school.

Components of Emotional Intelligence

Emotional intelligence involves several components that can be developed, nourished, and used increasingly within social situations to support and encourage student success. Peter Salovey and John Mayer (1990) define the basic characteristics of emotional intelligence as follows:

- Knowing one's emotions
- Managing one's emotions
- Motivating oneself
- Recognizing emotions in others
- Handling relationships

As we discuss the basic premises of each characteristic, we will also describe aspects of the Bully Busters program that address the development of emotional intelligence.

Knowing One's Emotions

As Bodine and Crawford (1999) assert, "Emotional self-awareness is . . . the cornerstone of emotional intelligence, serving as a building block for the other fundamentals of emotional intelligence" (p. 36). In other words, being able to recognize one's own emotions is necessary before one can express these feelings appropriately, identify the feelings of others, or comprehend what effect one's feelings may be having on one's interactions.

The Bully Busters program includes classroom activities to help children identify and name the emotions they have in situations relating to bullying interactions, as well as to other interactions with their teachers and peers. For example, the first activity in Module 1, "What a Feeling," is designed to help familiarize children with feeling words associated with various facial expressions, facilitating awareness of their own emotions and encouraging them to imagine the feelings of other children. Recognition is necessary before children can accept the feelings they have. Many children, as well as many adults, have been taught that some normal emotions are bad, especially anger. In the classroom activities, we help students own and recognize all feelings and then learn how they can gain more understanding and control over their emotions.

Managing One's Emotions

Managing one's emotions means recognizing and owning these feelings, then knowing what to do with them. Usually, emotions are appropriate and relevant to the occasion. For example, tension and nervousness when we drive in heavy traffic helps us exercise caution; pride in our families leads us to communicate to family members that they are valued. Difficulties may arise because an emotion is too intense for a given situation (e.g., traffic that creates so much nervousness that it causes a panic attack) or because people do not have the skills to manage the emotion. The goal of managing feelings is not to do away with or ignore them. Our emotions can help motivate us to act in ways that are more likely to result in positive outcomes.

Throughout the Bully Busters program, classroom activities give students an opportunity to consider alternative ways of handling emotional situations (e.g., "No Bullying Here," in Module 2). As noted, anger is a powerful feeling that is highly visible in the classroom and commonly associated with the bully-victim interaction. In actuality, anger is a feeling that is often secondary to emotions such as hurt, embarrassment, and fear (Bodine & Crawford, 1999). Managing the anger present in bully-victim interactions can be very challenging. During these times, it is easy for children to act impulsively and cause harm and embarrassment to others. However, students can work together to understand how their emotions guide their behaviors and can learn effective ways of handling intense emotions.

Motivating Oneself

As mentioned, emotions motivate us to do something—for example, to reach a goal, release tension or anger, or achieve happiness. Teachers and students can use their feelings either to motivate themselves or to impede their own progress. When bullies and victims understand the role of their feelings in the bully-victim interaction, they are more motivated to change the situation. The concept of learned helplessness applies to motivation (Seligman, 1991, 1995). Learned helplessness means that, through the repetition of negative experiences, an individual learns to feel powerless and hopeless, and therefore accepts the situation and makes little effort to change it. Such an orientation is common among the victims of bullying. Victims may feel powerless and may surrender time and time again to being bullied, consequently ensuring that the bullying will continue. If victims could learn to use their emotional and social resources, they would likely experience the emotion of hope—hope that the situation can improve with the help of their teachers and peers. Victims would then be motivated to change the situation and no longer succumb to bullying. Hope is key in motivation and a building block of emotional intelligence.

Recognizing the Emotions of Others

The ability to identify, recognize, and experience the feelings of others is known as empathy. A lack of empathy is dangerous because it allows individuals to engage in harmful and violent interactions with little care for others. The ability to empathize with others increases as children mature, but even young children are able to empathize with and understand others' feelings. However, often bullies are unable or unwilling to identify the feelings of their victims.

Bullies are frequently victimized themselves in other environments, including their homes, and so may get caught up in the immediate gratification of their own needs. Through their continual intimidation of other students, bullies get what they want and gain power and prestige. If bullies understood how they made their victims feel, they would likely find it more difficult to commit victimizing acts. A goal of the Bully Busters program is to help bullies identify the feelings of their victims and develop empathy. Activities focusing on empathy include "Identifying Others' Feelings," from Module 2, and "Name That Feeling," from Module 3.

Handling Relationships

Emotions are an essential component of interpersonal relationships. Through relationships, professional or personal, individuals communicate and respond to one another on an emotional level. Good relationships include emotional give and take, the ability to communicate ideas and feelings, and respect for other people's ideas and feelings.

Bully Busters activities help children, including bullies and victims, learn how to engage in more effective interpersonal relationships (e.g., "One for All," from Module 2). It is not necessary for all students to like one another and become friends. Instead, the goal is for children to learn how to work together and respect one another, even when they have different ideas, opinions, and desires.

If you understand these basic building blocks of emotional intelligence, you can better comprehend your own feelings, as well as nourish the emotional intelligence of your students. Your emotions can be used positively or negatively to influence the outcome of a situation. Can you recall a challenging situation that you feel you handled extremely well—in which you kept calm and responded in an appropriate and responsible manner? During this time, you likely had the ability to understand the situation, recognize how you and others were feeling, control your emotions, and, consequently, respond positively in the situation. This is the essence of emotional intelligence.

Take a moment to think back to a situation in which you were less successful—in which you were impulsive or reactionary. Afterwards, did you wonder why you acted in such a way? Were you caught off guard by your emotions? Was your reaction proportionate to the situation? Were you aware of others' feelings and possible perceptions of the situation? In these situations, our lack of emotional awareness makes it difficult to regulate our emotions as well as we may like.

Hurt, embarrassment, and anger are feelings that can have strong behavioral consequences. These are feelings often associated with being bullied as well as feelings that bullies themselves often experience. These feelings can fuel behaviors that are dangerous to the individual as well as to others. Often these feelings take hold so quickly that there is not much time to become aware of them, to consider their source, and to regulate a response to the situation. If understanding and taking control of emotions is challenging for adults, imagine how much more difficult the challenge is for children!

Emotional intelligence is not an innate characteristic; rather, it is a characteristic that can be encouraged and developed. Many children have wonderful abilities to understand and express emotions, as well as to be empathic to the feelings and experiences of others. Other children's emotional needs have been neglected. These children may not have had adults in their lives who were able to model the aspects of emotional intelligence.

Consider for a moment children who have grown up in homes in which there has been abuse or neglect. Emotions may run extremely high in these homes. Parents' responses may be inconsistent, and children therefore may have difficulty learning how to regulate their own emotions. Without appropriate models, they often rely on the only means they know, which may involve reacting in a physically violent manner.

Children who respond aggressively are unlikely to have a great awareness of their emotions and behaviors or how their emotions and behaviors may affect others. These students often misinterpret the intentions or actions of others.

> *As Juan was walking back to his desk, he accidentally hit the book on Peter's desk, knocking it to the floor. Peter felt a flood of anger: He believed that Juan had knocked his book off the desk on purpose. Peter jumped up and pushed Juan to the ground. Juan, stunned and embarrassed, scrambled to his feet, hurried back to his seat, and put his head on his desk.*

As this example shows, when children have difficulty understanding and recognizing their own and others' emotions, they are typically more likely to perceive the actions of others as provocative and purposefully hurtful (Crick & Dodge, 1994; Dodge, Pettit, McClaskey, & Brown, 1986). To a bully, an innocent bump in the hallway can be grounds for a verbal or physical fight. A glance by another student can instigate an aggressive response. In the scenario with Peter and Juan, Peter responded impulsively and did not empathize with Juan or understand his embarrassment.

How would this situation be different if Peter's emotional intelligence were nourished? First, Peter may not have perceived the situation as provocative because he would be able to generate other explanations for Juan's knocking the book off his desk. He may have been able to recognize that it was simply an accident. Peter may also have understood that the accident was embarrassing for Juan and even address an empathic comment to Juan (e.g., "Don't worry about it. It's OK").

DEVELOPMENTAL ASSETS

Beginning at an early age, we can help children acquire the resources that will help set them up for lifelong success. As seen in the increase of school violence, school communities cannot afford to wait until a crisis has occurred to act. We want to ensure that children are prepared with a sense of personal and social responsibility, social support, and conflict resolution skills.

The purpose of the Bully Busters program is to promote the healthy development of children in order to prevent future problems relating to bullying and other forms of aggression. With a similar preventive focus, the Search Institute, located in Minneapolis, has identified 40 developmental assets for elementary-age children (children ages 6–11). The institute's research with youth in Albuquerque and Minneapolis suggests that these assets serve as protective factors against high-risk behaviors, foster positive development, and increase hardiness or resiliency in children and adolescents. Findings indicate that youth with many of these developmental assets are happier and more successful than those with few. Specifically, findings indicated that youth with ten or fewer developmental assets were significantly more likely than the national average to experience alcohol use, tobacco use, sexual intercourse, depression/suicide, antisocial behavior, violence, and school problems (Benson, 1997).

Table 2 lists all 40 developmental assets by category and gives a brief definition for each. As the table shows, assets are defined as being either external or internal, and are further grouped by such categories as support, empowerment, commitment to learning, and social competencies. For more information, see *What Young Children Need to Succeed: Working Together to Build Assets from Birth to Age 11* (Roehlkepartain & Leffert, 2000).

All children can benefit from the development and nurturance of these developmental assets, and we have attempted to apply them in the Bully Busters program to encourage the healthy development of children and the establishment of bully-free elementary schools. The following discussion expands on the developmental assets and explains how they are relevant to the goals of preventing and reducing bullying and other forms of aggression.

Each asset is accompanied by an "asset challenge," giving you specific ways to apply your knowledge of the assets to promote students' strength and resilience. We encourage you to review each of the assets, then incorporate the asset challenges most appropriate for your situation into your teaching and other school activities. As always, these challenges serve as suggestions. Use your creativity and tap the creativity of your co-workers for other ideas.

External Assets

Asset Category: Support

Asset 1: Family support
Family support and love make a huge difference in the lives of children. Bullies sometimes have very little family support, and what they learn outside of school may encourage them to continue their bullying behavior. However, victims, particularly passive victims, often have lots of family support. Sometimes the support can be so much that a parent tries to do things for the child that the child is capable of or should be learning to do for himself or herself. Doing things for the child that he or she is capable of doing sends the child the message that he or she is incompetent. Children learn to feel successful and effective when they have the support and encouragement of their families to take new risks and learn new skills.

Family support is needed in interventions with bullies and victims, but teaching independence and taking care of oneself is also important. Our goal is to gain the support of families in helping their children and

TABLE 2   Developmental Assets and Their Definitions

Asset category	Asset name	Asset definition
EXTERNAL ASSETS		
Support	1. Family support	Family life provides high levels of love and support.
	2. Positive family communication	Parents and children communicate positively. Children are willing to seek advice and counsel from their parents.
	3. Other adult relationships	Children have support from adults other than their parents.
	4. Caring neighborhood	Children experience caring neighbors.
	5. Caring out-of-home climate	School and other activities provide caring, encouraging environments for children.
	6. Parent involvement in out-of-home situations	Parents are actively involved in helping children succeed in school and in other situations outside the home.
Empowerment	7. Community values children	Children feel that the family and community value and appreciate children.
	8. Children are given useful roles	Children are included in age-appropriate family tasks and decisions and are given useful roles at home and in the community.
	9. Service to others	Children serve others in the community with their family or in other settings.
	10. Safety	Children are safe at home, at school, and in the neighborhood.
Boundaries and expectations	11. Family boundaries	The family has clear rules and consequences and monitors children's activities and whereabouts.
	12. Out-of-home boundaries	Schools and other out-of-home environments provide clear rules and consequences.
	13. Neighborhood boundaries	Neighbors take responsibility for monitoring children's behavior.
	14. Adult role models	Parents and other adults model positive, responsible behavior.
	15. Positive peer interaction and influence	Children interact with other children who model responsible behavior and have opportunities to play and interact in safe, well-supervised settings.

This list is an educational tool. It is not intended to be nor is it appropriate as a scientific measure of the developmental assets of individuals. Copyright © 2000 by Search Institute. All rights reserved. Reproduced with permission from the Search Institute, 615 First Avenue N.E., Suite 125, Minneapolis, MN 55413.

Table 2 (continued)

Asset category	Asset name	Asset definition
Boundaries and expectations (*continued*)	16. Appropriate expectations for growth	Adults have realistic expectations for children's development at this age. Parents, caregivers, and other adults encourage children to achieve and develop their unique talents.
Constructive use of time	17. Creative activities	Children participate in music, art, drama, or other creative activities for at least three hours a week at home and elsewhere.
	18. Out-of-home activities	Children spend one hour or more each week in extracurricular school activities or structured community programs.
	19. Religious community	The family attends religious programs or services for at least one hour per week.
	20. Positive, supervised time at home	Children spend most evenings and weekends at home with their parents in predictable, enjoyable routines.
INTERNAL ASSETS		
Commitment to learning	21. Achievement expectation and motivation	Children are motivated to do well in school and other activities.
	22. Children are engaged in learning	Children are responsive, attentive, and actively engaged in learning.
	23. Stimulating activity and homework	Parents and teachers encourage children to explore and engage in stimulating activities. Children do homework when it's assigned.
	24. Enjoyment of learning and bonding to school	Children enjoy learning and care about their school.
	25. Reading for pleasure	Children and an adult read together for at least 30 minutes a day. Children also enjoy reading or looking at books or magazines on their own.
Positive values	26. Caring	Children are encouraged to help other people.
	27. Equality and social justice	Children begin to show interest in making the community a better place.
	28. Integrity	Children begin to act on their convictions and stand up for their beliefs.
	29. Honesty	Children begin to value honesty and act accordingly.
	30. Responsibility	Children begin to accept and take personal responsibility for age-appropriate tasks.
	31. Healthy lifestyle and sexual attitudes	Children begin to value good health habits and learn healthy sexual attitudes and beliefs as well as respect for others.

Asset category	Asset name	Asset definition
Social competencies	32. Planning and decision making	Children begin to learn how to plan ahead and make choices at appropriate developmental levels.
	33. Interpersonal skills	Children interact with adults and children and can make friends. Children express and articulate feelings in appropriate ways and empathize with others.
	34. Cultural competence	Children know about and are comfortable with people of different cultural, racial, and/or ethnic backgrounds.
	35. Resistance skills	Children start developing the ability to resist negative peer pressure and dangerous situations.
	36. Peaceful conflict resolution	Children try to resolve conflicts nonviolently.
Positive identity	37. Personal power	Children begin to feel they have control over things that happen to them. They begin to manage frustrations and challenges in ways that have positive results for themselves and others.
	38. Self-esteem	Children report having high self-esteem.
	39. Sense of purpose	Children report that their lives have purpose and actively engage their skills.
	40. Positive view of personal future	Children are hopeful and positive about their personal future.

schools to stop bullying and to help children acquire the skills and abilities to respond to other children in an effective, emotionally intelligent manner.

ASSET CHALLENGE

Talk to the parents of identified bullies and victims, and share the bullying situation occurring at school. Let them know that you are actively working on changing bullying so your class is safe for everyone. Advise the parents of victims that you are also encouraging these children to do more things for themselves and that doing so will help them feel good about themselves.

Encourage parents to talk with their child about the victimization, explore what the child feels he or she needs, and discuss new ways of responding to the bully. Ask parents if they can support you by having the child take more responsibility at home. Inform parents that if their child has responsibilities and meets them, he or she is more likely to have good self-esteem. Parents of bullies should be provided with information about steps being implemented at school and asked for their support. Share the list of 40 developmental assets with families.

Asset 2: Positive family communication

It is important for parents and children to be able to talk openly with one another and for children to be comfortable asking for help and advice from their parents. Especially when a child reaches the elementary school years, parents must understand his or her experiences at school, academically and socially, in order to relate to the child positively. Through positive communication, parents and children can have meaningful conversations, explore appropriate ways to deal with various situations, and learn about each other and their family roots. When parents are open and understanding, children are more likely to seek their help, support, and advice when they encounter situations at school like bullying.

ASSET CHALLENGE

Encourage parents to spend special time with their child to strengthen their bond and encourage open communication. Through notes or a letter home, encourage parents to spend 10 minutes a night with the child in an interactive activity the child picks. This activity communicates to the child that he or she is special and worth spending time with, and it gives parents and the child a time to talk and have fun with each other. Parents can also suggest fun projects to do together as a family—for example, creating family scrapbooks, doing puzzles, or drawing a poster-size family picture.

Asset 3: Other adult relationships

The support of caring adults has been identified as a crucial aspect of positive child development (Gregg, 1998). Adults other than parents are important sources of support when children are experiencing difficulty or facing new challenges. Teachers, coaches, scout leaders, and the like serve as role models for positive interactions and ways to solve conflicts peacefully. Many children do not have the opportunity to share their experiences with adults or to hear the stories and experiences of adults they respect. Through communication between children and adults, children can develop important and supportive relationships outside the family.

ASSET CHALLENGE

Take time to talk individually with your students. For example, you can hold child-teacher conferences to see how your students are doing at the beginning and end of each school quarter. The conference would not be evaluative, but would instead provide an opportunity for you to connect with your students on a more personal level. Building individual relationships with your students lets them know you care about what they are experiencing and that you are there to provide support. In particular, take time in your day to check in with potential bullies and victims. Checking in with them on a more personal level allows you to form a connection that demonstrates respect and caring. You can also share this responsibility by including community members. For example, invite PTA members, retired community members, high school students, parents, and others to spend lunchtime and/or recess with your students. Encourage these adults to sit with the students, eat with them, and talk with them about their lives.

Asset 4: Caring neighborhood

Caring neighbors create caring communities. By building connections with those around them, children can experience what it feels like to belong to a community and receive community resources and support. Bullying is learned in aggressive environments in which a child learns to feel powerful through the misuse of power. The bully-victim interaction does not occur in a vacuum, although the results of the interaction can lead to discouragement and isolation. Increasing support, guidance, and redirection inside the home and in outside environments can help bullies and victims better understand the interaction and find more positive ways to meet their needs.

ASSET CHALLENGE

Although home neighbors are important, at school students can meet their "school neighbors." Are the students in your class familiar with the teachers in the rooms next to yours? Do they feel comfortable going to another school professional to talk about an issue they may be experiencing? You can help children, especially children who are younger or new to the school, to get to know their school neighbors by hosting a get-together in your classroom where teachers and other school staff stop by and introduce themselves. You can also work to establish school mentoring programs, in which older students guide younger students through their early school years.

Building neighborhood connections can be difficult for families, even when they live only a few doors from one another. Many people do not know those who live near them. Children, accompanied by their parents, can be encouraged to meet the people who live next to them and learn something about them. Of course, children and parents will need to exercise caution in judging whom to meet and get to know.

Asset 5: Caring out-of-home climate

School and other activities that provide safe, encouraging, and caring environments foster children's growth. Children who connect and form meaningful bonds within the school environment may be more likely to experience academic success. When children are engaged in activities like ending bullying at school, they begin to develop a sense of ownership for the activities and are able to express their "expertise." When children feel they have a purposeful role in ending school bullying, they may be less likely to spend their time and energy on hurting others or ignoring those who are hurt. Like adults, children will perform best when they feel encouraged and supported at their "job."

ASSET CHALLENGE

Inform your students that you and the school are committed to helping create a safe and nonviolent place to learn. Let them know you want to find ways to eliminate violence at school. Your students are essential in creating a positive environment. Talk with your students about their role in preventing and reporting bullying and other forms of aggression. Let them know that you will be bringing in lots of activities so that they, too, can learn how to keep themselves and the school safe. Engaging students in this process allows them to feel responsibility for safety in the school as well as for their own behaviors.

Asset 6: Parent involvement in out-of-home situations

Children benefit when their parents are personally involved and aware of what is occurring in school and share their children's interests in hobbies and activities. Often the majority of conversations with parents of children labeled as bullies are in reference to these children's problem behaviors. It is difficult for parents to feel positive about the school and their children's school performance when they receive mostly negative information. In addition, it is possible that parents of aggressive children who themselves experienced difficulty in school do not feel they can help their children succeed in school. It is important for teachers to have regular contact with their students' parents in order to communicate that parent presence and support in school are needed and appreciated.

ASSET CHALLENGE

Take time to call parents whom you have little contact with during the school year. Let them know you want to touch base with them. Inform them of the positive characteristics you see in their child. Give them your telephone number, and encourage them to call you with any questions or concerns. Although many parents, especially single parents, may have limited time to commit to school, invite them to send in a note or call you to voice their opinions on school matters. If calling is difficult, send monthly classroom newsletters to all parents. Inform parents of what you are teaching in your classes, classroom news, and class values. List ideas and events parents can help with in your classroom or school. Continually express how important parents are in their children's education.

Asset Category: Empowerment

Asset 7: Community values children

Children learn to feel respected when they feel valued and they know they are cared for by meaningful adults in their families and the community. Ignoring the needs, behaviors, and communication of children is a form of disempowerment that sends the message that children are not valued. Most often, both children who bully and those who are victimized feel discouraged and devalued. When adults, particularly teachers and parents, ignore children's victimization, it communicates that they do not care. For some children, turning a blind eye may even confirm to them that they deserve the victimization. Paying attention to children and their needs is a way to communicate respect and caring.

Communicate with respect. Children know when they are respected, and, when they feel respected by you, they know that you believe in them and their future. Although it can be difficult at times, watch your tone of voice and avoid joining in common beliefs the class or school may hold about particular children. Specifically, when communicating with victims or bullies, let them know that your efforts are intended to help them feel better about themselves and learn to interact with others more effectively. Let them know that you have observed how they feel good about themselves when they do something proactive, like turning in work on time, doing well on an assignment, or starting a conversation with a peer.

Asset 8: Children are given useful roles

Children thrive when in the home, school, and community they are given age-appropriate and useful roles in which they can use their skills and express their opinions. Children—bullies and victims alike—need to see themselves as worthy and contributing members of the community. Aggressive and victimized children often feel that playing out the roles of bully and victim is the only means of getting the attention they need. Allowing children to adopt meaningful roles gives them the chance to obtain positive attention in a positive way.

Assign rotating roles to students in your classroom. These roles should be valuable to the classroom, and children should get positive feedback for their participation. Also encourage students to participate in community activities—for example, helping out at their church, joining the scouts, or participating in an extracurricular activity at school. These activities provide children the opportunity to build relationships and learn new skills both inside and outside of the school environment.

Asset 9: Service to others

Children are empowered in many ways. One way for them to feel empowered is to engage in activities that help them feel they are helping others within their schools, families, and communities. Helping others is beneficial and can foster altruism. Children can also derive great pride when they are of service to others.

Discuss the importance of doing things for the school and community. Talk with your students about why it is important to help others, and express pride in your students for thinking of the community. Your class can volunteer to help tutor younger students, keep the school playground clean, or visit a nursing home or children's hospital. Encourage students and families to get involved in their schools, neighborhoods, communities, or churches. For example, families can do a walk-a-thon for a charitable cause, work in a soup kitchen, collect food for donation, plant a tree, and so forth.

Asset 10: Safety

Safety is a basic need of all individuals. Children learn and function best when they are safe at home, at school, and in the neighborhood. When children live in fear or experience trauma, their primary focus is on finding safety. Developing positive learning skills and being open to positive relationships can be a priority only when children are feeling safe and can attend to learning.

ASSET CHALLENGE

You can foster students' success by helping to create an environment that reflects concern for the safety of children. Create a "Safe Room" sign, and put one on the outside of your classroom door and one at the front of your classroom. Let students know that you expect your classroom to be bully-free and that you will intervene when you see bullying behaviors. Ask to have the fact that your classroom is a "Safe Room" included in the morning announcements. Tell your students to spread the word to their classmates and children in other grades that if they need help with bullying or violence, they can come to you for support.

Asset Category: Boundaries and Expectations

Asset 11: Family boundaries

Children need clear rules, consistency, and boundaries at home to function successfully. They need to know their parents care for them, and parents show their caring by attending to their children, by putting forth the time and effort to create rules, and by consistently following up with appropriate consequences when those rules are broken. Children can become responsible for their own actions by learning the connection between behavior and consequences.

ASSET CHALLENGE

Encourage your PTA to organize programs on effective parenting and healthy homes. Invite community counselors or psychologists into the school to discuss child development, effective discipline, and parenting for children's school success. These presentations can be organized in conjunction with parent-teacher conferences. For parents who do not attend, send home any printed materials provided during the presentations.

Asset 12: Out-of-home boundaries

Children need consistent rules and consequences in school and other out-of-home environments. Rules and consequences for breaking them must be clearly defined. Children typically perform well when rules and consequences exist within a known structure. Consistency in rules and consequences between home and school helps children learn and attend to rules across these environments.

ASSET CHALLENGE

Work with your students to create classroom rules, then post these prominently in the classroom. Help students understand that you will be on the watch for people who are following these rules and will try to praise these students (i.e., "Catch them being good"). Also inform students that you will consistently follow up with those who break the rules. Apply all consequences fairly. Communication of rules and expectations to after-school program staff and others who work with children out of school is also helpful.

Asset 13: Neighborhood boundaries

"It takes a whole village to raise a child" is an aphorism commonly heard in American society. It implies that entire communities, not just families, must be concerned about the well-being of children. Together, communities can work to keep children safe, serve as additional sources of support, and help monitor children's behaviors. In today's world, many people do not want to get involved with matters of discipline or values concerning children other than their own. Many homes function independently, without interconnections and interactions among neighbors. However, it is an asset when neighbors do take responsibility for monitoring children's behavior.

ASSET CHALLENGE

Talk with your students about their neighborhoods. What is it like in their neighborhood? Whom do they talk to? Do they feel safe? Are their parents friends with neighbors? Does extended family live near by? This discussion will help you to understand the world your students live in when they leave the school grounds. Children should have someone nearby to go to in emergencies (in addition to knowing they should call 911 or another emergency number). Encourage students to identify someone, then have students talk with their parents to approve the choice (you may even ask parents to send you a note to that effect). Parents can then let the neighbor selected know that they have chosen him or her to be the person to go to in emergencies.

Asset 14: Adult role models

Parent-child interactions are the primary context in which children learn what behaviors are and are not acceptable. When parents and other adults model positive, responsible behaviors, these are the behaviors children learn. However, some parents may discipline their children harshly or even counsel their children, particularly boys, to be "strong" and "tough." Children learn from the adults around them how to handle conflict. Some may learn peaceful ways to resolve conflict, whereas others may learn to handle conflict through fighting, mean words, and demeaning others.

ASSET CHALLENGE

Write a letter to each of your students' parents. In the letter, inform parents that you are implementing an antibullying policy in your classroom to help make your school a safe, nonviolent environment. The purpose of your letter is to let parents know your expectations for children and to ask parents to convey the message that they expect their children to act appropriately and nonviolently at school. Inform parents that you are going to be strict and consistent about enforcing this policy in your classroom. Invite parents to join you in supporting this policy.

Asset 15: Positive peer interaction and influence

It is important for children to interact with other children who model responsible behavior and to have opportunities to play in safe, well-supervised settings. Children who are valued members of a peer group are less likely to be victimized. There is safety in numbers within the support system of the peer group. Children who are victimized are often isolated or excluded from others and therefore do not experience the encouragement of their peers. Because they have not benefited from peer-group experiences, they may not have learned the social skills necessary to interact with other children in an appropriate way. However, children can learn how to become members of a peer group and gain the skills and support they need to prevent them from being targeted by bullies.

ASSET CHALLENGE

Form buddy pairs. Attempt to pair the most socially competent students with classmates who are less social, unpopular, or quiet. Each week, have "buddy time," in which buddies can engage in an activity together—for example, playing a game, eating lunch, or talking about a special topic (e.g., favorite movies, what they like to do for fun, what they do after school). Each child should ask questions, listen to the other's response, and then give a response in return. The exchange helps both children form a relationship and practice the social skills needed in peer groups. After having students work in buddy pairs several times, have the children try switching roles. Have the child who is usually prosocial switch roles with the quieter or less socially competent student. Have the less socially competent child ask the other child questions, use eye contact, and smile. Ask the second child to respond in a positive way. This exercise gives children a chance to try on different behaviors; afterwards, the pair can talk about what it is like to be in the other person's shoes.

Asset 16: Appropriate expectations for growth

Children benefit if parents, caregivers, and other adults have realistic expectations for children's development at this age. Realistic expectations may be difficult if a child looks much older or younger than his or her chronological age or when a child's development is compared with that of siblings. Expecting too much can lead to the child's experience of frustration, whereas expecting too little can lead to a child's experience of helplessness and dependence. In both situations, children tend to display behaviors that interfere with their learning and the learning of other children in the classroom. When children feel frustrated or helpless, they are more likely to become irritable, angry, or tearful. At either extreme, the child is more likely to become involved in the bully-victim interaction, as either bully or victim. Understanding children's developmental abilities and holding appropriate expectations is important in fostering academic, cognitive, and social success.

Send a letter home to parents describing the developmental expectations of children in your grade. What are your expectations for children's schoolwork, level of autonomy, behavior, and social skills? During parent-teacher meetings, you can discuss where each child is in comparison with expectations for the grade level. Encourage further evaluation or psychological testing for children who fall below expectations.

Asset Category: Constructive Use of Time

Asset 17: Creative activities

When you are actively engaged in a task or hobby, you become focused on the activity and derive feelings of pleasure. However, if you are left to yourself for long periods of time with nothing to fill the void, it is likely that you will feel isolated, excluded, and sad. It is valuable for children to participate in music, art, drama, or other creative activities for at least 3 hours a week at home or elsewhere. Even more important is to introduce children to their own creative abilities and engage them in activities in which they can use various skills, expand their imagination, and express their talents.

ASSET CHALLENGE

Use multiple modes of teaching, and include music, art, and drama in the classroom. This exposure gives children a chance to feel successful in various domains and offers positive outlets for children who do not feel successful in traditional academic areas. Arts programs are often the first to be cut when there is a shortage of school funding. However, local community centers and park districts frequently offer art and music programs, as well as arts-based summer camps. Obtain brochures to send home to help children and families increase their knowledge of available programs.

Asset 18: Out-of-home activities

It is valuable for children to spend an hour or more a week in extracurricular school activities or structured community programs. Children learn norms for behavior from those around them. In some homes and communities, violence may be accepted. Exposing children to out-of-home activities (e.g., after-school programs, scouts) can be beneficial when these activities are structured, safe, and well supervised. In these contexts, children can learn positive ways of interacting with peers and adults.

ASSET CHALLENGE

As you identify potential bullies in your classroom, think of what their typical days are like. Who helps them get ready in the morning? Who spends time with them in the afternoon? What are their home environments like? Often children who bully do not have many financial resources. Can you talk to your school counselor and explore after-school activities these children could participate in? Could they be in athletics, a school organization, music, or tutoring? The goal is to increase the time potential bullies have in structured and prosocial interactions while decreasing the time they spend unsupervised, unstructured, and possibly exposed to the aggression of older peers or family.

Asset 19: Religious community

Research has suggested that children fare best when they are engaged in at least an hour a week in a religious program. Religious communities often provide instruction in the moral guidelines and values adhered to by the family and church community. Religious communities also provide an additional network of support and a strong connection to other children and adults who can serve as role models. Many religious communities also provide safe, well-structured social outlets for children.

ASSET CHALLENGE

Public schools today are not permitted to discuss or promote religious activities. However, religious beliefs frequently play a large role in children's overall belief system and understanding of right and wrong. In addition, many churches promote social cohesion, inasmuch as they are linked closely with their congregation's race or ethnicity. Becoming aware of your students' religious beliefs by listening to their discussions and being attuned to their experiences is important in that it provides additional insight into their attitudes and behaviors.

Asset 20: Positive, supervised time at home

Children need time at home in a safe, supervised setting. Children benefit when they spend most evenings and weekends at home with their parents in predictable, enjoyable routines. Often children are engaged in many extracurricular activities (or they may spend time in the streets with peers). Although structured extracurricular activities can be good, "downtime"—when children can relax, engage with family members, and enjoy hobbies—is invaluable. Family connections become increasingly more important as children mature and peers become more influential.

ASSET CHALLENGE

Parents who engage their children in multiple activities are attempting to ensure their children's healthy development and may not know the importance of quiet family time. Send a letter home to encourage parents to save time to spend with their children. In the letter you might suggest activities families commonly enjoy at home together as a family, such as preparing meals, taking walks in the neighborhood, playing games, or reading books.

Internal Assets

Asset Category: Commitment to Learning

Asset 21: Achievement expectation and motivation

When children are motivated to do well in school and other activities, they tend to do well. Believe in your students, their ability to overcome obstacles, and their ability to achieve. By sharing your expectations with your students, you help them set goals for themselves. Students who are believed to be hopeless, academically or behaviorally, will learn to become failures. Expect that your students will make the most of their classes, grow up to achieve their dreams, and respect one another along the way.

ASSET CHALLENGE

All teachers have general expectations for their students. However, consider what you hope and expect for each student. How can you help the student achieve this goal? Keep a journal on the students in your class. Make brief notes on what you hope for and expect each to achieve, academically and socially, by the end of the year. Take time to share your expectations with students individually, and let them know you are committed to helping them. Make sure to be realistic: Goals too high can be discouraging, whereas goals too low reflect a lack of confidence in children's abilities.

Asset 22: Children are engaged in learning

Engagement in learning occurs when children are actively involved in the learning process. Although school prepares children in many ways, the primary focus is on academic learning. Although some children will be easily engaged and find learning an easy task, others will be truly challenged. These children will be more difficult to get and keep involved. Students are more likely to engage in negative behaviors such as bullying or irritating peers when they are bored or frustrated. Creative use of a range of teaching methods can help to engage all children and decrease behavioral problems in the classroom.

ASSET CHALLENGE

Consider the various means by which children learn: physical experience, music, art, computers, games, and so on. Teachers do a wonderful job of finding creative ways to communicate new information to children. Pay attention to children who are at risk for poor academic performance, and refer them for testing and special placement, if appropriate. Take into account learning differences and disabilities when you teach. Also make sure children who need it are receiving tutoring or extra time with you or older students to help them master content and remain excited about learning. Encourage children to use what they have learned in the classroom outside of class by inviting them to look for examples of what they have learned, talk with family members about topics at school, and use their skills and knowledge throughout the day. If learning is fun, children will remain responsive, attentive, and actively engaged.

Asset 23: Stimulating activity and homework

When parents and teachers encourage children to explore and engage in stimulating activities, and children do homework when it is assigned, children feel more competent at school, and their motivation to complete future work increases. All children want to feel competent, and they select different roles at school to feel successful. Some children will naturally be engaged in school and identify themselves as "smart" and "good students." These children love to do well and receive rewards for doing well. Other children may not feel successful at school or with their schoolwork and activities. To compensate for their school problems—which they may perceive as failures—these children are likely to take on other roles to experience success. Aggressive bullies and provocative victims frequently occupy these roles because they bring power and attention, respectively.

ASSET CHALLENGE

Provide study time when students can work in small groups on academic tasks assigned as homework and can ask you for help when needed. Some children have very hectic home lives, in which homework is not valued, whereas other children have overindulgent parents who complete homework for them. Providing help at school while encouraging autonomy outside of school can be beneficial.

Asset 24: Enjoyment of learning and bonding to school

It is important for children to enjoy learning and care about their school. Children are great observers of their environments. They watch other children and adults, and learn from them. They also have interesting ideas, opinions, and experiences regarding bullying and school safety. Children will feel valued when their thoughts and experiences are validated and respected. When children feel valued and respected, and when they observe caring adults working to help them grow, they are more likely to feel a sense of belonging, take personal responsibility for what happens in the school, and work to fit in.

ASSET CHALLENGE

Talk with your class about bullying. Do they think bullying is a problem? Do they feel safe at school? What do they or would they do if they were bullied? How would they like their school to be? Let them know that you value their ideas and will share them with other teachers, counselors, or the principal. You can also create a suggestion/reporting box in your classroom. Inform students that if they have any concerns about bullying they can write a short note and put it in the suggestion box. Let them know you will check the box regularly and get back to them about their concerns.

Asset 25: Reading for pleasure

Healthy development is promoted when children and an adult read together for at least 30 minutes a day and when children are encouraged to enjoy reading or looking at books or magazines. Reading for pleasure offers children a great deal, including characters to relate to, solutions to tough problems, and an escape into imagination, not to mention enhanced reading and comprehension skills.

ASSET CHALLENGE

Create book challenges in your classroom, and allow children to select their own books to read. Offer a selection of books, recommended by your school librarian, that address issues related to bullying, fitting in, making friends, and dealing with learning disabilities. Encourage children to read their book selections when they complete their assigned work and during quiet time. Invite parents to read with their children at home and to visit the public library. Allow time for your students to share books they are reading with the class, telling about the story and what they think of it.

Asset Category: Positive Values

Asset 26: Caring

Most children have the capacity to offer love and enjoy being useful to others. Their behaviors are more likely to be helpful than harmful. Caring for others and bullying are contradictory behaviors. As your students come to understand the importance of caring for others and learn the skills they need to express their feelings, they will spend less time and energy invested in bullying interactions. Children who engage in aggressive behaviors like bullying may be accustomed to protecting and defending themselves, not recognizing their abilities to care for others or comprehending that caring for others is a positive way to get attention.

ASSET CHALLENGE

Discuss with students how people show they care for one another—for example, listening to what others have to say, sharing toys and treats, doing nice things for others, and helping others out when they have difficulties. In particular, invite students whom you know to be bullies or victims to participate in the discussion.

Asset 27: Equality and social justice

Young children typically view the world in terms of right and wrong or good and bad. In other words, they have a black-and-white view of moral justice. As they mature, they begin to understand that there are gray areas in life and to develop greater moral reasoning abilities. They are able to conceptualize equality and justice, and often begin to show interest in making the community a better place.

ASSET CHALLENGE

Talk with your class about fairness in their homes, school, and community. You can also introduce books about social issues to your class. Ask your school librarian to recommend books about historical figures, discrimination, and individual differences, and use these books to promote discussion about equality and social justice. Possible discussion questions include the following: Why is it important for situations in school to be fair? How do you feel when situations are unfair for you or those around you? What have you experienced in school that you feel has been unjust? and What would you want to change? You can also help your students think about other children in the world and how they are treated. What rights do they feel all children have? Often even very young children can be quite compassionate.

Asset 28: Integrity

Integrity is the ability to act on one's convictions and stand up for one's beliefs. It is valuable for children to begin to express integrity, to be true to what they believe is right despite conflicting messages and environmental stressors. When children believe that they have a right to be respected and a responsibility to respect others, they will not engage in behaviors that hurt themselves or others. They will act instead in ways congruent with their belief system. Encouraging children (especially bystander victims) to stand up for their beliefs can empower them to make a stand against bullying in the school.

ASSET CHALLENGE

Help your students identify what is important to them and what they believe. Talk with them about their rights and responsibilities and the importance of standing up for these principles. With students, brainstorm a list of rights and responsibilities, then post the list prominently. Read over the list each morning before class begins, as a reminder. Give your students permission to assert their rights and ask for help if their or others' rights are being violated. In particular, focus discussion on how children expect and need to be treated in school.

Asset 29: Honesty

Telling the truth in tough situations is difficult for children, especially if there are negative consequences for their honesty. However, it is important for children to begin to value honesty and act accordingly. Honesty is at the root of personal responsibility, trust, and healthy interpersonal relationships. Instilling the value of honesty helps children take personal responsibility for feelings and behaviors, and is at the foundation of their ability to work through, rather than avoid, challenging situations.

ASSET CHALLENGE

Develop a norm of honesty in your classroom. Share with students the negative consequences of being dishonest—for example, getting caught and having a small situation become a big problem or losing the trust of your teachers or parents. Encourage students to develop a sense of pride in being honest, and focus on the good feeling inside of them when they are honest. If you observe students being honest in tough situations, praise them publicly by saying, for example, "I know being honest was hard in this situation—it took a lot of courage!"

Asset 30: Responsibility

It is important for children to begin to accept and take personal responsibility for age-appropriate tasks. Bullies often blame others for their own aggressive actions. They may say things like "It's not my fault—Susan always looks at me funny" or "I didn't do anything wrong. He got what's coming to him." Although bullies may feel provoked, they are still responsible for their actions. As you help children accept and take personal responsibility, they can begin to recognize their own feelings and roles in aggressive interactions.

Bullying is a choice, and children are responsible for the consequences of their decisions. You can help bullies become responsible for their behavior by being honest with them about their actions and by exploring the effects of these actions on themselves and others. Work with bullies to identify provocative situations, describe the ways they choose to respond, and determine what they could do differently. Reflect on how they—and their victims—might have felt different if they had chosen a different response. With your guidance, you can help bullies make better choices.

Asset 31: Healthy lifestyle and sexual attitudes

As children mature, they will need to acquire good health habits and healthy sexual attitudes, as well as express respect for others. Even young children these days are exposed to drugs, alcohol, violence, and sexual activity, in the media if not in real life. Without a strong foundation, many children will give in to peer pressure or use negative means to cope with emotional difficulties. Elementary school is a crucial time for introducing prevention programs to reduce students' risk of participation in dangerous activities. During this time, children can develop a strong foundation and learn skills to deal with the pressures that inevitably lie ahead.

Work with other teachers in your school to conduct schoolwide prevention efforts. For example, older students can create plays for younger students about refusing to be bullied, resisting pressure to behave in a certain way, and avoiding dangerous behaviors. Younger students can make posters and signs advertising the plays to post around the school.

Category: Social Competencies

Asset 32: Planning and decision making

Many children will act first, then think and plan. By learning to plan ahead and by making choices at appropriate developmental levels, children can begin to make better decisions for themselves. Cognitively, young children are focused on the present; however, with guidance they can be encouraged to think about their future needs. Although planning and decision making are skills that children acquire as they mature, creating a strong basis for thinking before acting counteracts impulsivity. In addition, good decision-making skills help children feel more confident.

Consistently provide opportunities for children to use their decision-making skills. Walk them through the decision-making process. For example, before the end of the day, help children decide what they will need to bring home with them. Help them write down what they need in their notebooks or assignment books. When introducing new activities, encourage children to think about what they will need to use before they open their desks for supplies.

Asset 33: Interpersonal skills

We live in a social world. In order to be successful, individuals need to know how to interact effectively with others. Although knowledge and skills are important, these factors alone do not explain an individual's success. It has been noted that interpersonal effectiveness in adulthood, combined with knowledge and skills, is a key factor in an individual's success. For these reasons, it is critical for children to interact with adults and other children, make friends, express and articulate feelings in appropriate ways, and empathize with others.

ASSET CHALLENGE

Emphasize the elements of emotional intelligence in your classroom. The activities in the Bully Busters program can help you do this by encouraging children to understand themselves and how they influence others. Many of the activities provided encourage group and team work. These formats allow for more interpersonal connections as well as provide teachers with opportunities to give feedback on both effective and ineffective interpersonal interactions.

Asset 34: Cultural competence

Understanding and appreciating different cultures, ethnicities, and religious orientations is necessary in building respect and equality among classmates and within the community. It is valuable for children to know about and be comfortable with people of different cultural, racial, and/or ethnic backgrounds. Appreciating differences is a crucial component of children's respect for and understanding of one another. Bullies frequently select victims who are different in some way. Individual differences only fuel the bully-victim interaction to the extent that bullies and other students do not appreciate or accept diversity among their classmates.

ASSET CHALLENGE

There is a plethora of ways to increase understanding of diversity within the classroom. For example, make a point to share stories in your class that include characters of different races or ethnicities, cultures, family composition, and abilities. You might also hold a "culture fair" in your class, where all of your students can share food, clothing, and stories from their families and cultures. Also, when doing group work, create diverse groups according to gender, race or ethnicity, religion, and other differences to foster interaction, dialogue, and relationships among classmates.

Asset 35: Resistance skills

Children benefit when they develop the ability to resist negative peer pressure and dangerous situations. Negative influences include, among others, peer pressure to act out in class, not to do schoolwork, or to join in with school bullies. Children are resisting negative influences all of the time, although they often are recognized for their behavior only when they give in to a negative influence. Bullies exert a negative influence that can convince some children to bully with them and convince other children not to help the victims. Passive victims do not actively seek bullies' attention. However, other children may provoke the bully to get attention. In all of these cases, children are influenced to make certain decisions, sometimes at the risk of their own and others' safety.

ASSET CHALLENGE

If you make *bullying* an everyday word in your class and stress that bullying is unacceptable, children will feel better about coming forward or intervening when bullying occurs. Encourage kids to say, "Stop being a bully" when they see bullying. The bully, observers, and victims in your class will get the message that bullying is wrong and that you will support students when they say no or intervene in a bullying situation. Help your students recognize other negative influences they face as well. Does anyone try to get them to do things they don't want to do? Do they feel they have to do "bad" things so others don't make fun of them? Does anyone bother or interrupt them when they are trying to do their work? When any of these things happen, encourage your students to say, "We don't do that in our school!"

Asset 36: Peaceful conflict resolution

Bullies have a talent for resolving conflicts through violence or skillful manipulation of social situations. Although they are successful in the short term in getting what they want, they have done so in a way that hurts both themselves and the other parties in the conflict. They may feel bad later or experience other negative consequences for causing purposeful harm to another student. Bullies use violence to solve conflicts because that is what they know. All children, bullies included, need to learn to try to resolve conflicts nonviolently.

ASSET CHALLENGE

Engage students in peaceful conflict resolution, as many classroom activities in this manual direct. When you observe a conflict, take time to discuss the problem and brainstorm with the students how they could have handled the situation better. Continual application of the conflict resolution process will help students internalize these steps and begin to use them automatically, both in and out of school.

Category: Positive Identity

Asset 37: Personal power

It is important for children to feel they have control over things that happen to them and to manage frustrations and challenges in ways that have positive results for themselves and others. Sometimes children, especially those who are victimized, feel they are powerless to control what happens to them or to keep themselves safe. These children have good evidence that they do not have personal power or peer support. Feelings of helplessness and powerlessness are associated with depression and may contribute to a downward slide into greater social isolation, lack of peer support, and sadness. These characteristics only make children more attractive to bullies. We want all children to feel a sense of power in their lives, not in the sense of force, but as confidence that they have resources and people they can ask for help when they need it. Victimization is not the victims' fault. Victims can learn ways to use their power to keep themselves safe.

ASSET CHALLENGE

Personal power can be acquired and nurtured within peer relationships, but it is difficult to learn how other children handle situations successfully if you are not a part of a peer group. Encourage students to work in teams at school, where everyone has an equal role as contributor. Mix the groups so that sometimes bullies and victims work together collaboratively. At other times, pair energetic, socially skilled children with quieter and more isolated children. Encourage the more outgoing children to engage the potential victims. The goal is to pull victims into peer groups so they can experience being a part of a team. Open discussion among students about how they handle bullying situations. Encourage the bullies, as well as victims and others, to talk about what victims can do to stop bullying (bullies are typically victims in other situations). Generate a list of what students can do. Examine the list, and talk about which actions would be good for students to take (e.g., tell the teacher) and which would not be good (e.g., beating up the bully). Encourage the children by letting them know that each of them has the power to take these actions, and, although it can be difficult, they will feel good about themselves for taking action. Once again, remind them of your support.

Asset 38: Self-esteem

When children report having high self-esteem, they are able to make good choices for themselves and believe in themselves. When kids are continually picked on or bullied, it is hard for them to feel good about themselves or others. Instead, they often begin to believe the things their peers say about them. When the bullying interaction is ignored, these children are likely to believe that not even the teacher finds them worth caring about. Research suggests that self-esteem is one asset that boys tend to have more of than girls; this is particularly true for white boys and girls (Benson, 1997). Interestingly, there are no significant differences between the self-esteem of African American boys and girls, and their scores are consistently higher on self-esteem than for any other race or ethnicity.

ASSET CHALLENGE

Encourage all students, especially victims, to take minor risks, such as challenging themselves on a homework assignment or joining a new activity. Encourage them in areas in which you believe they will experience success. Be careful not to encourage them in areas in which you believe they will not achieve success; failures will only perpetuate their negative feelings. You can help them to identify their areas of strength by having them write you a letter, telling you about their special characteristics, even those that they don't think anyone notices. If children have difficulty with this exercise, you can spend some time assisting them in forming new interests or identifying strengths. As students try new skills, they will benefit from your support and guidance. It may be necessary for you to help them with each step in trying new tasks.

Asset 39: Sense of purpose

It is important for children to feel that they have a purpose and that they can use their skills and knowledge to achieve their purpose. Children can derive great benefit when they feel they are needed and have important skills to contribute. Many children who exhibit aggressive behaviors have become accustomed to protecting themselves and may not recognize ways they can help others or understand that doing so may bring them positive attention.

ASSET CHALLENGE

Identify potential bullies. Do they possess any special skills? For example, are they organized? Are they good leaders? Are they good at particular academic subjects or good artists? Enlist bullies and potential bullies as your helpers. You could ask them to prepare classroom materials (e.g., photocopying, stapling) or to help you rearrange the classroom, create a new bulletin board, tutor other students, or lead a class activity. As you do things together, talk with these children about their lives and ask them to name other students to help you. Let these children know how they have helped you, praise their work, and encourage them to help others, too.

Asset 40: Positive view of personal future

We want to build hope and optimism in our students. When children are hopeful and positive about their personal future, they tend to do well socially and academically. It is difficult for students, as well as adults, to feel motivated when they do not believe there is anything to work toward. Children who do well academically and are cooperative at school are continually encouraged about their future choices. Bullies often do not do well academically; on the contrary, they may get the majority of their attention in response to their negative behaviors. Our goal is to help bullies recognize that they have the power to make choices to ensure positive options and outcomes.

ASSET CHALLENGE

Tell all children that you believe in them. Take extra time with bullies to ask what they would like to be when they grow up. Do they know people who have this job? Do they want to stay in school? Let them know you expect them to be very successful if they set their minds to it.

MODULE

1 Increasing Awareness of Bullying

OVERVIEW

Children spend the majority of their day in school, and as additional services and supports are provided in the educational setting, they spend more time there. The ideal school environment promotes and supports children academically, socially, and emotionally. In this environment, children and teachers feel safe. As a teacher, you take on many roles, including being a key figure in creating and maintaining this safe community. Beyond sharing academic knowledge, you serve as a supporter, encourager, disciplinarian, advocate, and confidante. You are committed to nourishing students' growth by teaching them new academic skills. You also understand your equally important influence on students' skill development in nonacademic areas—in particular, in developing behaviors that support a safe, peaceful, and nonviolent environment. This module builds on the power of your influence by providing specific activities to increase awareness of bullying.

GOALS

- To consider various definitions of bullying and develop a personal definition of this term

- To understand and apply the "PIC" criteria for bullying

- To learn that behavior exists on a continuum from play to delinquent or criminal behavior

- To identify common bullying locations

- To consider aspects of the teacher's role in the prevention and remediation of bullying

BULLYING IN ELEMENTARY SCHOOLS

The term *bullying* is commonly used in schools and the media these days, although bullying is nothing new to schoolchildren. Bullying has been observed worldwide and throughout recorded time (Hazler, 1996; Ross, 1996). In fact, bullying and victimizing behaviors exist in the elementary school years, become more prevalent through the middle school years, and then decrease somewhat—but do not go away—in high school (Clarke & Kiselica, 1997; Olweus, 1996). Although the elementary school may be the first place children experience bullying, they may have been exposed to bullying in the form of violence in their homes and neighborhoods long before they attend school. Bullying is learned, and children begin their learning in the home. Sometimes they bring aggressive means of interacting with them when they enter school.

Did you know . . .

- The majority of children in school report experiencing bullying at some point during their school years. Seventy percent of students have experienced bullying at some point in their academic career (Hoover, Oliver, & Hazler, 1992).

- In a survey of 1,200 students from 85 schools, 98 percent reported that bullying occurs in their schools. Forty percent reported being bullied, whereas 76 percent said they had witnessed other students being bullied (Schroeder, 2002).

- In the United States, thousands of children refuse to go to school each day because of the fear of being bullied. As many as 160 thousand children miss school each day because of fear (Lee, 1993).

- Childhood bullying can have a severe effect on children's development throughout their school years and into adulthood. In fact, chronic peer abuse has been found to be a risk factor for adolescents' suicidal behavior (Carney, 2000).

- Kids who later will exhibit delinquency and criminal behavior can typically be identified by their teachers in elementary school. Signs of aggressiveness in the elementary school years are linked with later delinquency and antisocial behavior (Slaby, Roedell, Arezzo, & Hendrix, 1995).

DEFINITIONS OF BULLYING

What exactly is bullying? Over the years, researchers have studied the bully-victim interaction and have developed several definitions. Following are some definitions of bullying from the literature:

> A student is bullied or victimized when he or she is exposed, repeatedly and over time, to negative actions on the part of one or more other students. . . . [Bullying] is a negative action when someone intentionally inflicts, or attempts to inflict, injury or discomfort on another. (Olweus, 1994, p. 1173)

> A student is being bullied or picked on when another student says nasty and unpleasant things to him or her.

It is also bullying when a student is hit, kicked, threatened, locked inside a room, sent nasty notes, and when no one ever talks to him/her. These things happen frequently and it is difficult for the student being bullied to defend himself or herself. It is also bullying when a student is teased repeatedly in a nasty way. (Smith & Sharp, 1994, p.1)

Various researchers (Hazler, 1996; Hazler, Hoover, & Oliver, 1992; Ross, 1996) report that bullying includes the following elements:

Harm is intended.

There is an imbalance of power.

There is often organized and systematic abuse.

It is repetitive, occurring over a period of time; or it is a random but serial activity carried out by someone who is feared for this behavior.

Hurtful experiences by a victim of bullying can be external (physical) or internal (psychological).

The PIC Criteria: Purposeful, Imbalanced, and Continual

The formal definitions of bullying just provided are helpful, but it may still be difficult to determine exactly what bullying is and what bullying looks like in action. Many teachers find it difficult to differentiate between bullying and children's rough-and-tumble play, but differences do exist. In our *Bully Busters* book for middle school children, we defined bullying by using the "Double I/R" criteria: *intentional, imbalanced,* and *repeated* (Newman et al., 2000). When explaining bullying to younger students, we usually use the acronym PIC, which stands for *purposeful, imbalanced,* and *continual.* We use the PIC acronym with younger students because they seem to understand this definition better than the "Double I/R" criteria we use with middle school children.

Purposeful

Bullying incidents are not accidental. Rather, the bully purposefully inflicts harm upon the victim. We often see incidents where one child causes harm to another through exuberance. For example, a child who is jumping around the classroom in enthusiasm might bump into and hurt another child. Although the effect of the first child's exuberance on the injured classmate is pain, the same as if it were inflicted intentionally, this behavior is not bullying. Bullying occurs when one student purposefully harms another student or makes another student uncomfortable and does not express remorse.

Rough childhood play is common among children, and, although it can escalate into aggression or bullying, typically it does not. Most children do not want to hurt other children. When children are just playing, they have the mutual ability to stop playing or say that the play is becoming too rough or that they have been hurt. In these cases, the children respond immediately, and the rough play stops. When children are being bullied, they do not have these options; in fact, if they acknowledge that they are hurt, the bullying behavior may escalate.

Imbalanced

Bullying occurs in an interpersonal relationship characterized by an imbalance of power, physical or psychological. The imbalance can be reflected in power, strength, abilities, or influence. For instance, is there more than one bully, is the bully bigger or older, or does he or she have more social status? We sometimes find the example of a seesaw helpful in explaining to younger children the idea that a relationship can be imbalanced: When one child goes up, the other goes down.

Bullies are adept at identifying other students who lack the skills, abilities, or personal characteristics to defend themselves, and they are masters of the abuse of power and the use of coercion. In brief, bullies know their victims have less power and are unable to stop the bullying behaviors.

Continual

Bullying is not a one-time incident. Bullying interactions are carried out continually, over time. Although single acts of aggression need our attention, most students who experience an occasional unpleasant or even aggressive act in school are able to handle such incidents. It is when such incidents become continual that bullying is taking place and teachers must step in. Telling younger students that bullying happens more than once, a lot, or regularly helps them identify bullying behaviors.

BULLY BUSTERS SUPPORT TEAM THINK BLOCK

With your team, discuss the following:

1. What is your personal definition of bullying? Create a definition of bullying that applies to your school. How does your definition compare with the definitions in the bully-victim literature?

2. How does your school currently address bullying? Does this approach work? How are bullies and victims approached? Brainstorm ways your school could uniformly address bullying.

3. Has your school issued a policy demanding nonviolence? Does everyone—including teachers, substitute teachers, parents, and students—know and agree that violence is unacceptable in your school, and are they committed to intervening?

Is It Bullying?

Apply the PIC criteria to each of the following scenarios to determine whether or not bullying is taking place.

Tisha, a second grader, comes home from school in tears every day. Each day on her way to and from school, Miranda, a fifth grader, shouts names at her. Tisha always tries to sit in the front of the bus and keep her head down, but Miranda gets other kids to join her in the name-calling.

Will shows up in the nurse's office several times a week right before lunch and always before gym class. He usually complains of stomachaches or headaches and asks to lie down for a while. The classroom teacher overhears one student telling another student how two boys in gym class continually try to steal Will's pants and make fun of him as he tries to get them back. These boys also have the same lunch period as Will.

You observe that several of the students in your class disregard Sheila, but you are not sure why. Sheila always seems so sad, and frequently she is absent from school. One day when Sheila is absent, you catch Sam putting a handful of dirt and rocks in Sheila's desk. When you question Sam, he says, "What's the big deal? Nobody likes her, and a few of us always keep on her!" "What do you mean?" you ask Sam. "Well, for instance, Mia and Cara try to pull Sheila's ribbons out of her hair every day, and sometimes they even get her lunch!"

○○○✲○○○

All of these scenarios represent bullying situations. In each case, the behavior is done purposefully, reflects an imbalance of power (at least two bullies are picking on the victim or the bully is older or of higher status), and has occurred continually (more than once).

BULLY BUSTERS SUPPORT TEAM THINK BLOCK

To help you understand the differences between bullying and rough play, work with your team to assess behaviors you have witnessed in your classrooms and on your school grounds. As each team member shares an incident, discuss how the situation did or did not meet the PIC criteria for bullying:

P: Was the behavior purposeful, to inflict harm on another?

I: Was there an imbalance of power between the students, such that one could be defined as a bully and the other a victim?

C: Was the behavior continual? That is, did it happen more than once?

A Continuum of Behavior

The active behaviors students engage in can be placed on a continuum ranging from play to criminal activity. As Table 3 shows, bullying takes a number of forms:

- *Physical bullying:* Bullies physically harm a victim. This type of bullying is action oriented and includes any type of behavior that intentionally inflicts bodily harm (e.g., hitting, pushing, punching, kicking).

- *Emotional bullying:* Bullies emotionally harm a victim. This type of bullying is word or verbally oriented and includes using words to humiliate or hurt the victim (e.g., name-calling, teasing, racial slurs, insults).

- *Relational bullying:* Bullies attempt to harm the relationships of the victims. This type of bullying is peer oriented and includes peer exclusion and rejection through rumors, lies, embarrassment, and manipulation. This type of bullying is closely associated with emotional bullying and occurs most frequently among girls.

- *Bystander victimization:* Bullies indirectly harm innocent bystanders. This type of bullying is bystander oriented. These students watch the bullying occur but do not feel they have the power to confront the bully or fear that they may be the bully's next target.

For you to intervene appropriately and effectively, it is important to understand where on the continuum a particular behavior falls. We know from experience that if a bully is allowed to get away with small acts of aggression, misbehavior will escalate. The key to intervening successfully is to gain awareness into what behaviors are bullying behaviors.

Most children kid around with one another, call one another names, and take part in physical horseplay. Distinguishing bullying from typical childhood play is crucial for teachers. The difference often lies in the relationship between the bully and victim, and in the intent of the interaction. In addition to the PIC criteria, some helpful hints to differentiate between play and bullying include the following:

- In play, children usually do not use their full physical strength, whereas those who bully often do use their full strength.

- In play, children often regroup after they play, whereas they part ways following bullying.

- In play, children often choose their roles and engage in role reversals (e.g., good guy–bad guy), whereas in bullying roles often remain stable (i.e., victim and bully).

When you observe student interactions in which one child is always the focus of attention, in which students do not regroup after the activity, or in which one or more children use their full strength, the situa-

TABLE 3 Continuum of Behavior

Play	Bullying	Delinquent or criminal behavior
Rough-and-tumble play	*Physical bullying:* Bullies physically harm a victim.	Use of weapons
Joking		Major physical harm
Sports activities	*Emotional bullying:* Bullies cause emotional harm.	Serious threats
Playful teasing	*Relational bullying:* Bullies attempt to harm the relationships of victims.	Sexual abuse
		Theft
		Property damage
	Bystander victimization: Bullies harm these victims indirectly.	
Managed by classroom discipline, character education programs, and/or teacher support groups.	Addressed as bullying problems through the interventions of teacher support groups, administrative support, class and/or school bully reduction programs.	Managed by administrators or community personnel such as police, juvenile courts, and/or other authorities.

tion is more likely bullying than rough-and-tumble play. Another element differentiating bullying and play is the voluntary nature of the process: Victims of bullying do not voluntarily participate in activities in which there is an imbalance of power.

COMMON BULLYING LOCATIONS

It is often presumed that bullying is more likely to occur to and from school than at school. Although it is true that bullying often does occur away from the school, especially on the school bus, this situation is less common than bullying within the school setting. A major predictor of where bullying occurs is unsupervised and unmonitored time, and many bullies have such periods of time at school. Because victims are more accessible within the school setting, bullies often engage in considerably more aggression at school than in other places. Within the school environment, common locations for bullying include hallways, classrooms, rest rooms, playgrounds, cafeterias, locker rooms, and bus loading zones.

A useful activity for identifying places bullying is occurring in your school is to obtain a map of your school and use thumbtacks of three different colors to designate areas where victims have been bullied, areas where students have witnessed bullying, and areas where students feel safe.

If you are aware that bullying exists, then you have the ability to help change the situation. Victims and bullies alike need their teachers' support and guidance. However, many teachers have told us that they are uncertain about their role in addressing bullying dilemmas. Beliefs that commonly maintain bullying, some questions teachers frequently ask us about bullying, and some general learning goals for teachers are next described.

Teacher Beliefs That Maintain Bullying

A difficulty teachers sometimes have when trying to reduce bullying is holding beliefs that are not supportive of change. If they regard bullying as simply child's play or fear that intervening will make the victim's situation worse, it is doubtful that they will feel it is appropriate to intervene.

Because we are likely to behave in a way that is consistent with our beliefs, it is necessary to challenge beliefs that are not helpful. As a teacher, your heightened awareness of bullying in your classroom will improve your ability to change the situation. Having knowledge of beliefs that maintain the status quo also can help you establish your role as an active change agent. Following are some common erroneous beliefs.

Bullying is just a normal part of childhood
In fact, bullying is aggression against one or more other children and is normal only in the sense that most children behave aggressively until they are socialized to respect others, treat others kindly, and realize that hurting others is inappropriate.

Children outgrow bullying
Actually, the evidence is clear that unless attention is paid to the problem, there is little likelihood that children will outgrow bullying. Unless action is taken by adults or influential peers, bullying continues and in many cases escalates into violence, delinquency, or criminal behavior.

Some children are just born rough
Some children are more active, and some are more aggressive, but bullying behavior is learned and maintained in the social situation (school, classroom, neighborhood) and can be stopped there as well.

Teachers cannot intervene in bullying situations because they lack adequate training and skills
Although it is true that teachers may lack training and skills, they can take action to develop these skills through programs like Bully Busters and can address the problem rather than ignore it.

It is pointless for teachers to intervene because they can't change the way bullies are treated at home, where they learn to be aggressive

Although children may learn to react aggressively at home or in their neighborhoods, they can also learn to be nonaggressive in school. Aggression is an adaptive way of dealing with a rough environment. When children form meaningful bonds within the school community and perceive the school environment to be supportive, they are less likely to respond aggressively.

Frustrations at school cause bullies to behave aggressively

School problems are common in children who bully or are otherwise aggressive because they are less likely to attend to school matters, pay attention in class, and spend time on their schoolwork. Bullies do frequently experience school difficulties and frustrations. However, school difficulties typically follow the aggressive behavior, not precede it. School is just one of many contexts that can influence the development of bullying behaviors.

Intervening will only result in continued or increased bullying

In fact, the opposite is more accurate; the more bullying is ignored, the more likely it is to occur.

It is best to ignore bullying incidents

This position sends the message to bullies that they can continue to do as they have and a message to victims that they are on their own and vulnerable to bullying, therefore confirming students' beliefs that their teachers are unaware of or insensitive to the problem.

It is OK to intervene only once in a while

As with other situations, when bullies learn they can usually get away with their behavior, they tend to continue or even accelerate their efforts.

Commonly Asked Questions about Bullying

In becoming aware of issues relating to bullying, teachers often ask us questions like these.

What if you do not see the bullying incident but have a hunch that bullying may be occurring?

The relationship teachers form with their students is very powerful. Usually, your students will want to have a trusting relationship with you. If you are concerned that a student is being victimized, take the time to nourish your relationship with that student, and provide a safe place for him or her to disclose the bullying.

Should I look for any signs to indicate bullying may be occurring?

Like Will in the scenario described earlier, many children experience secondary symptoms of victimization. Secondary symptoms include physical complaints; absenteeism; active avoidance of particular school activities; and emotional reactions such as sadness, depression, or anxiety.

How does bullying differ from typical childhood play?

During childhood play, there is not a purposeful intention to harm another student. At times, a child may be harmed physically or emotionally, but this harm comes accidentally. If that same child is "accidentally" harmed several times by another child, you will want to explore the situation to determine if it is in fact bullying.

What if I don't see the bullying incident?

Some bullies are adept at secretive mischief and act aggressively only when others are not around. Look for the signs of aggression (e.g., a child has an injury or avoids places like rest rooms), and pay attention to requests for help.

General Goals for Teachers

Children look to teachers for support and encouragement, and teachers have the power to make significant differences in children's lives. As you proceed through the remaining modules in this manual, work to achieve the following:

- Increase your knowledge and skills by reading the material in this manual and other sources, and believe in your ability to use the skills you acquire to intervene in and prevent classroom bullying.

- Recognize that if you cannot effectively intervene, you can remove yourself from the situation long enough to review it and consult with other members of your Bully Busters Support Team. If necessary, you can help students seek assistance from other school personnel (e.g., school counselor, principal, other teachers).

- Let students know you are aware of bullying incidents by introducing the topics of bullying and victimization. Integrate activities like the ones described in this manual into your curriculum to enhance your students' awareness and understanding of bullying.

- Serve as a change agent. Monitoring and altering your own behavior can facilitate positive changes in your students' behavior. Monitoring your students' behavior will help you become more aware of bullying incidents, thus allowing you to intervene and facilitate change.

- Recognize the different forms of bullying and victimization, as well as the differences between male and female bullies. Work to identify every instance of bullying (even minor incidents).

- Learn prevention strategies specifically related to the problem of bullying and victimization, and integrate prevention activities into the curriculum.

- Establish an open-door policy to encourage students to feel safe seeking out and speaking with those in authority.

- Master the skills necessary to intervene in bullying situations—for assisting bullies, victims, and bystanders.

- Seek out other resources to help prevent and reduce bullying: Attend bullying prevention workshops and seminars, join teacher support groups, participate in group problem solving, and access Internet sites on the topic.

- Believe that with the knowledge and skills to prevent and intervene in classroom bullying, you can make a difference in your students' lives.

Module 1: Content Review

The following statements relate to the learning goals of this module. Ask yourself if you feel confident that you can answer yes to each item. If not, please review the material and discuss any difficulties among your Bully Busters Support Team.

1. I understand definitions of bullying and have a clear idea of my own personal definition of this term.

   Yes ❑ No ❑

2. I recognize the "PIC" (purposeful, imbalanced, continual) criteria for bullying and can evaluate situations on the basis of it.

   Yes ❑ No ❑

3. I am aware that behavior exists on a continuum from play to delinquent or criminal behavior.

   Yes ❑ No ❑

4. I can name some common bullying locations.

   Yes ❑ No ❑

5. I have considered the role of teachers in preventing and intervening in bullying situations.

   Yes ❑ No ❑

6. I have challenged teacher beliefs that maintain bullying and understand general goals toward which to work.

   Yes ❑ No ❑

Bully Busters: A Teacher's Manual for Helping Bullies, Victims, and Bystanders (Grades K–5)
© 2003 by Arthur M. Horne, Christi L. Bartolomucci, and Dawn Newman-Carlson.
Champaign, IL: Research Press. (800) 519–2707.

A Reminder . . .

CLASSROOM INTERACTION AND AWARENESS CHART

Use the CIAC to describe any bullying behavior you observe (and that students report to you, if you wish). A copy of the CIAC and a weekly summary sheet appear in Appendix A.

THE BIG QUESTIONS

Honestly appraise your progress by asking yourself the Big Questions. There are no right or wrong answers.

In relation to increasing awareness of bullying in my school:

1. What is my goal?

2. What am I doing?

3. Is what I am doing helping me achieve my goal?

4. *(If not)* What can I do differently?

PERSONAL GOALS FORM

The Personal Goals Form, on the next page, is designed to help you tailor the content of this module to your own students and situation. Please take a moment to fill out the form now.

Module 1: Personal Goals Form

Goals

- To consider various definitions of bullying and develop a personal definition of this term

- To understand and apply the "PIC" criteria for bullying

- To learn that behavior exists on a continuum from play to delinquent or criminal behavior

- To identify common bullying locations

- To consider aspects of the teacher's role in the prevention and remediation of bullying

1. My personal definition of bullying is as follows:

2. I have observed incidents of bullying. *(Please record incidents on the CIAC.)*

    ____ Number of times I intervened   ____ Number of times I chose not to intervene

    Other observations:

3. I will review the classroom activities for this module and select ones appropriate for my class. *(Please list.)*

4. I will accept the challenges associated with the developmental assets discussed in chapter 2. *(Please list the specific assets and describe what you plan to do.)*

5. I will give my students feedback about the bullying incidents I have observed and encourage discussion of bullying and related issues. We will discuss these topics:

6. I will share my experiences in applying the information in this module with other teachers and administrators, as well as with my students' families. *(Please specify who and when.)*

7. I plan to meet with my Bully Busters Support Team. *(Please specify when and list what issues and questions you will raise.)*

Bully Busters: A Teacher's Manual for Helping Bullies, Victims, and Bystanders (Grades K–5)
© 2003 by Arthur M. Horne, Christi L. Bartolomucci, and Dawn Newman-Carlson.
Champaign, IL: Research Press. (800) 519–2707.

Classroom Activities

ACTIVITY 1.1: WHAT A FEELING (GRADES K–5)

This activity familiarizes children with feeling words associated with different facial expressions, allows them to become more aware of their own emotions, and encourages them to imagine the feelings of children who bully and children victimized by bullies. It includes two versions of the Feelings Chart, one appropriate for grades K–2 and the other appropriate for grades 3–5.

ACTIVITY 1.2: STORY TIME (GRADES K–5)

Children's literature is useful in developing students' awareness of bullying and in giving them the opportunity to consider issues involved in bullying. This activity suggests a structure for using literature in this way and provides a bibliography of children's books from which to choose.

ACTIVITY 1.3: THAT'S GARBAGE (GRADES K–5)

This activity helps students understand the power of mean words, recognize when they say mean words, and learn how to make more appropriate comments to peers. Students color and/or write down mean words on a drawing of a garbage can, then symbolically throw their mean words away in a real trash can.

ACTIVITY 1.4: WANTED: REWARD GIVEN! (GRADES 3–5)

In this activity, students draw what they think a bully looks like. Group discussion of their drawings helps them clarify what bullying is, allows them to share their observations about bullies, and encourages a common understanding of what constitutes bullying behavior.

What a Feeling

OBJECTIVES

- To increase students' ability to recognize feelings and increase their feeling-word vocabulary

- To help students identify feelings associated with bullying and victimization

- To help students understand that bullying causes all children to feel bad

MATERIALS

- Copies of the Feelings Chart appropriate for your grade level (Grades K–2 or 3–5)

- Three different-colored crayons, markers, or pencils for each student

- Chalkboard or easel pad

DIRECTIONS

1. Introduce the lesson by explaining that today you will be talking about feelings, particularly the feelings of bullies and victims.

2. Distribute the Feelings Chart, one per student. Explain the purpose of these charts by saying something like this:

   This chart has been created to help you understand different types of feelings. We are going to talk today about the feelings you often experience. We are also going to talk about how we think bullies may feel when they bully and how victims may feel when they are bullied. Our goal is to begin to identify different types of feelings that we all feel at times and to better understand the feelings of bullies and victims.

3. Distribute crayons, markers, or colored pencils, instructing each student to take three different colors.

4. Have students pick a color to represent the feelings they think bullies experience when they are bullying others and then color in the circle labeled "Bully's feelings" on the chart. Instruct students to pick a different color to represent feelings they believe students who are victimized commonly feel. Ask students to color in the circle labeled "Victim's feelings."

5. Instruct students to take the color representing bully feelings and, on the chart, circle feelings that they think bullies may have. Inform them that there are no right or wrong answers.

6. Then instruct students to take the color for victim feelings and circle the feelings they believe victims may experience.

7. On the chalkboard or easel pad, title two columns "Bully's feelings" and "Victim's feelings." Ask the students to share the feelings they circled as being commonly experienced by bullies and those they circled as being commonly experienced by victims. Write the responses as students generate them.

8. Process the differences and similarities in the feelings circled by asking the discussion questions. As you discuss, summarize the feelings identified for the two groups. Explain that, although at times we all experience these negative feelings, bullies and victims are more often likely to experience these negative feelings.

9. Explain that the class is going to work more on recognizing feelings and learning how feelings and actions affect other people's feelings and actions. Share with students that the goal is to help bullies and victims feel better about themselves.

10. Ask students to keep their Feelings Chart handy—in a notebook, an assignment book, or their desks—to help them become more familiar with feeling words.

DISCUSSION QUESTIONS

- Do you think the lists of feelings we made describe bullies and victims well? Are there any other feeling words you would like to add to each list?

- Do you notice any differences in the way bullies and victims feel?

- Are there similarities in how bullies and victims feel? Why or why not?

- Do you think bullies or victims are satisfied with the way they are feeling?

- How do you think bullies and victims can change the way they are feeling?

- When you see someone being bullied, which of these feeling words describes how you feel?

Feelings Chart: Grades K–2

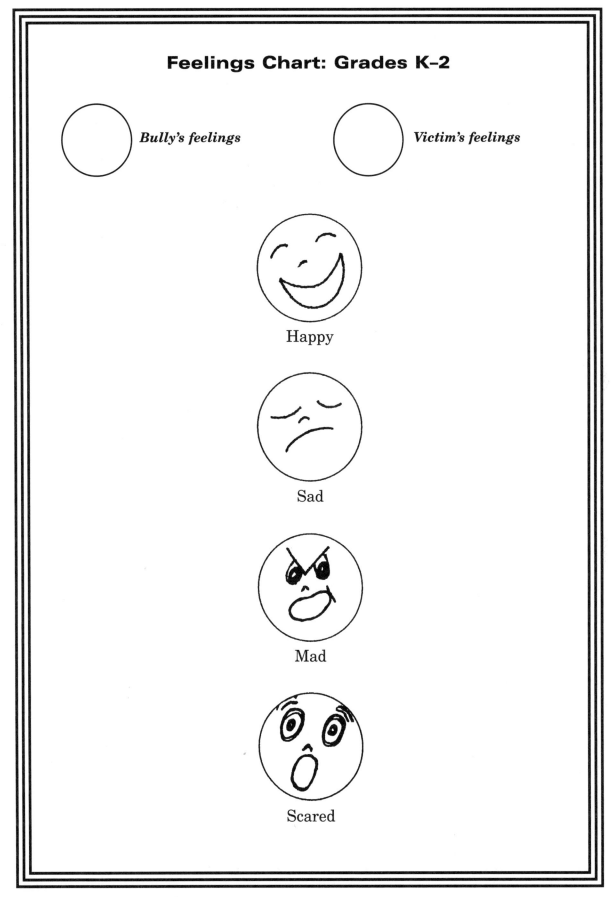

Bully's feelings   Victim's feelings

Happy

Sad

Mad

Scared

Activity 1.1

Bully Busters: A Teacher's Manual for Helping Bullies, Victims, and Bystanders (Grades K–5)
© 2003 by Arthur M. Horne, Christi L. Bartolomucci, and Dawn Newman-Carlson.
Champaign, IL: Research Press. (800) 519–2707.

Feelings Chart: Grades 3–5

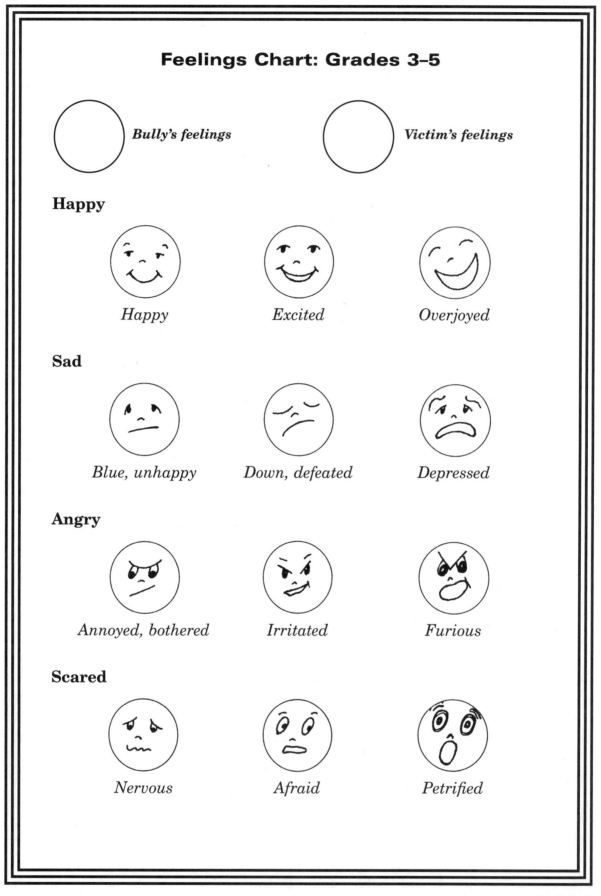

( ) **Bully's feelings**   ( ) **Victim's feelings**

Happy

Happy   *Excited*   *Overjoyed*

Sad

Blue, unhappy   *Down, defeated*   *Depressed*

Angry

Annoyed, bothered   *Irritated*   *Furious*

Scared

Nervous   *Afraid*   *Petrified*

Activity 1.1

Bully Busters: A Teacher's Manual for Helping Bullies, Victims, and Bystanders (Grades K–5)
© 2003 by Arthur M. Horne, Christi L. Bartolomucci, and Dawn Newman-Carlson.
Champaign, IL: Research Press. (800) 519–2707.

Story Time

OBJECTIVES

- To increase students' recognition, appreciation, and tolerance of individual differences in physical size, disability status, race/ethnicity, or other characteristics

- To help students recognize that it is unfair to target people for bullying and mistreatment because they are different

- To encourage children to value one another's uniqueness

MATERIALS

- A story chosen from the list at the end of this activity or any other story you feel is relevant to the topic of bullying

DIRECTIONS

1. Have students gather in a circle, either on the floor or in their chairs. (You may even want to take your students to the school media center to meet.)

2. Introduce the story, and let students know you want to share it because it has something to say on the problem of bullying.

3. Read the story aloud to the class. (If it is a long book, you may choose to read a chapter at a time.)

4. Discuss the story as a group, using the questions provided as well as any you devise that concern specific events in the story.

DISCUSSION QUESTIONS

- What did you notice in the story? How did you feel when you heard the story?

- Who were the victims in the story? How did they feel?

- Who were the bullies in the story? How did they feel?

- Why did the bullies bully the victims?

- Did anyone stick up for the victims? Who, and how did that happen?

- How would you have helped the victims in the story?

- How were the bullies treated? Was this a good or bad way to treat them?

- What was the outcome for the bullies and the victims?

- What was special about each of the characters?

NOTE

This is a great activity to tie into your curriculum. Are there stories of people or events in history that you discuss in your class that involve bullying or exclusion based on a particular characteristic? Examples include the story of Anne Frank and her family, persecuted for their faith, and the story of Ruby Bridges, the first African American female to attend a desegregated school.

A Tall Tale of Bullies: A List of Stories

To create this list, we drew on our own experience, consulted with teachers, and reviewed booklists such as *They're Never Too Young for Books,* by Edythe McGovern and Helen D. Muller (Buffalo, NY: Prometheus Books, 1994). This list is meant to serve as a starting point, but feel free to use other books. You can ask your school media specialist and fellow teachers for their opinions and take suggestions from students who might like to share a story on the topic with the class. To ensure that they are appropriate for your group, we encourage you to review these books before selecting them for your class.

Ada Potato, by Judith Caseley (New York: Greenwillow, 1989)

Angel Child, Dragon Child, by Michelle Maria Surat (New York: Scholastic, 1990)

A Bad Case of Stripes, by David Shannon (New York: Blue Sky Press, 1998)

Bear Party, by William Pene Du Bois (New York: Viking, 1963)

Benjamin and Tulip, by Rosemary Wells (New York: Dial, 1973)

Best Friends for Frances, by Russell Hoban (New York: HarperCollins, 1969)

Blackboard Bear, by Martha Alexander (New York: Dial, 1969)

The Brand New Kid, by Katie Couric (New York: Doubleday, 2000)

A Cake for Barney, by Joyce Dunbar (New York: Orchard Books, 1987)

Chrysanthemum, by Kevin Henkes (New York: Greenwillow, 1991)

Don't Call Me Names! by Joanna Cole (New York: Random House, 1990)

Feelings, by Aliki (New York: Greenwillow, 1984)

Franklin Is Bossy, by Paulette Bourgeous and Brenda Clark (New York: Scholastic, 1993)

Franklin Says Sorry, by Paulette Bourgeous and Brenda Clark (New York: Scholastic, 1999)

Hooway for Wodney Watt, by Helen Lester (Boston: Houghton Mifflin, 1999)

Hound and Bear, by Dick Gackenbach (Boston: Houghton Mifflin, 1976)

I'm Terrific, by Marjorie Weinmann Sharmat (New York: Holiday House, 1977)

I Know What I Like, by Norma Simon (Morton Grove, IL: Albert Whitman, 1971)

It's Okay to Be Different, by Todd Parr (Singapore: MT Books, 2001)

King of the Playground, by Phyllis Reynolds Naylor (New York: Atheneum, 1991)

The Recess Queen, by Alexis O'Neill and Laura Huliska-Beith (New York: Scholastic, 2002)

Today I Feel Silly and Other Moods That Make My Day, by Jamie Lee Curtis (New York: HarperCollins, 1998)

Yoko, by Rosemary Wells (Hong Kong: Hyperion Books for Children, 1998)

That's Garbage

OBJECTIVES

- To help students recognize mean words and give them an opportunity to talk about how mean words make them feel

- To help students understand how saying mean things can hurt someone's feelings

- To encourage students to make the decision to discard mean words and say nice things instead

MATERIALS

- Copies of the That's Garbage worksheet

- Markers, crayons, or colored pencils

- A garbage can

- Chalkboard or easel pad

- *Optional:* The book *Elbert's Bad Word,* by Audrey Wood (San Diego: Harcourt, Brace Jovanovich, 1988) or another story that has "mean words" as the theme

DIRECTIONS

1. Explain that today you are going to talk about mean words that people sometimes say to one another.

2. If you wish, read and discuss *Elbert's Bad Word* or another story including mean words.

3. Give each student a copy of the That's Garbage worksheet, and distribute the art supplies.

4. Instruct students to color the garbage can and, depending on ability, write mean words inside the can. If students are unable to write or spell the words, you can circulate and assist them.

5. When students are finished, instruct all of the students to hurry and "zip their mouths" so that the words they wrote can't get back in.

6. Hold the garbage can, and let each student come to the front of the room, rip his or her paper up, and throw it in the trash. When everyone is finished, place the garbage can outside the classroom and inform the students that the custodian will remove all of the mean words for good.

7. Ask students to brainstorm kind things to say, making a list on the chalkboard or easel pad.

8. Use the discussion questions to process the activity.

DISCUSSION QUESTIONS

- Have you ever used a mean word? What happened? How were you feeling? Can you think of something else you could have said?

- How do you feel when you hear someone use a mean word?

- What should you do when you hear someone use a mean word?

- What can we do to keep mean words out of our classroom?

NOTE

You can suggest that students tell someone who is saying something unkind, "That's a mean thing to say" or tell you so you can help the offending student learn not to say the mean words.

That's Garbage

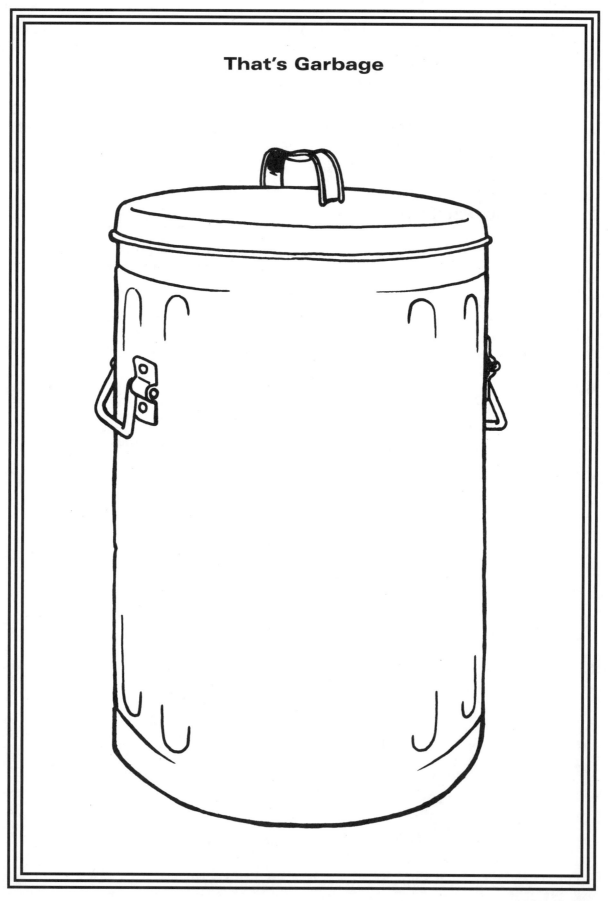

Activity 1.3

Bully Busters: A Teacher's Manual for Helping Bullies, Victims, and Bystanders (Grades K–5)
© 2003 by Arthur M. Horne, Christi L. Bartolomucci, and Dawn Newman-Carlson.
Champaign, IL: Research Press. (800) 519–2707.

Wanted: Reward Given!

OBJECTIVES

- To increase students' awareness, understanding, and identification of bullying behaviors

- To help students create a picture and definition of bullying within their classroom

- To enlist students in becoming active in creating a nonviolent school environment

MATERIALS

- Copies of the Wanted: Reward Given! poster

- Crayons, markers, or colored pencils

- Chalkboard or easel pad

- A sheet of poster board

- Marker

DIRECTIONS

1. Introduce the activity by telling the class that today you are going to begin talking about what bullying means.

2. Distribute the art supplies and copies of the Wanted: Reward Given! poster to students.

3. Ask the students to create their own definition of bullying by drawing a picture of a bully, then adding symbols and/or words to describe bullying. *It is important to tell students not to name other students.*

4. When the students are finished, allow each one to share his or her drawing and definition of bullying.

5. On the chalkboard or easel pad, record the features of bullying that students identify most frequently, then discuss these features with the class in order to achieve a consensus definition.

   Sample features: "big," "mean," "thinks he (or she) is cool," "tries to get attention," and "hurtful."

Sample definition: "Bullying is happening when one person (boy or girl) or a group of people say mean words to another person or harm the person over and over again."

Although the preceding responses are typical, your group's responses will be uniquely theirs. It is important to encourage creativity.

6. Make your class's definition of bullying public by writing it on a piece of poster board, then hanging the poster on the classroom wall. You could possibly make a "Wanted" bulletin board where you hang the children's pictures to remind them of their definition of bullying.

7. Process the activity by asking the discussion questions.

DISCUSSION QUESTIONS

- What happens when students are bullied?

- How do students feel when they are bullied?

- Do you ever see students being bullied? What do you do?

- Do you think bullies know that they are bullies? How do you think they feel?

- Why do you think some students bully?

NOTE

This is a powerful exercise. Teachers and students tell us that they like and benefit from it. However, it can be difficult for students who bully. When students describe bullying and talk about how it makes them feel, it may be the first time a name is put to this behavior. The goal is not to make bullies feel bad: Bullies have learned bullying behavior from situations that may have been very hurtful to them. Instead, the goal is to help all students recognize bullying behaviors for what they are.

Bully Busters: A Teacher's Manual for Helping Bullies, Victims, and Bystanders (Grades K–5)
© 2003 by Arthur M. Horne, Christi L. Bartolomucci, and Dawn Newman-Carlson.
Champaign, IL: Research Press. (800) 519–2707.

MODULE

2 Preventing Bullying in Your Classroom

OVERVIEW

Bullying interactions are most prevalent in middle school and high school (U.S. Department of Health and Human Services, 2001), but the elementary school years are an ideal time to begin the prevention of bullying. These years are critical in helping children form lasting beliefs regarding nonviolence (Samples & Aber, 1998). Much of this manual concerns ways to intervene with children who bully and children who are victimized. However, it is essential that teachers have the knowledge and know-how to keep bullying from occurring in the first place.

Although the focus of this program is both preventive and remedial, it is always better to prevent a problem than it is to treat it after it has happened. The "Lifeguard versus the Swim Teacher" and the "Mechanic versus the Gardener" are two analogies that demonstrate this point. With respect to the first, it is important to have a lifeguard to save the lives of swimmers who are in trouble in the water, but it is even more important to teach children to be strong swimmers to keep them from getting in trouble in the first place. As relates to bullying, we must create safe school environments and develop strong skills in our students to prevent bullying interactions from occurring. As for the mechanic versus the gardener, mechanics fix things that are broken; they attend to problems and try to repair damage. Gardeners enjoy helping plants grow, providing the nurturing environment they need. J. Jeffries McWhirter says, "Rather than the hasty tinkering of the mechanic, nurturing life requires the patience of the gardener. The technological rush of society leads us to be mechanics. We believe teachers should work as gardeners, nurturing and tending to the healthy development of children. Doing so eliminates the need to fix problems later" (McWhirter, McWhirter, McWhirter, & McWhirter, 1998, p. 3). The preventive approach, rather than therapeutic treatment after the fact, pays great dividends.

GOALS

- To understand the importance of prevention in eliminating bullying at the classroom and school levels

- To become aware of school and teacher characteristics that affect bullying and learn ways to establish positive relationships with children who bully

- To understand the importance for preventing bullying of establishing and enforcing clear classroom rules

- To become aware of what kind of responses to conflict can increase and decrease bullying behavior

PREVENTION IN THE CLASSROOM

Primary prevention can be realized in the classroom as "an intervention intentionally designed to reduce the future incidence of adjustment problems in a currently normal population as well as efforts directed at the promotion of mental health functioning" (Durlak & Wells, 1997, p. 117). Lewis and Lewis (1983) indicate that prevention assumes that "equipping people with personal and environmental resources for coping is the best of all ways to ward off maladaptive problems, not trying to deal with problems that have already germinated and flowered" (p. 6). Conyne (1987) notes that primary prevention focuses on collaboration and empowerment rather than on individual remediation.

Primary prevention is a powerful tool in guiding students' development. In the schools, where children are working hard to learn new academic and interpersonal skills, prevention efforts center on creating a supportive environment in which students may acquire skills that lead to a healthy lifestyle, characterized by responsibility and sensitivity to others.

As a teacher, you may find yourself questioning the feasibility of applying preventive techniques in your classroom. Education and mental health programs have emphasized prevention for more than half a century, yet our society as a whole has allocated few resources for the prevention of childhood pathology, aggression, and violence. Until recently, our focus has been directed toward children at risk for academic failure rather than those identified as at risk for behavioral problems. However, rising interest in school prevention programs has paralleled the increase in school violence.

Frequently, children engaged in bullying interactions are faced with a plethora of challenges, both academically and behaviorally. The Bully Busters program emphasizes children's personal strengths and targets their specific challenges. By engaging in primary prevention, you will be working with students to hone their strengths and defend against maladaptive behaviors such as violence. Just as we need to continue our efforts with students at risk academically, we also need to direct increased attention toward children at risk for emotional and behavioral problems.

A number of reasons exist for the lack of support for school prevention programs focusing on bullying, including the following beliefs:

- Childhood bullying is a normal and natural part of childhood development and interactions, and children will "grow out" of childhood bullying.

- Children naturally grow up to be healthy adults.

- Childhood bullying and school aggression are not large enough problems to warrant prevention programs.

- Money allocated for special programs to address bullying are not cost effective.

- Schools should focus on academics and not address children's social and behavioral needs.

- The teaching of appropriate behavior is a family matter.

It is important to recognize that acting on assumptions like these may impede teachers' work in the classroom. Specifically, such assumptions may lead teachers to overlook acting-out behavior, resulting in classroom disruption and less-than-effective teaching.

Building students' strengths decreases the likelihood of aggressive behavior both now and in the future. If elementary school students have a positive and safe school environment where they are able to build a firm academic and social base, they will be more likely to call upon their skills throughout their years of schooling. As children are establishing a strong academic foundation that will serve them throughout their school years and into the adult world of work, other programs can provide them with the social skills, communication skills, and conflict resolution skills that will guide them in their interpersonal interactions.

PREVENTION AT THE SCHOOL LEVEL

As adults and school professionals, we have a right to work in an environment that is safe and secure. At school we expect the same: a sense of safety and security. We expect to be able to walk down the halls without having fellow teachers push or shove us, without having anyone take our lunches or our wallets—we even expect to be able to use the rest rooms without being harassed or injured. Providing the same level of safety and security for our students is essential. Because school is legally required, students are entitled to feel safe; in addition, they need to feel safe before they can learn the academic and social skills that will help them to succeed in life.

Two factors are associated with schools that protect the safety of all those in the school environment: administrator characteristics and a zero-tolerance policy.

Administrator Characteristics

Certain characteristics of the school administration are associated with greater or lesser degrees of aggression in the school (Goldstein, 1999). Specifically, schools characterized by low aggression generally have administrators who exhibit the following qualities:

- They are highly visible and available to students and teachers.

- They have a finger on the pulse of the school—in other words, they know what is occurring in their school environment.

- They recognize problems in the school and rapidly take steps to address them.

- They have created fair and consistent responses to the needs and complaints of students and teachers, and are quick to respond to these grievances.

- They support and empower teachers and school personnel to meet the needs of their students.

Schools characterized by high rates of aggression and violence generally have administrators who exhibit the following qualities:

- They provide guidelines for teachers and students that are either too strict and rigid or too lax.

- They are impersonal in their interactions and separate themselves from the issues and needs of their teachers and students.

- They provide inconsistent means of addressing school problems and responding to problems.

- They overuse punishment and exercise harsh discipline with teachers and students.

- They provide weak or inconsistent support of faculty.

Zero Tolerance

The cardinal rule in the prevention of bullying is to establish a zero-tolerance policy. A zero-tolerance policy means that no bullying or aggression of any kind will be tolerated on the school premises. This policy position may be difficult for some educators to imagine, especially if they accept childhood aggression and bullying as a natural part of the maturation process.

Children typically test limits to see what they can do without getting in trouble. This means children can take part in many indirect or minor aggressive acts without receiving consequences. A school's tolerance of aggression can lead some students to become increasingly aggressive toward others. The level of "acceptable" aggression becomes higher and higher, while students are continually victimized. With a zero-tolerance policy, you eliminate the ambiguity of knowing what aggressive acts to address. Children clearly and consistently receive the message that no aggression or bullying is tolerated.

Some school faculty and staff have reacted negatively to the idea of a zero-tolerance policy because, in some programs, the zero-tolerance concept has been carried to an extreme, applying inflexible consequences for any rule infraction. Examples include expulsion of students for bringing a ceremonial sword to "show and tell," even with the teacher's prior permission; taking medication not dispensed by a nurse; and fighting back in self-defense when attacked by a group of bullies. These consequences reflect rules that do not allow for professional decision making on the part of educators.

We strongly support the concept of zero tolerance for bullying, and we also support the opportunity for educators to exercise their professional judgment in determining the appropriateness of consequences. In one school that had implemented the Bully Busters program, we saw

Module 2: Preventing Bullying in Your Classroom

how the zero-tolerance message had been inculcated into the school culture in a positive way. A class was lined up to go to recess. At the end of the line, one boy started flicking the ears of the boy in front of him. The victim was ignoring the insult, though it was obviously painful. Another student saw what was happening and walked over to the bully and said, "You are new to our school, so you don't know the rules. We don't do that in our school, and you must stop it now." The bully looked embarrassed and stopped, and the incident was dropped. In this case, the zero-tolerance policy had been adopted by the students as a valuable part of their school culture and was practiced by all.

As adults, we hold different expectations for adults and for children. Although varying abilities, maturity, and so forth may warrant such differences, aggression is an area in which expectations should be consistent. If we will not tolerate aggression in the workplace, we should not tolerate it in our children's schools.

BULLY BUSTERS SUPPORT TEAM THINK BLOCK

Have you created a zero-tolerance policy in your school? Take some time with your team and examine the Big Questions as they relate to this issue. Walk through the questions, evaluate your actions, and discuss what changes you can make to achieve your goals.

1. What is my goal? *To have zero tolerance for bullying in my classroom.*

2. What am I doing? *Do you ignore examples of bullying? Do you ignore students telling you about bullying or teasing that you don't see or observe? Do you tell students to learn to handle these problems? Or do you take immediate action, address concerns, and make an effort to understand what happened, even if you were not present?*

3. Is what I am doing helping me achieve my goal? *If you are ignoring the problems, does that help you to achieve your goal of zero-tolerance of bullying? If you avoid addressing bullying that you don't personally see, does that simply mean the bullies become sneakier? Is this helping you achieve your goal?*

4. *(If not)* What can I do differently? *With your team, identify specific steps you can take. In addition, review all of the Bully Busters modules to learn other ways you can achieve this goal.*

Schoolwide Commitment to Reduce Aggression

It is important for school faculty to establish a schoolwide orientation toward reducing bullying and other forms of aggression. If one or two teachers attempt to bring about change in their classrooms, but the school norms allow bullying to continue, change will be very difficult. Children need to receive a consistent message that aggression is unacceptable. Although it is important for individual teachers to make their own personal commitment to reducing violence, they need the support of their fellow teachers and school administration. Otherwise, children will receive mixed messages: They cannot bully in Mr. Johnston's class, but they find that same behavior is acceptable in Mr. Garrison's class or when Ms. Spring is on recess duty. Efforts to create unity throughout the school are integral. When students are supported by empowered teachers and administrators, the school will be much more successful in creating a safe and violence-free environment.

TEACHER CHARACTERISTICS

In addition to aspects of the broader school environment, the following teacher characteristics affect the bullying situation.

Teacher Self-Efficacy

Teacher self-efficacy is the belief that one can successfully bring about desired outcomes with one's students (Bandura, 1986; Gibson & Dembo, 1984). Teachers who believe they can make a difference *do* make a difference. In interviews with teachers, we have found that those teachers who have a high sense of self-efficacy have fewer bullying incidents in their classrooms. If teachers have appropriate skills and adequate incentives, their sense of self-efficacy is a major determinant in how they choose classroom activities, how much effort they put forth, and how long they will sustain effort when dealing with difficult students. In fact, teacher self-efficacy may be the single most powerful explanatory variable in student performance. Teachers must not only believe that the interventions they are suggesting can be effective, they must also have confidence in their ability to implement these interventions effectively. Teachers with a high sense of self-efficacy take personal responsibility for their students and their students' learning; when their students fail or have difficulty, they examine their own performance and look for ways they might make their teaching more effective.

Presentation Style

How teachers present themselves to students can make a difference in how students respond, both to teachers and to one another. Teachers can elicit students' interest and increase their authority if they convey confidence through their posture, gestures, and tone of voice. Teachers with low levels of classroom bullying vary their presentation style to avoid monotony. They also walk around the room and make eye contact with students; doing so increases the group's feeling of cohesion and also allows teachers to monitor classroom behavior.

The physical presence of the teacher is particularly important with bullies and victims. Initially, highly aggressive students will indicate a dislike for having the teacher be close by and touching them, but when the teacher demonstrates caring and support—a fair relationship rather than a punitive one—they generally respond much more positively to the teacher's presence.

"FAMOUS" Teachers

As an elementary school teacher, you are charged not only with meeting the academic needs of your students, but also with meeting many of their social and emotional needs as well (Pianta, 1999). These two areas of learning are often intertwined.

We use the acronym FAMOUS to help teachers codify the attributes they require to meet the emotional and behavioral needs of students, particularly students involved in the bully-victim interaction. These teachers build positive relationships with their students, helping to create a supportive environment, ideal for learning.

FAMOUS stands for the following:

*F*air and firm

*A*rranges rules and consequences

*M*odels positive and respectful behaviors

*O*pen and trustworthy

*U*nderstands students' diverse needs and experiences

*S*hows genuine interest

How can you become a FAMOUS teacher? Next described are the characteristics of FAMOUS teachers and several examples of how a FAMOUS teacher interacts with students.

Fair and Firm

Students need to trust that you have their best interests at heart. By being fair and firm, you communicate to your students that you care about them. Because you care about them, you apply your rules consistently. When you are being fair and firm, it usually means you have clearly defined the rules of the classroom; that you are paying attention to students' behaviors, attitudes, and feelings; and that you are applying your rules across different situations. When students break the rules by engaging in bullying behaviors, you are right there, encouraging them to take responsibility for their actions and believing they will do better next time.

You can be *fair and firm* by doing the following:

- Consistently reinforcing rules with all students

- Monitoring your reactions to all students and not engaging in favoritism

- Taking a step back, examining situations objectively, and only then proceeding

Arranges Rules and Consequences

Many problems arise when students misunderstand rules or believe rules are not enforceable. Children function best when they experience clear and consistent consequences. When rules and consequences for breaking them are clearly stated, students learn rules faster, are less likely to act out against their teachers for being unfair, and are able to take more responsibility for their actions. Students can understand how their behaviors lead to certain outcomes and are better able to discuss what they would like to do differently next time.

You can *arrange rules and consequences* in these ways:

- Creating, explaining, and openly displaying rules that are important for your classroom

- Acknowledging that there are consequences for breaking the rules and implementing the consequences for negative behaviors

- Working with other teachers and school personnel to create consistent schoolwide rules and consequences

Models Positive and Respectful Behaviors

Teachers serve as models for their students (Bandura, 1986; Besag, 1989), and students often look to their teachers for guidance and for a code of conduct for treating others. In fact, schools have a "hidden curriculum" of social expectations known by all but not openly discussed. How teachers behave and react is as important as the behaviors they reinforce—all are witnessed by students. Teachers set precedents and guide behaviors in the classroom. Modeling positive behaviors facilitates the development of positive behaviors in students.

You can *model positive and respectful behaviors* in these ways:

- Communicating with students in a positive, encouraging, and respectful manner

- Using and discussing proactive conflict resolution skills

- Respecting and being sensitive to students with diverse behaviors and ideas

Open and Trustworthy

All of your students, and particularly students engaging in bully-victim interactions, may be experiencing stress. Creating an open and trustworthy alliance with your students will encourage them to come to you with challenging situations, be they academic problems or situations in which they are victimized. It is important to let students know that they can talk to you privately about any topic and that you will make the effort to help them. You may be the only adult in some students' lives who offers stability, consistency, and safety.

You can be *open and trustworthy* by acting in the following manner:

- Encouraging students to seek you out and talk with you any time

- Letting students know that you are interested in their personal as well as their academic experiences

- Informing students that you will keep their stories private and that, together, you will seek out additional help if necessary to ensure their safety

Understands Students' Diverse Needs and Experiences

Your classroom is likely to reflect a diverse student population with differing needs and experiences. Each child in your class has his or her own unique set of educational, emotional, and social needs, and each child looks to you in a different way to meet these needs. Although some children will reach out and confide in you, others may be much harder to reach. It is often this latter group who have relationship difficulties and who may not be sure how to form positive relationships with peers or adults. Some children who bully may not have been taught to be emotionally sensitive and have a tendency to remain guarded. It is usually students who are most disconnected or who actively push you away who are most likely to need your help.

You can *understand students' diverse needs and experiences* in these ways:

- Talking with students individually and attempting to understand their perspectives on different situations

- Speaking with family members to get a more comprehensive picture of students' needs and goals

- Sharing challenges with other teachers and exploring together how you can meet students' needs

Shows Genuine Interest

Students who feel a connection with their teachers and peers are more likely to stay in school and eventually to graduate. Think what a difference it makes to you when someone notices your hard work, your long hours, or simply something special about you. Showing a genuine interest in your students communicates to them that you are paying attention to them, you are glad that they are in your class, and you think they are special. Furthermore, genuine interest is essential in building positive relationships with your students.

You can *show genuine interest* in these ways:

- Providing individual attention to students in your class, especially if you notice something different about them (e.g., mood, school performance, energy level, dress)

- Asking students how their day is going and listening to their responses

- Recognizing, commenting, and giving feedback on students' schoolwork, behaviors, and efforts

Another step toward creating the classroom of your choice is to be certain that you have a clear understanding of how you perceive yourself in the classroom compared to how others may see you. Teachers who are perceived congruently—that is, their view of themselves and their students' view of them are consistent or congruent—have more effective classrooms.

Teacher Empathy

Being empathic means being able to understand how others feel and to communicate that understanding to them. Empathy is a core component of effective teaching (Pianta, 1999) and an essential ingredient in classrooms that are peaceful, powerful, and positive.

Children who are empathic tend not to be aggressive. They are aware of the feelings of others and strive to understand how it would feel to be in another person's shoes. Teacher empathy is equally, if not more, important in creating classrooms where children feel safe and accepted. Frequently, teachers and other school professionals can become overwhelmed or frustrated by the concerns or behaviors of children. At times, adults can lose touch with how children see and experience the world. At these times, adults' behaviors toward children change and may reflect negatively on the child.

When a child is acting out, withdrawn, isolated, or aggressive, ask yourself, What is this child experiencing? How does this child feel in my classroom? and How is this child coping with the environmental stressors he or she faces? At times, it is easy for adults to assume that children should feel a certain way, given a particular situation, but it is important to think instead in terms of the individual child and how that child may experience the situation. It is not easy to suspend your own thoughts and beliefs and focus on the world through the eyes of a child, but it is critically important. As a teacher, you are striving to create an environment where children can learn, achieve goals, and build the confidence and competence to negotiate their school years. Understanding and responding to children both emotionally and academically can help to create an ideal learning environment.

Brooks and Goldstein, authors of the book *Raising Resilient Children* (2001) suggest that, as professionals, we need to appreciate the power of empathy. They suggest an empathy activity to help professionals explore how they want to be perceived and how they are actually perceived by their students. We have expanded on this self-awareness exercise in the following activity. This activity takes considerable time to complete, but it is worthwhile. Usually, we have teachers identify characteristics themselves, without asking students or colleagues to respond. However, some teachers have sought the feedback of their students and colleagues. It is good to know how we differ from our ideals and to consider changes we can make to more closely approximate our ideal.

BULLY BUSTERS SUPPORT TEAM THINK BLOCK

Complete the following statements on your own, then discuss your responses with your Bully Busters Support Team.

1. If I were an ideal teacher, I would . . .

2. In the present, my teaching characteristics are . . .

---

3. My students would characterize my teaching as . . .

4. My colleagues would characterize my teaching as . . .

5. Changes I would like to make are . . .

BUILDING GOOD RELATIONSHIPS WITH TOUGH KIDS

With some children, you will easily form relationships. These children usually present few problems in class. You may have a very challenging time connecting with other children in both a personal and professional manner. Generally, these children are not involved in school processes, have difficulty getting along with peers, and may use bullying or aggression to get what they want.

When children display negative behaviors that demand the attention of their teachers, it is easy for teachers to become frustrated and even to engage in power struggles. Yet power struggles are exactly what fuel a negative relationship with students. Children who display negative behaviors—behaviors often associated with bullying—are accustomed to being treated in a negative manner. They may expect that adults in their lives will not respond to them positively. In fact, they may engage in negative behaviors that make it difficult for teachers and other adults to treat them with the warmth they need.

Bullies and other aggressive youth need positive relationships with teachers, just as their victims do. A relationship characterized by caring concern, constructive feedback, and respect is necessary for all children. But how do you form positive relationships with students who do not appear to want them? Here are some "do's and don'ts":

Do . . .
- Communicate respectfully.

- Pay attention to the student, not just the behaviors.

- Catch the student doing something good; acknowledge positive behaviors.

- Find ways to work with each student individually.

- Create and agree on individualized plans to address behavior problems.

Don't . . .
- Engage in a power struggle in which you are forced to do something drastic.

- Make a public scene about negative behaviors (the student will likely see the negative attention as better than no attention at all).

- Ignore behaviors or give in to coercive behaviors because you pity the student.

- Take the student's behaviors too personally. (Overpersonalization can interfere with your ability to form a positive relationship and will certainly increase your potential for frustration and burnout.)

> **BULLY BUSTERS SUPPORT TEAM THINK BLOCK**
>
> Take a minute to think of what is important to you in your closest relationships. How do you expect to be treated? How do you know that another person cares about you? What do you not tolerate in these relationships?
>
> Now think of a student or students with whom you have a positive and respectful relationship. Why do you have this relationship? Is the child or children more agreeable, sociable, likeable, or respectful?
>
> Now think of a student or students with whom you have not yet been able to form a positive and respectful relationship. What characteristics or behaviors may make forming this relationship challenging?
>
> Discuss your thoughts with your Bully Busters Support Team.

ESTABLISHING AND ENFORCING CLASSROOM RULES

In chapter 1, we touched on the importance of establishing and enforcing clear classroom rules, but it is worth underscoring the importance of rules again here, as they relate to prevention. Here are some "rules for rules":

- Define and communicate classroom rules for students in specific and behavioral terms (e.g., "Raise your hand before asking a question").

- Tell students what to do (e.g., take turns, talk over disagreements) rather than what not to do (e.g., don't fight, stop yelling).

- Keep rules short and few in number, and post them where they can be seen clearly.

- Encourage students to take an active role in rule development, modification, and implementation. Rule adherence is better when students have participated in this process.

- Be able to give a rationale for why each rule is needed. A good rationale for having rules in general is that because everyone is required to be in school, we are responsible for making sure school is a safe place for everyone.

- Develop and implement rules early on, from the start of the school year.

- Make certain the rules are fair and that they apply equally to all students.

- Be certain the rules are understood. When students don't understand, rules are difficult to enforce.

- Spell out reasonable consequences in advance. Just as adults don't like "surprise consequences" for their behavior, students want to know what the consequences will be.

- Apply the rules and consequences consistently. We don't want traffic tickets that vary according to the police officer's mood: We want predictability, as do students.

In identifying consequences, it is important to identify undesirable behaviors (e.g., teasing, name-calling, pushing, taunting). This should be part of a class discussion: Why are these behaviors undesirable? What can we do instead of these behaviors, particularly to lead us to work together more cooperatively and show respect? What should happen if these behaviors do occur? After the class has had this discussion, establish consequences that fit the offenses. Implement consequences directly following an offense; do not keep a running tally of offenses, then implement a consequence. Finally, direct the negative consequences toward the undesirable act, not the student. A teacher might say, for example, "Janel, because you teased Pat, you will need to take a time-out."

ADDRESSING CLASSROOM CONFLICT

Kreidler (1984) has delineated six potential sources of conflict in the classroom:

- *A highly competitive atmosphere,* in which students learn to work against rather than with one another

- *An intolerant atmosphere,* characterized by cliques, scapegoating, intolerance of racial or cultural differences, and lack of support for classmates, leading to isolation and loneliness

- *Patterns of poor communication,* in which students and teachers do not listen to each other and have no forum for expressing emotions and needs

- A classroom in which students have not learned *self-control*

- *Lack of conflict resolution skills*

- *Misuse of power* by the teacher

Teacher Misuse of Power

Throughout this manual, we stress the importance of teachers' modeling appropriate behaviors for their students. Teachers continually model appropriate behavior of all kinds, including behavior associated with conflict. Yet teachers and other school professionals are also susceptible to engaging in aggressive or bullying behaviors with each other or with their students. This usually happens when teachers are angry or frustrated with the behaviors occurring in the classroom. Inevitably, when teachers respond in this manner, conflict and tension in the classroom increase (Kreidler, 1984).

As explained in Module 1, bullying occurs when one person with power purposefully inflicts harmful behaviors on another person with less power, repeatedly and over time. All children and adults need power, yet in the classroom teachers typically hold the power. Most students accept the power differential between themselves and their teachers. Problems arise, however, when teachers abuse this power. Teachers resort to bullying their students when they feel there are no other methods to gain or regain control in the classroom or when they find themselves in the middle of a power struggle with their students. In a power struggle, neither the teacher nor the student wants to back down.

The Conflict Cycle

Sometimes teachers get stuck in conflict cycles with their entire class or with a particular student. These cycles are hard to break because of the tenacious nature of the behavior on the part of both students and teachers. It takes hard work to interrupt these patterns. The first step is to identify the existence of the conflict cycle and understand its nature. The following is one common conflict cycle:

1. A small misbehavior escalates if the teacher gives a warning and doesn't follow through on it or tries to ignore the behavior.

2. The student becomes more disruptive; the noise level and physical acting out increase, and the teacher starts to get frustrated.

3. The teacher repeats the warning without following through with a consequence, and the student's misbehavior now gets larger.

4. The student thinks he or she has "gotten" the teacher.

5. The teacher gets angry. He or she loses control and may even yell; punishment, which may involve the whole class, is meted out.

6. The student calms down behaviorally but builds up a resentment and starts planning more passive-aggressive behaviors.

7. The student starts the small behavior again, yet this time it gets large quicker because the limits are not clear.

8. The teacher gets angry again. The student now becomes openly defiant and disrespectful.

9. The teacher punishes, sometimes coming up with some "really serious punishments."

It is essential to stop this cycle at the beginning. Once you give a warning in response to a small problem, you must follow through with the appropriate consequence. Do it assertively and privately, and make sure that you watch for and encourage the student's appropriate behavior throughout the day.

Understanding Your Response to Conflict

Every teacher is unique and has an individual way of managing conflict and bullying situations in the classroom. Each teacher is influenced by his or her own experiences with conflict. Kreidler (1984) has developed a method to assess the manner in which teachers approach conflicts in their classroom. Specifically, he has identified the following different approaches:

- *No-nonsense approach:* I do not give in to students. Students need firm guidance in learning acceptable versus unacceptable behavior (e.g., make a disciplinary referral, tell students to sit down and begin their assignments).

- *Problem-solving approach:* I set up a situation in which the students and I can solve the problem together (e.g., try to find out what the real problem is, encourage students to find alternative solutions).

- *Negotiating approach:* I teach the students to listen to one another and assist them in reaching a compromise (e.g., mediate, help students understand one another's points of view).

- *Smoothing approach:* I prefer my classroom to be calm and peaceful whenever possible. Often student conflicts are insignificant, so I try to redirect students (e.g., divert attention from the conflict, get everyone involved in doing something else).

- *Ignoring approach:* I indicate limits and allow students to work out conflicts on their own. It is important that they learn the consequences of their behavior (e.g., let students fight it out as long as no one gets hurt, tell them to settle it on their own time).

With the exception of the ignoring approach, all of these ways of responding to conflict are valid. We do not in any way support or encourage the ignoring approach. Too often, it allows bullying to continue and gives students the impression that the teacher sanctions the behavior or does not care about their safety.

BULLY BUSTERS SUPPORT TEAM THINK BLOCK

What is your way of handling conflict? Teachers have told us that identifying their approach toward dealing with specific bullying incidents helps them to adjust their style and reach even more effective outcomes. With your Bully Busters Support Team, discuss your approaches to conflict. Ask yourselves the following questions:

1. In what situations would each of these approaches to conflict be most useful?

2. Are there certain approaches you would recommend using over others?

3. Which approach do you use most often?

4. Which approaches would you like to use more often?

Module 2: Content Review

The following statements relate to the learning goals of this module. Ask yourself if you feel confident that you can answer yes to each item. If not, please review the material and discuss any difficulties among your Bully Busters Support Team.

1. I understand the importance of efforts to prevent bullying in the classroom and school.   Yes ❑   No ❑

2. I can name the characteristics of the school administration and of teachers that help to prevent bullying.   Yes ❑   No ❑

3. I know what to do and not do to build positive relationships with children who bully.   Yes ❑   No ❑

4. I understand why developing and enforcing clear classroom rules is important in preventing bullying behavior.   Yes ❑   No ❑

5. I can describe the conflict cycle and can identify my own pattern of response to conflict.   Yes ❑   No ❑

Bully Busters: A Teacher's Manual for Helping Bullies, Victims, and Bystanders (Grades K–5)
© 2003 by Arthur M. Horne, Christi L. Bartolomucci, and Dawn Newman-Carlson.
Champaign, IL: Research Press. (800) 519–2707.

A Reminder . . .

CLASSROOM INTERACTION AND AWARENESS CHART

Use the CIAC to describe any bullying behavior you observe (and that students report to you, if you wish). A copy of the CIAC and a weekly summary sheet appear in Appendix A.

THE BIG QUESTIONS

Honestly appraise your progress by asking yourself the Big Questions. There are no right or wrong answers.

In relation to preventing bullying in my classroom:

1. What is my goal?

2. What am I doing?

3. Is what I am doing helping me achieve my goal?

4. *(If not)* What can I do differently?

PERSONAL GOALS FORM

The Personal Goals Form, on the next page, is designed to help you tailor the content of this module to your own students and situation. Please take a moment to fill out the form now.

Module 2: Personal Goals Form

Goals

- To understand the importance of prevention in eliminating bullying at the classroom and school levels

- To become aware of school and teacher characteristics that affect bullying and learn ways to establish positive relationships with children who bully

- To understand the importance of establishing and enforcing clear classroom rules

- To become aware of what kind of responses to conflict can increase and decrease bullying behavior

1. My personal understanding of how I can help to prevent bullying in my classroom is as follows:

2. I have observed incidents of bullying. *(Please record incidents on the CIAC.)*

   ____ Number of times I intervened   ____ Number of times I chose not to intervene

   Other observations:

3. I will review the classroom activities for this module and select ones appropriate for my class. *(Please list.)*

4. I will accept the challenges associated with the developmental assets discussed in chapter 2. *(Please list the specific assets and describe what you plan to do.)*

5. I will give my students feedback about the bullying incidents I have observed and encourage discussion of bullying and related issues. We will discuss these topics:

6. I will share my experiences in applying the information in this module with other teachers and administrators, as well as with my students' families. *(Please specify who and when.)*

7. I will meet with my Bully Busters Support Team. *(Please specify when and list what issues and questions you will raise.)*

Bully Busters: A Teacher's Manual for Helping Bullies, Victims, and Bystanders (Grades K–5)
© 2003 by Arthur M. Horne, Christi L. Bartolomucci, and Dawn Newman-Carlson.
Champaign, IL: Research Press. (800) 519–2707.

Classroom Activities

ACTIVITY 2.1: ROOM RULES (GRADES K–5)

Including students in the decision-making process relating to behavior management helps them establish "ownership" of classroom rules. This activity gives students a chance to provide their input and serves to clarify classroom expectations.

ACTIVITY 2.2: NO BULLYING HERE (GRADES K–5)

It is important to convey the idea that students' classrooms are "safe zones" in which bullying will not be tolerated. In this activity, students work in small groups to create posters with no-bullying messages. They then place them in areas of the school where bullying commonly takes place. Versions for grades K–2 and 3–5 are included.

ACTIVITY 2.3: THE DROP BOX (GRADES 3–5)

Children often need "permission" to report instances of bullying. This activity gives them a way to bring bullying to your attention, anonymously if they wish. Students write a note each morning about their concerns about bullying or other matters, then drop the note in a box. You can then discuss these concerns as a class and act on the information as appropriate.

ACTIVITY 2.4: ONE FOR ALL (GRADES 3–5)

In this activity, students take on specific roles and, through role-playing, attempt to accomplish a team goal. In the process, they become aware of the different roles in the bullying interaction (bully, victim, bystander) and see for themselves the negative impact of bullying on the team's ability to work together. (The activity may become rowdy, but it helps students see and feel as others do.)

ACTIVITY 2.5: IDENTIFYING OTHERS' FEELINGS (GRADES 3–5)

This activity gives students the opportunity to read several scenarios on a worksheet, then write feeling words to show what emotions the characters in the scenarios may have been having. By comparing responses,

they increase their awareness of others' feelings and begin to realize
that different people can feel different ways about the same situation.

Room Rules

OBJECTIVES

- To explain classroom rules and the reasons for them

- To help students feel ownership of classroom rules

- To illustrate that consequences for certain behaviors exist and will be applied fairly and consistently

MATERIALS

- Chalkboard or easel pad

- Several sheets of poster board

- Markers

- Your personal list of essential classroom rules

DIRECTIONS

1. Consider the rules you feel are important in your classroom and why you believe these rules are necessary.

2. Go over the rules, one at a time, with the class. Discuss why each rule is important to have in the classroom and what the consequence will be for breaking the rule.

3. Help your students feel ownership for the rules by including them in the discussion. Ask:

   Do you believe these rules are important? Why do you think so?

   What happens to the students, the teacher, and the class as a whole when a rule is broken?

   Do you think the consequences for breaking certain rules are fair?

   Are you willing to help your classmates follow the rules by telling another student (or reminding yourself) that he or she is breaking a rule? *(Emphasize that this is not being a tattletale, but helping to take responsibility for the classroom.)*

   What rules would you like to add to the list?

   Why do you think these rules are important?

4. On the chalkboard or easel pad, make a final list of rules for the classroom, including your rules and the rules students have added to your initial list.

5. Give students the poster board and markers, and have them create posters to illustrate the rules. (Students in the lower grades may need help with lettering.) If you wish, you can have small groups work together on the posters.

6. Process the activity by asking the discussion questions; display the posters prominently in the classroom.

DISCUSSION QUESTIONS

- How did you like helping to make the rules for our classroom?
- Why is it important to have rules?
- How do our class rules protect class members?
- Is it better to have a lot of rules or very few rules?
- Do you feel that you are more or less likely to follow the rules that you helped to create? Why or why not?
- How do you feel about helping a teacher enforce the rules?

No Bullying Here

OBJECTIVES

- To increase the visibility of any bullying occurring in your school
- To promote awareness of bullying throughout the school
- To help students feel ownership for the prevention of bullying

MATERIALS

- Prepared posters for students to decorate (grades K–2)
- Several sheets of poster board (grades 3–5)
- Markers

DIRECTIONS

1. Discuss with your students the idea that bullying must be stopped so everyone can feel safe at school. Provide examples of bullying behaviors: teasing, pushing, making fun of others, excluding others from play, and so forth.

2. Divide the class into groups of three or four students each.

3. Choose the procedure appropriate for your grade level:

    Grades K–2: Give each group a poster you have predesigned (on the model of those described for grades 3–5). Instruct the groups to decorate the posters as they wish.

    Grades 3–5: Give each group a sheet of poster board and some markers. Instruct each group to design a poster with a no-bullying message. For example:

    No Bullies Here

    Students against Bullying

    The word *bullies* with an *X* through it

4. Allow each group time to share their poster with their classmates.

5. Discuss with the class where they think bullying happens the most. Ask students whether they would like their posters to appear in these areas.

6. Post or have students post the no-bullying messages throughout the school.

DISCUSSION QUESTIONS

- How do you feel about "advertising" for a no-bullying school?

- How do you think the posters will affect other students, including bullies?

- Do you think other students will want to join in to create a no-bullying school?

- Why is it important for our school not to allow bullying?

- Whose responsibility is it to make sure bullying does not happen at our school?

- How many of you are committed to helping your classmates not get bullied?

NOTE

Request that an announcement be made to the whole school to explain that the no-bullying posters have been put up to help all students become aware that bullying is not allowed. You and your peers on the Bully Busters Support Team can also make "safe-place" signs to hang on your classroom doors and post throughout the school so students will know that they can come to you for help with these issues. (Include names and room numbers on these signs.)

The Drop Box

OBJECTIVES

- To increase students' comfort in informing the teacher about bullying situations in the classroom

- To assure students that their concerns about bullying in the classroom will be addressed

MATERIALS

- A shoe box with a hole cut in the lid

- Copies of the Notes to My Teacher page (one note for each student; cut each page into individual slips)

DIRECTIONS

1. Introduce the activity to the students by saying something like the following:

   Bullying happens when one student who has more power harms another student. That is why it is very important to have a teacher or another adult help you if bullying occurs. I would like to help you stop bullying in our classroom. I want you to know that I will be here for you to talk to and that I won't be mad at you for talking to me about bullying. I will not consider anyone a tattle-tale if they are helping to keep our classroom a safe place to learn.

2. Give each student a Note to My Teacher slip, then do as follows:

   Explain that you will give students a copy of this note every day and that you would like them to take a few minutes to write you a brief message.

   Tell them that the notes can be about anything, not just bullying, and that they can sign their names or not, as they wish.

   Show them the drop box, and let them know that after they have written their messages, you will bring the box around so they can deposit their notes.

Let them know that you will read their notes and begin to work on any bullying problems the class might be having. (If the problem continues, they can let you know by writing that in the note the next day.)

3. At the end of each week, save time to talk to your students about any major, ongoing concerns they may have about bullying, and let them know what steps you have taken to solve these problems.

DISCUSSION QUESTIONS

- How do you feel about writing me a note every day about bullying or anything else that is on your mind?

- Do you think writing me a note will be easier for you to do than talking to me?

- If you feel uncomfortable talking to me or another adult in person about bullying, why do you suppose this is?

- Is it tattling to tell me or another adult about a bullying problem you know about?

- How do you think I can use the things you tell me to make our classroom a safer, better place for learning?

NOTE

If students reveal in their notes that they are experiencing high levels of stress related to bullying or to other issues, you may decide to invite the school counselor or social worker to your class or make individual referrals as appropriate.

Notes to My Teacher

A note to my teacher

A note to my teacher

A note to my teacher

A note to my teacher

Activity 2.3

Bully Busters: A Teacher's Manual for Helping Bullies, Victims, and Bystanders (Grades K–5)
© 2003 by Arthur M. Horne, Christi L. Bartolomucci, and Dawn Newman-Carlson.
Champaign, IL: Research Press. (800) 519–2707.

One for All

OBJECTIVES

- To give students an opportunity to recognize how their behaviors affect other students

- To help students identify ways they can work together so everyone "wins"

- To encourage students to become aware of how they can support victims, or other students in need, in their class

MATERIALS

- Copies of the One for All Roles (a copy for each group of four students; cut each page so one role appears on each slip of paper)

- Scissors

- Small rubber balls (or large gumballs)

- Plastic spoons

DIRECTIONS

1. Divide students into groups of four. Tell the students that they are going to do a team activity and their jobs are to act out a role that you will assign them.

2. Call one group at a time to the front of the class, and give each group member one of the four roles. Instruct students not to share their roles with other group members. (It may be helpful to give the class bully, if there is one, the helper bystander's role in order to put him or her in a position to help the student in the victim role.)

3. Instruct each group to line up in a row. Give each team member a plastic spoon.

4. Inform the group that, as quickly as they can, they must pass the ball from one end of the line to the other and back to the beginning again without dropping it.

5. After each group has had a chance to come to the front and do the exercise, process the activity by asking the discussion questions.

DISCUSSION QUESTIONS

- What problems did you notice on your team?

- Could your team have finished faster? How?

- What did you notice about each person on your team?

- How did each person's behavior affect the team?

- What could you do to help your teammates?

- What role would you have most liked to play?

One for All Roles

### *Bystander*	### *Bully*
You always do what you are supposed to do and follow the rules of the game.	You move around a lot, get out of line, bang into the other people on your team, and call them names.
### *Victim*	### *Bystander*
You constantly drop the ball. You just can't keep it on your spoon.	You are a helper. You help the teammate who can't keep the ball on the spoon.

Bully Busters: A Teacher's Manual for Helping Bullies, Victims, and Bystanders (Grades K–5)
© 2003 by Arthur M. Horne, Christi L. Bartolomucci, and Dawn Newman-Carlson.
Champaign, IL: Research Press. (800) 519–2707.

Identifying Others' Feelings

OBJECTIVES

- To encourage students to identify how others might feel in different challenging situations

- To allow students to connect their behaviors with various emotional consequences

- To illustrate that different people can feel different ways, even if they are in the same situation

MATERIALS

- Feelings Charts appropriate for grades 3–5 (completed during Activity 1.1)

- Copies of the Feeling Situations worksheet

- Pencils or pens

DIRECTIONS

1. Ask students to take out the Feelings Chart they completed during Activity 1.1.

2. Discuss the feelings identified on the chart by reading each word aloud and asking students if they have heard the word or can recall a situation in which they experienced that emotion.

3. Distribute the Feeling Situations worksheets, and explain that the group will be considering each situation and thinking about how the main character in the situation may have felt.

4. Read (or have volunteers read) each scenario on the worksheet. Following each item, ask students to identify and write feeling words to show how they think the main character might have felt. Let students know that they can use their Feelings Chart to help identify the feelings. If it is tricky to think of how the characters might feel, they can think about how they might feel in that same situation.

5. When all the items have been read, discuss the different feeling words students chose for each situation. Ask, "Would you feel the

same way in the situation that you believe the character to be feeling?"

6. Point out different responses among students, and discuss how people can feel different ways about the same situation. For example:

> Justin and Daniel were showing their science project to the class, and their presentation didn't go as planned. The class started laughing at them. Justin became very angry, but Daniel felt sad and started to cry.

7. Use the discussion questions to process the activity.

DISCUSSION QUESTIONS

- Was this activity easy or hard for you? Why?

- Can there be more than one right answer to how a person may feel in a situation?

- What is it like for you to think about how other people may be feeling?

- Next time you are in a tough situation, do you think you can try to understand how the other person may feel?

NOTE

If a challenging situation exists in your class, you may wish to create a scenario about it to help your students identify the feelings they are having and begin to resolve the issue peaceably.

Feeling Situations

Feeling situation	Feeling words
1. Billy woke up in a bad mood. He didn't want to go to school, he didn't do his homework, and he didn't feel like talking to anyone.	
2. Kayla won first prize in the science fair for her seed project, which she did almost all by herself.	
3. Charles had his pet dog since the day he was born. When he got home from school, his mother told him that his dog died earlier in the day.	
4. Jana was selected as the class's "Very Important Person" because she always tried to help her classmates with their work and even stopped a fight at lunch time.	
5. Jonas sat at lunch all by himself, and he could hear the boys at the other table calling him names. Once in a while the boys would even throw food at him.	
6. Lola woke up in the middle of the night, everything was very dark, and she thought she heard a strange noise at the end of the hall.	
7. Everyone was going to the birthday party—everyone except Brianna, who didn't get an invitation. She heard her classmate say that whales were not allowed to go to parties.	
8. Andy was walking out of the rest room when he saw two bullies headed straight toward him.	
9. Marcus was on the playground when two older boys came up to him and pushed him around until he fell on the ground.	

Activity 2.5

Bully Busters: A Teacher's Manual for Helping Bullies, Victims, and Bystanders (Grades K–5)
© 2003 by Arthur M. Horne, Christi L. Bartolomucci, and Dawn Newman-Carlson.
Champaign, IL: Research Press. (800) 519–2707.

M O D U L E

3 Building Personal Power

OVERVIEW

To create a positive climate for learning and to prevent and reduce bullying, students and their teachers need personal power. In brief, personal power comes with practice: Children build confidence in themselves by learning they have the skills to handle challenging situations and by experiencing success, especially as it relates to certain areas: anger management, conflict resolution, and relationships. As students gain confidence in themselves, their abilities, and their surroundings, they are more likely to achieve their potential. This module focuses on ways you can foster students' development in these areas, toward the goal of creating a bully-free learning environment.

GOALS

- To understand the importance of personal power for students, especially as expressed in strong, healthy narratives; positive risk taking; and feelings awareness

- To learn how personal power relates to anger in bullies, victims, and bystanders

- To consider the importance of effective conflict resolution and problem solving for the development of personal power

- To understand how using school families and appropriate laughter can enhance personal power

WHAT IS PERSONAL POWER?

Over the past decade, an energizing movement toward identifying and building on the personal power of children has been under way. A focus on strengths (e.g., Seligman, 1995), healthy development (e.g., Benson, 1999), and resilience (e.g., Brooks & Goldstein, 2001) is important in preparing today's youth to maneuver successfully through life's challenges.

Building a sense of personal power is like building a firm base for academic skills. Children must be exposed to and taught skills that help them to feel their actions have meaning. They need to practice interpersonal skills and receive feedback in much the same way they do for their academic work. Although each child has his or her own level of social capability, all children can benefit from learning the skills that promote healthy and nonviolent interactions with others.

BULLY BUSTERS SUPPORT TEAM THINK BLOCK

When you think of personal power, what characteristics come to mind? Take a moment to think of the qualities in yourself—as well as in your friends, family members, and students—conducive to success in life. Briefly list these qualities, then discuss with your team.

Numerous characteristics have been identified as essential in developing healthy and resilient children. Three ways to encourage children's resilience are by promoting strong, healthy narratives; by encouraging them to take positive risks; and by promoting their awareness of feelings.

Strong, Healthy Narratives

Even young children have a sense of themselves in comparison with other students. You may see children's sense of self expressed in the form of acting out when they are frustrated at being unable to perform their academic work as well as other students. You may see other children express their sense of self by raising their hands immediately every time you ask a question, with confidence that they have the right answer. Yet other children, even as young as 4 and 5, may have developed a feeling that they are "bad kids" from their experiences at home and at school.

All of these children have created a "story," a personal narrative about themselves that is reinforced on a day-to-day basis. The child who is confident and encouraged is often rewarded by being called upon and given praise for answering questions correctly. A child who does not feel prepared to answer a question may not raise his or her hand and will not experience that feeling of success. Children who are mistreated, neglected, or exposed to chaotic or disorganized homes may not learn how to interact positively. They may receive inconsistent discipline and little praise or positive feedback at home. These children reenact their behavior at school, where they are again reprimanded. As a result, they come to expect negative feedback and begin living up to others' expectations that they are troublemakers.

Each of the children in the following examples has a different personal narrative.

Becky is the "voice" of the class. If there is a problem, she is sure to be the one to let you know. She is a straight-A student and is confident that she will make As on all of her work. When asked what she will be when she grows up, Becky says, "The first woman president!"

Brian comes to school each day disheveled, his papers crumpled in his bag and his hair a mess. Brian never has his work done, and you can never get a parent to sign the papers he does bring home. Although Brian is smart, he always seems distracted and uninterested at school.

Amber is always getting in fights. If another child looks at her wrong on a bad day, she will yell or start pushing. She always seems angry, but you are not sure why. The other kids try to avoid her, fearful of what she will do.

Becky's personal narrative is quite positive, but the personal narratives of the other two children are not. Yet all children want and need the same things: They need to feel love and that people are invested in them, to experience success, to have role models to guide the way, and to receive attention and constructive feedback to help them develop in a healthy manner. Some children will excel and thrive on the praise they receive from their good works, whereas others will gain your attention by continually being out of their seats and causing a commotion. In both instances, the children are seeking to engage you, and they incorporate your feedback into their stories about themselves.

Children's personal narratives are constantly being constructed, and educators can have a significant impact on them. Elementary school is an ideal time to help children who see themselves as poor students experience success; for children who see fighting as the only solution to become positive problem solvers; and for children who appear self-assured and confident to continue to experience situations that challenge them to grow and develop.

BULLY BUSTERS SUPPORT TEAM THINK BLOCK

Take time to think of each child in your class. Think of children who are very successful, both academically and socially. How do the narratives of strong and healthy kids "read"?

1. What are the major themes of each child's story?

2. What is it about these children that makes them feel a sense of personal power?

3. Do they have support at home?

4. Do adults in their lives take time to do special things with them? Do they have role models?

Now think about the children who have a rough time in your class and what kind of personal narratives they have constructed for themselves.

1. What are the major themes of each child's story?

2. What is it about these children that makes them lack a sense of personal power?

3. Do they have support at home or other positive adult role models?

4. What purpose do these children's negative behaviors serve in your classroom?

5. Are there alternative ways for these children to meet their needs?

Positive Risks

Encouraging children to challenge themselves personally and academically within a safe and supportive environment can help them develop genuine self-confidence. Consider the child who frequently says he or she can't do something when you know the child can. This child can benefit from gentle support and encouragement in working through and succeeding at difficult tasks.

You can help children succeed by doing the following:

- *Be aware of the child's abilities and developmental stage.* Pushing children beyond what they are capable of doing can lead them to feel misunderstood and frustrated.

- *Have high expectations for performance.* Although we should not push children beyond their abilities, it is equally wrong not to expect children to perform to their ability levels.

- *Be supportive and encouraging.* Some children may be more cautious or anxious in approaching new tasks. This is OK, but be aware that they may need more coaching to achieve success. Work closely with these children, giving verbal support and providing guidance as needed.

- *Be patient.* The development of self-confidence is a gradual process in which children benefit from multiple experiences of success.

- *Work with parents.* Inform a child's parents that you are working with their child to increase his or her self-confidence in a particular area. Let them know how important it is for children to feel they can accomplish tasks and fulfill responsibilities on their own. Invite parents to join you in working with the child to build self-confidence.

Feelings Awareness

As discussed in chapter 1, students behave in a way that is consistent with how they feel about themselves. Often, students are reminded to "behave themselves" without addressing the underlying feelings that lead to the behavior. To help students establish better control over how they behave, they first need to become more aware of how they feel.

Most children receive instruction on how to behave but receive little instruction on how to identify their own and others' feelings. Sometimes children are told to monitor or control their feelings with expressions like "Chill out," "Cool it," or "Get yourself under control." Although the person giving such directions probably means well, the directions are generally too vague for students to understand. Our experience is that time spent helping children to identify their own and others' feelings and to understand the role emotions play in behavior is very worthwhile.

ANGER MANAGEMENT

Anger is a common and natural feeling. However, many people are afraid of anger because it is a very powerful emotion. Anger can be fueled by a number of other feelings, such as frustration, sadness, or hurt. Anger also can motivate people to act out violently or aggressively toward others.

Anger in Bullies, Victims, and Bystanders

All of the parties involved in a bullying situation can feel anger—sometimes very strong anger, even rage. Bullies often are children who have observed anger and aggression in their homes, schools, and neighborhoods and who are particularly aware of aggression in the media and in the larger community. Victims also experience anger, as a result of being in a one-down position and feeling powerless to stop the bullying. Victims of bullying often do not have an acceptable outlet for their anger, so these feelings fester inside until the children who are victimized release their emotion, either toward others or toward themselves. Recently, through media coverage of school shootings, we have heard the debilitating, and at times fatal, effects of victims' anger. Bystanders also can have feelings of anger, the result of observing their peers being treated poorly, feeling powerless to change the situation, and lacking hope that their school can be made safe.

Different Ways of Expressing Anger: Using Animal Examples

Identifying anger and learning to manage this emotion in a positive way are skills that will benefit all students throughout their schooling and into their adult lives. Both adults and children express and manage their feelings of anger differently. Some children express their anger through overt verbal or physical aggression. Other children have learned that it is not "nice" or acceptable to express anger in these ways and may deny their feelings or keep them bottled-up inside. Others fear both their own anger and that of others.

Talking openly about the feeling of anger with students can help normalize this emotion and communicate that it is an emotion children can learn to manage. For children, a good (and fun) way to explain different responses to anger is to introduce the topic in a friendly and non-threatening manner, through stories about animals. The following animal characters illustrate different ways of handling anger. Reading these descriptions to children can give them the opportunity to identify and discuss their own expression of this emotion. Using puppets to play the different characters can be very effective.

Katie Clam: Anger Trapped Inside

Some children hold their anger in and don't express their feelings when they become angry. Instead, their angry feelings build and build. This can be good in some ways because it prevents conflicts from occurring. However, it can be bad because anger usually builds and builds until something happens, sometimes even a small thing that wouldn't ordinarily make you feel angry, and then there is an anger explosion! Like Katie Clam, some people really "clam up" when they are angry and refuse to talk at all. Eventually, Katie

Clam has so much anger inside she has to force her shell open to deal with it.

Leonard Lion: Roaring Anger

Some children's anger may be very violent. An upsetting situation might occur, and these children may immediately become angry—yelling, name-calling, or hitting other children. Some children say that they "see red" and don't know why they act the way they do. Like Leonard Lion, these children yell and roar when they are mad. Sometimes even the smallest little annoyance causes them to let out a roar!

Molly Mouse: Angry? Not Me!

Some children are not comfortable with feelings of anger and say they don't feel anger at all. They may have been taught in their homes that it is not appropriate to feel angry. Although everyone feels anger at times, these students may try to ignore their angry feelings. Like Molly Mouse, some people never make a squeak about how mad they are—instead, they scurry away!

Linus Lobster: Snappy, Snappy Anger

Sometimes children will do things that make others students very angry. Sometimes they do this on purpose, like name-calling, and sometimes they do this accidentally, like bumping into someone. For some reason, these angry students who are called names or bumped into do not feel comfortable talking about their feelings. Linus Lobster is like this sometimes. He gets angry but doesn't express his anger to the person who angered him. Instead, Linus Lobster snaps at anyone who comes near him rather than the person who really made him mad.

Wise Olive Owl: Let's Talk

Some children have learned how to talk about their angry feelings with others. Sometimes they can even sit down with the person they are angry with and talk about the situation, what made them upset, and what the two of them could do to make the situation better. Learning to talk about conflicts is a skill all children can learn. Like Wise Olive Owl, children can learn to recognize angry feelings and talk about their problems with one another.

CONFLICT RESOLUTION

Another area of personal power is effective conflict management. Here are some important facts about conflict:

- Conflict between people is natural and often based on individual differences.

- The outcome of conflict can be good, bad, or neutral.

- Positive conflict resolution can lead to personal growth, learning, appreciation of differences, and change.

- Positive conflict resolution strategies can create situations in which everyone involved wins.

- Unresolved conflicts will not go away; they will reappear and may escalate into serious aggression or violence.

Frustration is a primary source of conflict in childhood and motivates a great deal of aggressive behavior. Family issues, peer issues, or school difficulties may contribute to children's frustration. At school, a high level of frustration can often lead to acting-out behaviors, which sometimes allow the child to avoid academic tasks or other responsibilities.

All students, but especially bullies and victims, need to learn positive ways to resolve conflict. Bullies and other aggressive youth often resolve conflict in harmful ways. Many children do not think about the negative consequences of solving a conflict in this manner. Often children, especially younger or more aggressive children, act before they think through their options. Although bullies may feel as though they have prevailed through their use of power, in actuality both bullies and their victims lose. Bullies lose because their inability to control their emotions leads to further school troubles and the assignment of negative labels. Victims lose because the emotional or physical threat of harm causes emotional scarring.

Peacemakers versus Peacebreakers

Bodine and Crawford (1999) state that "Conflict resolution education equips individuals to act as peacemakers; peacemakers are emotionally intelligent individuals" (p. 150). Specifically, Bodine and Crawford say that peacemakers have the following qualities:

- See themselves as responsible for the safety and productivity of their school world

- Feel connected to their school world and value the ways they can make their school world better with the help of those around them

- Are willing to become involved in activities and behaviors that help one another

According to Bodine and Crawford, peacebreakers possess a different set of qualities. They tend to act in these ways:

- Seek retaliation

- Use aggression to solve conflicts

- Do not take personal responsibility for problems or conflicts; often blame others for the conflict or outcome

- Have not established alternative ways to address conflict

Bullies are "peacebreakers." They do not have or use positive conflict resolution skills. Instead, bullies continually resort to coercion and violence to handle conflict. Bullies often blame their victims, saying their victims deserve the bullying because they have some characteristic the bullies feel they cannot tolerate. Conflict management skills can help bullies begin to feel connected to their school and responsible for the effects of their behaviors on others.

Although victims may not be peacebreakers, like bullies, they lack the skills to take on the role of peacemaker. Victims (especially provocative victims) often respond to bullies in a manner that seems to invite bullying. Victims typically do not feel empowered to address conflicts between themselves and their aggressors. They often feel unsafe at school and, in addition, that they are not valued or perceived as contributing members of the school. Furthermore, victims often do not believe they are able to help themselves or others in bullying situations.

A Foundation for Effective Conflict Resolution

Effective conflict resolution involves certain knowledge and abilities that both children and adults can acquire. The child development literature associates the following with effective conflict resolution and interpersonal success:

- An understanding that nonviolence and respect are essential for managing conflict

- The development of emotional intelligence (i.e., the ability to look at one's own feelings and to consider how others involved may feel; Goleman, 1995)

- The ability to control emotions and behaviors (Bodine & Crawford, 1999)

- The ability to communicate feelings and thoughts to others

- The ability to listen to others

- The ability to brainstorm numerous options in handling a conflict

    Another useful skill is the ability to ask oneself the Big Questions:

1. What is my goal?

2. What am I doing?

3. Is what I am doing helping me achieve my goal?

4. *(If not)* What can I do differently?

As you are teaching, think of ways you can incorporate the Big Questions into your daily lessons. For example, if you are teaching reading, you might apply the Big Questions to a conflict in a story you are reading to the class. Specifically, you could ask your students to take these steps:

1. Define the conflict.

2. Identify who is involved in the conflict.

3. Describe how they think each participant feels in the conflict.

4. Think of good ways for the participants to handle the conflict.

5. Decide whether the approach chosen will work.

BULLY BUSTERS SUPPORT TEAM THINK BLOCK

With your team, discuss the following questions:

1. What are some common conflicts in your classroom? What do you do when they occur?

2. How have you seen other teachers handle conflicts? Describe a positive and negative approach that you have observed.

3. What feelings do you have when you are in a conflict? Do you manage these emotions as effectively as you would like, or do you think you need additional skills?

4. If you need additional skills for managing emotions in conflicting times, what would they be and who might help you learn them?

Successful Problem Solving

The Bully Busters program has as one of its goals helping students learn a strategy for problem solving that will assist them in making good decisions and dealing with conflict in a positive way. All problem-solving strategies involve stepping back from the problem situation, calming down, reflecting on what has happened, and choosing a plan that will result in a positive outcome. They also commonly include, as a final step, an evaluation of the success or failure of the plan employed.

BUILDING CONNECTIONS: THE POWER OF RELATIONSHIPS

Children learn and grow through supportive and nurturing relationships. Relationships that communicate caring and respect foster healthy growth, whereas those characterized by conflict or pathology can lead to disconnection and isolation. Children who are isolated, either by other children or by choice, are primary targets for bullies. These children do not have the social support network they need to protect themselves or to help them learn and improve their social skills. When children are tied into social networks, not only do they naturally benefit from the friendships, they also have an open forum for feedback and problem solving as well as people to turn to for help when it is needed most.

Through your daily classroom activities and instruction, you can maximize opportunities to establish and nurture connections between yourself and your students, as well as among students. For example, you can have your students perform classroom activities in pairs or small groups, assign class projects that involve the whole school, and invite community members or school volunteers into your classroom to participate in activities.

Building School Families

One especially effective way to build connections among children is to create "school families" composed of younger and older students. We have observed beneficial effects from having older students take on the role of "big brothers" or "big sisters" to younger students. Older members of the school family can serve as guides, teachers, and mentors to the younger students. Each year, new students can be added to the families. Each family can also have an adult role model to help coordinate their time together. These adults can be school professionals, but they may also be volunteers from the community. These families can offer support and help decrease feelings of isolation at school. All students can benefit from belonging to their families and can be empowered by helping one another through the years.

Including Humor and Laughter

The quotation "Play is the work of children" has been attributed to Jean Piaget, and there is truth to this idea. Too many children see school as a place where fun is set aside at the classroom door. Including humor and laughter in the classroom is one way to help students develop personal power and stronger relationships.

Encouraging Laughter and Fun in the Classroom

The saying "Laughter is the best medicine" is an important message to all of us. Sometimes in the stress of daily life, children and adults alike forget to have fun. With our busy lives, it is easy to remain task-focused and overlook time for good old-fashioned fun. Even very young children can begin to take life too seriously. Sometimes the intensity of the school day, numerous after-school activities, or stressful events at home cause laughter to take a backseat in children's daily lives.

Children can find humor in imaginative play, through being silly, or by inventing new and different characters in class skits.

What you can do . . .

- Take time to have fun with your students. During long weeks or stress-filled days, take a break to read your students a funny story or show a funny movie.

- Allow students to have a "joke time," when they can share jokes they have learned or read jokes from children's joke books. (Before joke time, remind students that jokes should not make fun of other students or groups of people.)

- Take note of the students in your class who are and are not laughing. Who is not laughing? Why is this? Some students simply have a different sense of humor, but others may be experiencing depression or reacting to troubling events in their lives. If you notice that certain children look sad, are withdrawn, or have difficulty laughing or engaging in fun activities, seek help from your school counselor, psychologist, or social worker. These children may need individual intervention from you or the school counselor.

Giving Children Permission to Laugh at Themselves

It can be very embarrassing when a child makes a mistake, especially if the class and teacher notice the mistake. Some children will see their mistakes, negative interactions with others, or even clumsiness as indications of personal failure. Children, as do adults, tend to focus on these "failures" and are unable to see them in perspective. Everyone makes mistakes, everyone is clumsy at times, and we all have bad days. It is what we do at these times that makes a difference. Some children will proceed as if nothing happened, "blowing it off," whereas others will berate themselves, hang their heads, and withdraw. More aggressive children may externalize their feelings by blaming others.

Children and adults can learn how to laugh at themselves to minimize anxiety or discomfort. For example, as you watch the morning news, you may notice that even news readers, who are typically skilled at clear articulation, will get tongue-tied. When this happens, many news readers will make a joke or laugh and continue with their presentation. This lets listeners know that they realized what happened but that it doesn't affect their ability to say what they have to say.

What you can do . . .

- Serve as a role model by laughing appropriately at yourself. Some children will have mastered this skill. Others may make jokes about themselves that bring them negative attention. The goal is to teach children when and how they should laugh at themselves.

- When you notice a child appropriately laughing at a mistake, praise that child publicly for handling this challenging situation.

- Ask your students to find something each day that is funny about themselves or their lives.

Knowing When Not to Laugh

It is also important to help children learn when not to laugh. Laughing together is one thing; for example, a group of friends may laugh at something one of them said or did. Laughing with the group is different from laughing at someone outside the group. When the latter occurs, the laughter may be accompanied by pointing and whispering, and it may make someone else feel ridiculed.

What you can do . . .

- Make a class rule that informs your students that making fun of or laughing at other children is not acceptable or tolerated in your class.

- Keep a watchful eye. If you observe children inappropriately laughing at another child, intervene immediately.

You can also share examples like the following with your class:

> *Christian is walking to the front of the class and trips on his shoelace. He drops all of the papers in his hands, and the class breaks out in an uproar. Christian is not hurt, but he is embarrassed.*

As a teacher, you could calmly say to the class, "We help our classmates—we don't laugh at them. How can you help your classmate?" You could also help the class see the situation from Christian's point of view by asking, "What could Christian do that would help him deal with this embarrassing situation in a confident way?" Have the class brainstorm, then evaluate possible responses: For example, Christian could run out of the room, but how would that help? He has to come back. Maybe Christian could take a bow for his performance. In this way, he could take control of the situation by making a joke of it himself.

Module 3: Content Review

The following statements relate to the learning goals of this module. Ask yourself if you feel confident that you can answer yes to each item. If not, please review the material and discuss any difficulties among your Bully Busters Support Team.

1. I understand the importance of enhancing students' sense of personal power.   Yes ❑   No ❑

2. I know that students can derive a sense of personal power from having strong, healthy personal narratives; positive risk taking; and becoming aware of their own and others' feelings.   Yes ❑   No ❑

3. I have considered the differences in the behavior of children who have strong, healthy narratives and those who do not.   Yes ❑   No ❑

4. I understand the role of anger in the bully-victim relationship and can explain different ways to respond to anger by using animal examples.   Yes ❑   No ❑

5. I know that effective conflict resolution skills, including problem-solving skills, are essential to preventing and reducing bullying and have thought about ways to integrate these skills into my classroom.   Yes ❑   No ❑

6. I know that personal power derives from quality relationships with others and that I can strengthen my relationships with my students by building school families and encouraging laughter and fun in the classroom.   Yes ❑   No ❑

Bully Busters: A Teacher's Manual for Helping Bullies, Victims, and Bystanders (Grades K–5)
© 2003 by Arthur M. Horne, Christi L. Bartolomucci, and Dawn Newman-Carlson.
Champaign, IL: Research Press. (800) 519–2707.

A Reminder . . .

CLASSROOM INTERACTION AND AWARENESS CHART

Use the CIAC to describe any bullying behavior you observe (and that students report to you, if you wish). A copy of the CIAC and a weekly summary sheet appear in Appendix A.

THE BIG QUESTIONS

Honestly appraise your progress by asking yourself the Big Questions. There are no right or wrong answers.

In relation to building students' personal power:

1. What is my goal?

2. What am I doing?

3. Is what I am doing helping me achieve my goal?

4. *(If not)* What can I do differently?

PERSONAL GOALS FORM

The Personal Goals Form, on the next page, is designed to help you tailor the content of this module to your own students and situation. Please take a moment to fill out the form now.

Module 3: Personal Goals Form

Goals

- To understand the importance of personal power for students, especially as expressed in strong, healthy narratives; positive risk taking; and feelings awareness

- To learn how personal power relates to anger in bullies, victims, and bystanders

- To consider the importance of effective conflict resolution and problem solving for the development of personal power

- To understand how using school families and appropriate laughter can enhance personal power

1. My own definition of personal power is as follows:

2. I have observed incidents of bullying. *(Please record incidents on the CIAC.)*

   ____ Number of times I intervened   ____ Number of times I chose not to intervene

   Other observations:

3. I will review the classroom activities for this module and select ones appropriate for my class. *(Please list.)*

4. I will accept the challenges associated with the developmental assets. *(Please list the specific assets and describe what you plan to do.)*

5. I will give my students feedback about the bullying incidents I have observed and encourage discussion of bullying and related issues. We will discuss these topics:

6. I will share my experiences in applying the information in this module with other teachers and administrators, as well as with my students' families. *(Please specify who and when.)*

7. I will meet with my Bully Busters Support Team. *(Please specify when and list what issues and questions you will raise.)*

Bully Busters: A Teacher's Manual for Helping Bullies, Victims, and Bystanders (Grades K–5)
© 2003 by Arthur M. Horne, Christi L. Bartolomucci, and Dawn Newman-Carlson.
Champaign, IL: Research Press. (800) 519–2707.

Classroom Activities

ACTIVITY 3.1: NAME THAT FEELING (GRADES K–2)

This activity promotes personal power by helping students identify common feelings others may have in various challenging situations. Knowing what others are experiencing and feeling can empower students to manage their own feelings and behavior more effectively.

ACTIVITY 3.2: WHAT WOULD YOU DO? (GRADES K–2)

This activity includes a handout illustrating, in picture form, different ways of responding to difficult situations. Students are asked to identify the "best way" and "worst way" of handling each situation. In doing this, they become more conscious of alternatives and their consequences.

ACTIVITY 3.3: CAN YOU HEAR ME NOW? (GRADES K–5)

This activity helps children acquire personal power by learning active listening skills and making assertive "I feel" statements. They can use these statements in tough situations to tell others how they are feeling and what they would like to have happen.

ACTIVITY 3.4: MY GIFT TO YOU (GRADES 3–5)

In this activity, students identify their own characteristics, then work in small groups to share this information about themselves. In the process, they come to appreciate and accept one another's unique characteristics and begin to develop tolerance for individual differences.

Name That Feeling

OBJECTIVES

- To help students increase their abilities to recognize emotions

- To encourage students to consider the emotional consequences of various interactions

- To allow students the opportunity to feel comfortable identifying and talking about feelings

MATERIALS

- Copies of the Name That Feeling worksheet

- Pencils or pens

DIRECTIONS

1. Distribute copies of the Name That Feeling worksheet, and instruct students to look at the feeling faces.

2. Ask the class to name the feeling for each face and then, individually, to trace the feeling word under the feeling face.

3. After they have finished, read each situation in the right-hand column, one at a time. After reading each situation, ask students to identify the feeling that goes along with it, then draw a line from the situation to the feeling face.

4. Facilitate discussion by asking the following questions.

DISCUSSION QUESTIONS

- When have you felt happy? Sad? Scared? Mad?

- What do you look like when you feel happy? Sad? Scared? Mad?

- How do others know when you are happy? Sad? Scared? Mad?

- What do you like to do when you are happy? Sad? Scared? Mad?

Name That Feeling

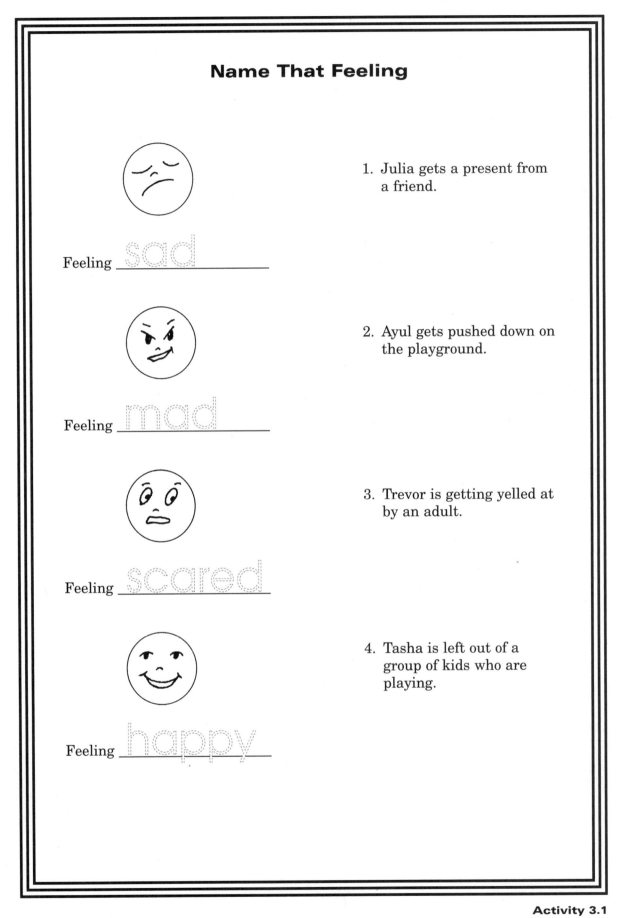

Feeling _sad_

1. Julia gets a present from a friend.

Feeling _mad_

2. Ayul gets pushed down on the playground.

Feeling _scared_

3. Trevor is getting yelled at by an adult.

Feeling _happy_

4. Tasha is left out of a group of kids who are playing.

Bully Busters: A Teacher's Manual for Helping Bullies, Victims, and Bystanders (Grades K–5)
© 2003 by Arthur M. Horne, Christi L. Bartolomucci, and Dawn Newman-Carlson.
Champaign, IL: Research Press. (800) 519–2707.

What Would You Do?

OBJECTIVES

- To encourage students to develop problem-solving skills, necessary in handling bullying and other tough situations

- To help students learn alternative ways to manage aggression

- To increase students' awareness of and control over responses in these situations

MATERIALS

- Copies of the What Would You Do? worksheet

- Pencils or pens

DIRECTIONS

1. Give each student a copy of the What Would You Do? worksheet. Direct students' attention to the first situation, then read the situation aloud (i.e., "Ray hit Benjamin").

2. Explain that the three pictures that go with this first example show different ways the student who was bullied could respond. Go over what is happening in each picture so the possible responses are clear.

   Situation 1: Ray hit Benjamin.

   > A. Benjamin tells the teacher. *(best)*
   >
   > B. Benjamin hits Ray Back *(worst)*
   >
   > C. Benamin yells at Ray.

3. Once students understand the possible responses, ask them to identify the picture that shows the best way to handle the situation by circling it, then to identify the worst way by drawing an *X* over it.

4. Follow the procedure in Steps 2 and 3 for the remaining two situations.

   Situation 2: A fifth grader stole a second grader's lunch.

   > A. The second grader cries.

B. The second grader tells the teacher. *(best)*

C. The second grader kicks the fifth grader. *(worst)*

Situation 3: David called Rita a name.

A. Rita calls David a name back.

B. Rita hits David. *(worst)*

C. Rita tells David, "Go away." *(best)*

DISCUSSION QUESTIONS

- How do you decide how you want to handle a tough situation?

- Is it easy or hard to make a good choice?

- What happens if someone hits you and you hit the person back? Do you also get in trouble for hitting?

- Do you know anyone who handles tough situations well?

- Whom can you go to for help if you are in a tough situation?

What Would You Do?

1. Ray hit Benjamin.

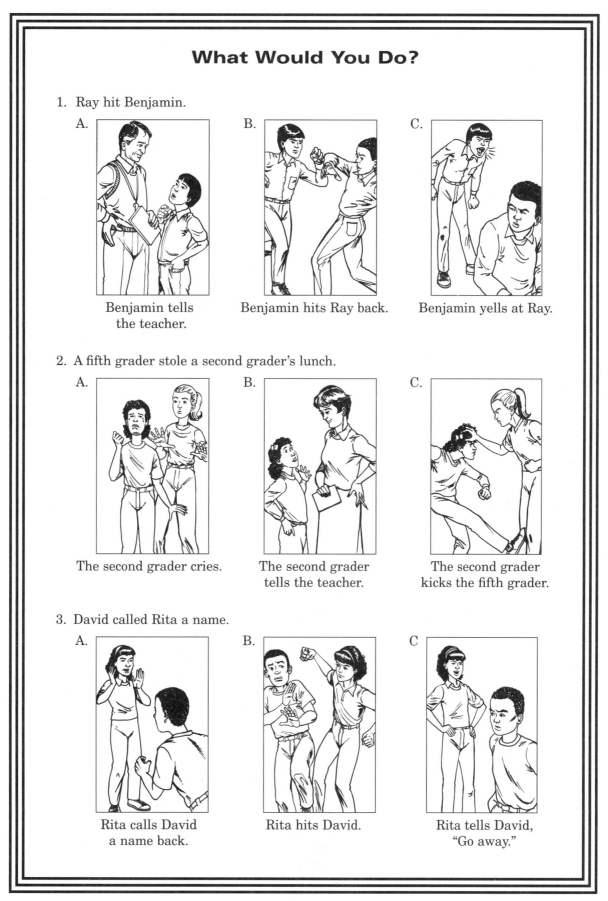

A.

Benjamin tells
the teacher.

B.

Benjamin hits Ray back.

C.

Benjamin yells at Ray.

2. A fifth grader stole a second grader's lunch.

A.

The second grader cries.

B.

The second grader
tells the teacher.

C.

The second grader
kicks the fifth grader.

3. David called Rita a name.

A.

Rita calls David
a name back.

B.

Rita hits David.

C

Rita tells David,
"Go away."

Activity 3.2

Bully Busters: A Teacher's Manual for Helping Bullies, Victims, and Bystanders (Grades K–5)
© 2003 by Arthur M. Horne, Christi L. Bartolomucci, and Dawn Newman-Carlson.
Champaign, IL: Research Press. (800) 519–2707.

153

Can You Hear Me Now?

OBJECTIVES

- To help prevent bullying problems from developing by encouraging students to develop active listening skills

- To show students how to express their needs more effectively by using "I feel" messages

- To give students the opportunity to practice using assertive statements

MATERIALS

- Chalkboard or easel pad

DIRECTIONS

1. Introduce the topic of assertive communication. You might say something like this:

   > Today we are going to be talking about talking. How we talk to others is a very important part of getting along. Sometimes when we are in hard situations, when we are being bullied or we are feeling angry, we don't know what to say or do. Today we are going to learn how to talk to someone when we are in such a situation.

2. Ask students whether they have ever heard the word *communication*. Discuss, then summarize by saying something like this:

   > When people communicate, there are at least two people involved, the talker and the listener. The talker is the person telling something to the other person, and the listener is listening with his or her ears to hear what the talker is trying to share. Let's talk about what each of these people can do to help communication go smoothly.

3. Discuss the role of the listener, pointing out that good listening involves using *active listening skills*. While describing each of the following skills, act it out for your students:

Eye contact: Looking at the talker, giving the talker your attention *(Point to your eyes.)*

Body language: Facing your body toward the talker, sitting still, nodding your head *(Exaggerate these movements.)*

Mouth closed: Not interrupting the talker, waiting your turn to talk *(Pretend to zip your mouth shut.)*

4. Role-play these elements to show their importance. First demonstrate inappropriate listening by having a student start talking to you about some topic. Look around instead of at the speaker, face away, and/or interrupt. Ask the students how you did, then role-play active listening skills instead.

5. Discuss the role of the speaker, saying something along these lines:

> What we say and how we say something can make a tough situation better or worse. Sometimes when we are feeling angry or frustrated or scared, it is hard to say things in a calm manner. Sometimes we might want to call the other person names, blame the other person for our feelings, interrupt the other person, or say something mean, but all of these things can make the situation worse. As the talker, it is your job to send a clear message.

6. Explain to students that you will be teaching something called an "I feel" message, which they can use when they are in a tough situation and need to tell another person how they are feeling and what they would like to have happen. Write the following on the chalkboard or easel pad.

I feel _____ when you take my toy.

I feel _____ when you don't pick me for your team.

7. Give examples like the following:

> Suppose Max pushes in front of you in the lunch line. Instead of pushing Max or saying, "Max, you always cut in front of me in line," you could say, "Max, I feel angry when you cut in front of me in line."

> Instead of telling Jasmine how mean she is for not playing with you, you could say, "Jasmine, I feel sad when you won't play with me at recess."

8. Next give students an opportunity to practice active listening skills and "I feel" messages. Read the following statements aloud, then ask for volunteers to rephrase them as "I feel" messages. (Sample answers are given in italics.)

Stop pushing me. *(I feel mad when you push me.)*

Give me my toy. *(I feel mad when you take my toy.)*

You're stupid. *(I feel sad when you call me names.)*

I'm not going by myself. *(I feel scared to go by myself.)*

9. Conclude by asking the discussion questions.

DISCUSSION QUESTIONS

- When you are talking with someone, how do you like him or her to act? What do you like that person to do when you are talking?

- How do you feel when someone talks to you in a mean way or blames you for something?

- How did you feel when you heard the "I feel" messages? Did those messages sound better than saying it the other way?

- Do you think you could use an "I feel" message with a bully or someone who is doing something that you did not like? When could you do that?

My Gift to You

OBJECTIVES

- To help students recognize their own special qualities
- To allow students to see one another as unique
- To foster an appreciation of differences, as well as similarities, among classmates

MATERIALS

- Copies of the My Gift to You worksheet
- Pencils or pens

DIRECTIONS

1. Introduce the lesson by explaining that today you are going to talk about individual differences and learn something about the special qualities each student has.

2. Give each student a copy of the My Gift to You worksheet. Explain the purpose of the activity by saying something like the following:

   There are many things about each of us that make us special. We call these things "characteristics." Sometimes we have the same characteristics as other people, but sometimes our characteristics are very different. When all of our characteristics come together, they make each of us a very special person. Every person is special in his or her own way.

3. Read, or have students read, each item on the worksheet aloud, and ask students to fill in the blanks to finish the sentences.

4. When students have completed the worksheet, separate the class into groups of four. Have group members share their answers with one another.

5. After 5 or 10 minutes, ask the class to reassemble, then ask the discussion questions.

DISCUSSION QUESTIONS

- Did you find things you had in common with your group?

- What does it mean to be special?

- What did you learn about your classmates in this exercise?

- Why is it important to appreciate people's differences?

- Why is it good for people to like the way in which you are special?

My Gift to You

1. In my family, there are _____ people.

2. My favorite thing to do after school is _____.

3. I like to _____.

4. When I grow up I want to be a _____.

5. It makes me very happy when _____.

6. My favorite animal is a _____.

7. Most people don't know that I _____.

8. I was born in _____.

9. It hurts my feelings when _____.

10. I get so mad when _____.

11. My favorite story is _____.

MODULE

4 Recognizing the Bully

OVERVIEW

In order to achieve the goal of reducing and preventing bullying, we need to be able to recognize and understand children who bully. Bullies typically are seen as problem children and labeled negatively throughout their school years, but it is important to realize that they have learned aggressive means of interacting with others to meet their social and emotional needs—and that they deserve our help and attention. Before we can intervene to improve their behaviors and social interactions, we must be able to recognize bullies and understand the process whereby their bullying behaviors have developed.

GOALS

- To understand differences between the bully and the well-adapted child

- To learn how bullying behaviors develop and are influenced by child characteristics, family interactions, school environment, community, and culture

- To understand the relationship of learning and behavioral consequences to bullying

- To identify three types of bullies: aggressive, passive, and relational

- To become aware of typical differences between male and female bullying

THE AGGRESSIVE VERSUS THE WELL-ADAPTED CHILD

In recognizing bullies, it is helpful to understand how the behavior of the aggressive child differs from that of the well-adapted child. Table 4 compares characteristics of the aggressive child and the well-adapted child. Although these two representations are extremes, and it is very unlikely that any child will have all of the characteristics of either extreme, these differences appear at many levels.

TABLE 4 The Aggressive versus the Well-Adapted Child

The aggressive child	*The well-adapted child*
• Often sees the world through paranoid eyes and interprets others as instigating conflict.	• In a warm and caring social environment, learns to consider the perspectives and feelings of others.
• Manages conflict through aggression.	• Values working together.
• Uses force to solve problems.	• Solves problems through collaboration and cooperation.
• Lacks trust, respect, tolerance, and appreciation for others.	• Is willing to listen and work with others to come up with mutual solutions.
• Reacts to others negatively, based on misinterpretations of others' behaviors.	• Respects others and appreciates differences.
• Expects others to buckle under his or her force.	• Feels responsible for his or her behavior.

THE DEVELOPMENT OF BULLYING BEHAVIORS

Bullying does not occur in isolation. It is the result of interactions in a variety of systems, including the home, school, community, and society at large. The development of the bully can best be understood in the context of the various influences on the bully.

The development of children is influenced by a number of factors: the individual child's genetic, cognitive, and temperamental characteristics at birth; the child's interactions within the family, with peers and others in the school environment, and with neighbors and others in the community; and the child's cultural background. All children learn by observing and experiencing the outcomes of their interactions—positive and negative—in the world. Some children learn effective living skills through their observations and interactions; others learn coercive and aggressive behavior.

Child Characteristics

Children are born with certain genetic characteristics—eye and skin color, for example. Characteristics at birth also include temperament and intellectual and cognitive attributes. Any parent of more than one child—and all teachers—can tell that children come with a variety of individual characteristics. Some children are temperamentally more calm and easygoing, friendlier, and more optimistic and happy, whereas others are more irritable, distant, and prone to conflict.

Each child develops his or her own set of personality traits (e.g., temperament, sense of self-worth, resilience); physical characteristics (e.g., tall, strong); and behaviors (e.g., aggressive, immature, thoughtful). These qualities serve to influence the child's early family interactions as well as interactions with other children. Although characteristics such as eye color and height are fixed, and children may be born with predispositions toward certain behaviors based on temperament, predispositions

Module 4: Recognizing the Bully

are not destined to be expressed in behavior. Children learn behavior through their interactions with others, and this includes bullying and other forms of aggressive behavior.

Family Interactions

Children's behavior is greatly influenced by the home environment and by parent-child interactions. For example, if family members respond coercively to a child predisposed to be fussy, the child is likely to develop aggressive, bullying tendencies. The child develops and maintains bullying behavior as a result of the interactions he or she has with family members and others: The behavior is learned, not predetermined.

The bully at school is often the victim at home and has caretakers who use physical discipline; provide little supervision; are hostile, rejecting, authoritarian, or inconsistent in their parenting; lack effective problem-solving skills; and teach their children to strike back when provoked (Batsche & Knoff, 1994; Fleischman, Horne, & Arthur, 1982; Floyd, 1985; Horne & Sayger, 1990; Patterson, 1982, 1986; Voors, 2000). Aggressive children have family members who tend to be inconsistent and use such ineffective discipline practices as coercion and harsh punishment (Olweus, 1978; Patterson, 1986). In addition, family members and caretakers of aggressive children tend to provide inadequate emotional support and are likely to display a lack of warmth or caring (Olweus, 1993).

Family interactions are often influenced by many stress factors, including marital conflict, single-parent households, and low income. Such factors may contribute to the development of bullying behavior (Horne, 1990; Lowenstein, 1978; Stephenson & Smith, 1987). When families experience stress, it is hard for parents to find the time and patience to focus on the child and model effective means of interacting. Furthermore, many parents have not learned how to communicate their feelings or deal with conflict without force, intimidation, or violence. This limitation in turn interferes with their ability to teach such skills to their child.

When studying the impact of temperament on future behavior, it is evident that some children are more active at birth, have more difficulty relating to others, and are harder for parents and teachers to manage (Forehand & Long, 1996; Horne & Sayger, 1990; Martin, 1988). The likelihood of difficulty in the home with environmental stresses is multiplied exponentially when the child's temperament is also difficult. Even when the child is an infant, parents can interpret the child's behavior as a purposeful attempt to irritate them, when in actuality the child may be signaling needs that must be met, as all babies do. The tension between parents and child can develop very early and only increases as the child ages and environmental stressors increase.

In the home environment marked by high stress and conflicted relationships, children do not frequently experience open displays of affection, appropriate parenting skills, or unconditional love. Further, they do not learn positive means of resolving conflict; rather, conflict may be ignored until it becomes violence. These children may not have contact with individuals who attend to their emotional needs, help them express their feelings, or model ways they can control their emotions. Instead, they may learn that expressing emotions is "wimpy" or that it is desirable to resolve their conflicts by force. Some children may be physically harmed if they do not stand up for themselves in an aggressive way when in conflict with others. Consequently, it may be difficult for these children to identify and express their feelings, experience empathy for others, or learn positive and healthy ways to exist in relationships.

This explanation is given neither to blame nor to excuse families. Rather, it is offered to emphasize the challenges often present in the homes of aggressive children and the importance of including parents in bullying interventions. Although changing the family environment is a monumental task—and usually beyond the abilities of schools and teachers—teachers and parents can work collaboratively to bring about change in the beliefs and behaviors of children.

Family involvement is essential in changing the behavior of children who bully. We value the inclusion of families and encourage you to identify ways you can involve parents in your efforts to prevent and decrease bullying. Change is most likely to occur if the child receives consistent messages across the home and school settings. For particularly challenging families, it will be important to bring in the school counselor, psychologist, or social worker for more intensive and ongoing interventions.

The School Environment

In the school environment, children's behavior is influenced both by adults (teachers, principals, counselors, etc.) and by their peers. Educators have never intentionally promoted aggression in schools, yet aggression and bullying behavior are traditions in American schools (Wilezenski et al., 1994), and the bullying behaviors of children seem to be deeply embedded in the school culture (Young, 1994). In many schools, bullying, although not intentionally endorsed, is often legitimized. This perception is fostered by the disciplinary philosophy of some schools and demonstrated by the unwillingness of some teachers, administrators, and counselors to attend to and intervene in bullying or other types of student conflict. Nonintervention by school personnel may be perceived as approval of the aggressor, thereby tacitly reinforcing aggression. Bullies may wonder, "If what I was doing was wrong, wouldn't the teacher say something?" When bullying is ignored, both bullies and victims get the message that bullying is acceptable school behavior (Fried & Fried, 1996; Hoover et al., 1992).

Children who are not prone to aggression and violence in their homes or neighborhoods are unlikely to engage in bullying at school. These children acquire positive strategies to communicate differences and resolve conflicts, and they learn to care about and respect others through these positive interactions. But children who experience parental coercion, without consistent warmth and with few or no negative consequences for aggressive behavior, become susceptible to using aggression and violence in the school. Intimidation tactics are what they know, and they know that these tactics can gain them the power and attention they desire.

At school, acceptance and rejection by peers also affects the development of bullying behaviors. If a child develops appropriate social skills and is able to interact effectively with other children, then the future is positive. The child will likely be accepted by a supportive peer group. However, if the child fails to develop these social skills, the child is likely to be rejected. When rejected by peers, he or she may resort to socializing with peers who are available, and these peers may be others rejected by the group. The rejected group is likely to engage in aggression and other forms of antisocial behavior. Bullying also allows children who are either bored with school or not doing well to be good at something, prove their courage and dominance over other children, and feel superior (Ross, 1996). In addition, it eliminates the need to form friendships with other children.

Children who become bullies are attempting to gain the recognition and attention they crave and have not experienced in healthy relationships. These children do the best that they can, use what they know, and recognize that bullying others can get them what they want and need. Although we have little influence to change family factors, we can work together to understand what factors lead to bullying and help children who bully have a more positive experience while at school, find new ways of interacting with their peers, and learn more appropriate behaviors. The great news is that teachers are in a powerful position to prevent and reduce bullying behaviors: They do this by facilitating the development of more adaptive skills, more effective means of problem solving and conflict resolution, and more positive relationships.

The Community

The neighborhood in which one resides is influential in the development of bullying behaviors. In some neighborhoods, the concept of "survival of the fittest" predominates. Children may believe there are only two choices: fight or lose. With this belief system, how can they win? In addition, the attitude of the community can have a significant effect on the type of interpersonal relationships considered acceptable (Fried & Fried, 1996). Sanctioning or increased tolerance of bullying may reflect the community's inability or lack of interest in supporting alternative solutions (Young, 1994).

Children who bully may learn their bullying tactics from other children in the neighborhood; they may even be the victims of bullying in their neighborhoods. Older children in the community may serve as role models to younger and more impressionable children. These children, impressed by the strength and perceived popularity of their own oppressors, begin to imitate bullying behavior with children yet younger than themselves.

Many communities are not safe for children. As Benson (1997) has noted, many factors, common and accepted, hinder children's development—for example, low socioeconomic level and the availability of alcohol, drugs, and weapons, as well as abuse and violence. Benson and his colleagues at the Search Institute do not recommend accepting violent and unhealthy communities as they are. Rather, they encourage the community to take a stand and join together to raise responsible, caring, and successful children.

Culture

The cultural context exerts a profound influence on the development and maintenance of bullying and other aggressive behaviors. Embedded in the cultural context are attitudes that sanction and reinforce bullying, such as the motto "Stand up for yourself." This is underscored by the role of the media in shaping the values of American culture. For example, in television programs, bullying and aggression often are rewarded. Such portrayals further reinforce the acceptance of bullying as a social norm (Fried & Fried, 1996; Horne, Glaser, & Sayger, 1994). In addition, there is a general consensus that active and aggressive behavior is a normal and desirable characteristic for American children (Olweus, 1991). On the whole, the American culture stresses individualism and competition rather than collectivism and collaboration.

Children begin to learn early that in order to get ahead in the world they may have to step on others' toes. But is this really the message we want to communicate to children? Many people succeed by understanding themselves, understanding others, and learning how to maximize their potential (Goleman, 1995). In actuality, children who are most likely to succeed as adults are children who feel a connection, a sense of belonging, and a personal responsibility to their families, schools, and community (Benson, 1997). It is through healthy connections that children learn how to interact effectively with others and achieve success throughout their childhood and adult lives.

THE BULLY-DEVELOPMENT MODEL

Another way of looking at the influences of the child, family, neighborhood, school, and community is provided in our own model of bully development, shown in Figure 5. The *culture* is a contextual variable that umbrellas the entire model. In brief, culture encompasses societal norms, which are highly influential in bullying. The society at large has a profound influence in determining what is acceptable within that culture. In simplified terms, the predominant culture impacts the *community,* affecting *family demographics. Disrupted family management* may combine with certain *child personality traits* to result in *weak conventional bonding* with the child, associated with *hostile parent/child interaction* and an *inconsistent parenting* style. These interaction styles may influence how the child's *temperament* is manifested in behavior, which in turn influences that child's *cognitive ability* to interpret environmental cues. For example, the child might misinterpret a pat on the back as a push or shove, an act of aggression, or a threat. This potentially leads to *bullying behaviors* inside and outside of the school. The bullying behaviors are often positively *reinforced by peers*: Spectators may

Figure 5 The Bully-Development Model

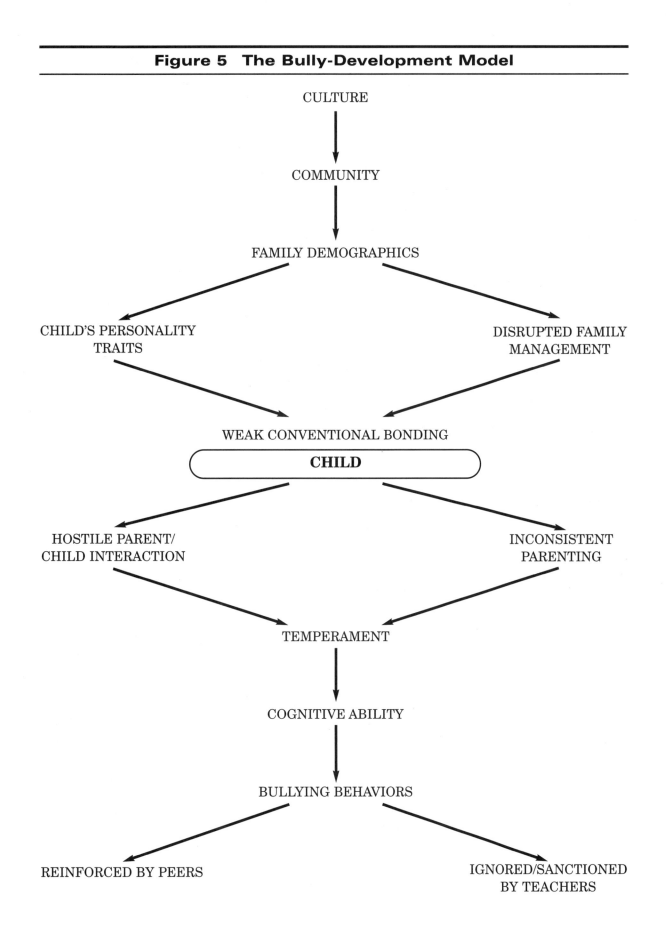

CULTURE

COMMUNITY

FAMILY DEMOGRAPHICS

CHILD'S PERSONALITY
TRAITS

DISRUPTED FAMILY
MANAGEMENT

WEAK CONVENTIONAL BONDING

CHILD

HOSTILE PARENT/
CHILD INTERACTION

INCONSISTENT
PARENTING

TEMPERAMENT

COGNITIVE ABILITY

BULLYING BEHAVIORS

REINFORCED BY PEERS

IGNORED/SANCTIONED
BY TEACHERS

express interest and admiration for the manipulations of the bully. In addition, it is not uncommon for bullying to be *ignored or sanctioned by teachers* who mistakenly believe that the children involved will "work it out on their own." Imagine as an adult becoming involved in a conflict with a much larger person on a downtown street in your town or city. Imagine further that a police officer comes to the scene and says, "You look like adults—you two work this out," then walks away, leaving you face to face with this large, menacing person. This is often the situation our children encounter. This general tolerance of bullying then contributes to the societal acceptance of bullying in our *culture*. In this continuous feedback loop, then, bullying behaviors amplify, resulting in more and more school violence.

FACTORS ASSOCIATED WITH BULLYING BEHAVIORS

As discussed, children learn bullying and aggression through their interactions within a variety of contexts. Bullying behaviors are learned in a social situation and are influenced and maintained through interactions with others. During these interactions, several factors help to explain how children learn bullying behaviors. These factors include different means of learning and different types of behavioral consequences. As you consider how these factors shape bullying behavior, also recognize that these same forces allow for the development of positive and emotionally intelligent responses.

Learning

Children learn bullying behaviors directly or vicariously through interactions in a variety of social contexts, including the home, school, neighborhood, community, and larger cultural context. Children learn prosocial, caring, empathic, and emotionally intelligent behaviors in the same way and in the same contexts.

Direct learning is learning experienced directly, specifically by "doing." For example, if one child pushes another child off a swing, then immediately gets to use the swing, the first child has learned directly that using force can get the child what he or she wants. *Vicarious learning* is learning experienced indirectly, by observing another's behavior and the consequences of that behavior. Children learn vicariously by observing behaviors in real life and depicted in movies, video games, television, and other media. Consider the previous example, in which one child pushes another child off the swing, then gets to use the swing immediately. A child observing this interaction witnesses the first child getting what he or she wants through the use of force. The observing child may learn vicariously, through his or her observation, that force is a powerful way to get what one wants.

Behavioral Consequences

The consequences of a behavior—reinforcement or punishment—determine whether the behavior will be maintained or extinguished. The bully's perception of reinforcement or punishment for bullying behaviors determines whether he or she will continue to bully. Likewise, a child's perceptions of the consequences of peaceful, supportive, and cooperative behaviors will determine whether he or she continues to interact with others in this manner or chooses a different means of interaction.

Positive Reinforcement

Positive reinforcement increases the frequency of a behavior through reward. Most people, adults included, work very well when positively reinforced (i.e., rewarded) for their behaviors. Employees may work harder when they know they will be given a financial bonus. Teachers may know that if they share their ideas with the principal in a particular manner, the principal will be more likely to agree. Bullies are no different: When bullies get their way, they are being positively reinforced and are more likely to continue to engage in the same behavior. The reinforcement may be direct (e.g., getting to use playground equipment), or it may be cognitive (e.g., getting pleasure out of being able to make a person do things he or she would not otherwise have done).

Positive reinforcement is particularly valuable in decreasing bullying because, when students are engaging in more positive behaviors, they are engaging in fewer negative ones. Therefore, it is important to "catch students being good."

Negative Reinforcement

Negative reinforcement increases the frequency of a behavior by removing an aversive, or unpleasant, stimulus. A teacher's ignoring bullying behavior is an example of negative reinforcement: In this case, the aversive response to the bully's behavior would be getting in trouble with the teacher. When the bully recognizes that the teacher will not respond, the bullying will likely continue or increase because there are no conditions present that would make the bully want or need to stop bullying. Other children can also provide negative reinforcement for bullying. When peers who have previously condemned bullying behavior begin to ignore bullying, the removal of their negative response maintains or increases the bullying behavior.

Punishment

Punishment decreases the frequency of a behavior and occurs when children endure a negative consequence for negative behaviors. When consequences bullies don't like follow bullying behavior (e.g., being placed in time-out or removed from the classroom), the intention is punishment. The difficulty in using punishment is making sure the response is, in fact, punishing. Sometimes bullies look on typical punishments as reinforcers instead. For example, being sent to the principal's office may be seen as a privilege if it promotes a "tough guy" image. If punishment is working, the behavior will decrease. If the behavior is maintained or increases, the response is not an appropriate punishment.

Behavioral principles are always at work, and employing behavioral techniques in the classroom can be a powerful method of reducing bullying behavior. Determining an appropriate program of reinforcement and punishment requires reflection and collaboration among school professionals. (Additional discussion of behavioral principles appears in Module 6, "Recommendations and Interventions for Bullying Behaviors.")

> ## BULLY BUSTERS SUPPORT TEAM THINK BLOCK
>
> Meet with your team to share your experiences using behavioral principles with your students. Ask yourselves the following questions:
>
> 1. What experiences would you say were successful? Unsuccessful?
>
> 2. Have you tried to use punishment with a bully only to find that it increased the negative, aggressive behaviors? How did you handle this?
>
> 3. When was the last time you "caught a student being good"?
>
> 4. How might you reinforce positive behaviors in your daily classroom routine?

TYPES OF BULLIES

Bullies come in many shapes and sizes. As discussed in Module 1, bullying can be difficult to identify and to differentiate from rough play. What makes bullying even trickier to identify is that it does have different faces. There are three primary types of bullies: aggressive, passive, and relational. In addition, there are differences in boys' and girls' typical patterns of bullying.

The Aggressive Bully

The aggressive bully:

- Is the most common type of bully

- Initiates aggression toward peers

- Is characterized as fearless, coercive, tough, and impulsive

- Has an inclination toward violence and a desire to dominate others (Olweus, 1996; Ross, 1996)

- Shows little expression of empathy toward victims (Olweus, 1994)

- Openly attacks victims

- Enjoys having control over others

- Often sees the victim's behavior as provocative regardless of the victim's intentions

- Often views the world through a paranoid lens (Ross, 1996)

Common behaviors of the aggressive bully include the following:

- Pushing or hitting

- Threatening physical harm

- Stealing money, lunches, or materials

- Trapping victims in hallways or bathrooms

> *Tybias knows he is the biggest kid in the fourth grade, and he is not afraid to use his size to frighten younger and smaller kids. Tybias especially likes to pick on Charles. Tybias continually orders Charles to do things for him, such as carry his book bag, give him his lunch money, or take something from the teacher's desk. If Charles refuses, Tybias will push him or put him in a headlock. Tybias has been known to try to lock Charles in the bathroom on several occasions.*

Tybias's behavior is bullying because it fits the PIC criteria, discussed in detail in Module 1: It is *purposeful, imbalanced,* and *continual.* Tybias is an aggressive bully because he uses physical threats and force to intimidate Charles.

The Passive Bully

The passive bully:

- Is less common than the aggressive bully

- Tends to be dependent on the more aggressive bully

- Can be insecure and anxious

- Seeks the attention and acceptance of the aggressive bully

- May value the norm of aggression and violence

- Is likely to join in bullying if he or she sees bullying is rewarded

- Without the bully, lacks a defined social status among peers

- Is referred to as a "follower" (Olweus, 1996; Ross, 1996)

Common behaviors of the passive bully include the following:

- Being present and supporting the aggressive bully's actions

- Copying the actions of the aggressive bully

- Using indirect methods to bully others, such as social exclusion and name-calling

- Typically, not initiating aggressive bullying without the aggressive bully's presence

> *Sandra is a quiet and petite fourth grader who is already very serious about excelling at school. One group*

*of boys in her class, led by Billy, teases her daily about
being a brownnose and a goody two-shoes. Billy often
comes very close to Sandra and whispers mean words to
her while the rest of the group forms a circle to block
anybody from seeing what Billy is doing.*

Billy's followers are engaging in passive bullying. Although they are not actively calling Sandra names, they are supporting Billy's behaviors. Again, Billy's behavior fits the PIC scheme: It is *purposeful, imbalanced,* and *continual.*

The Relational Bully

The relational bully:

- Is the most common type of bully among females

- Is effective in girls' social groups (Crick, 1996)

- Often attempts to gain social status and power through the exclusion of others

- Intentionally isolates peers from social activities and events

- When upset with a peer, "gets even" by excluding the person from the peer group (Crick, 1996)

- Manipulates social relationships to get something (Crick, 1996)

Common behaviors of the relational bully are as follows:

- Spreading rumors or lies about a peer

- Attempting to get others to dislike the peer by telling stories (Crick, 1996)

- Excluding others from social activities on the playground, at the lunch table, or during after-school events

- Threatening not to be friends with a peer unless the peer does what the bully wants (Crick, 1996)

  *Lola wanted Janie to stop being friends with Sasha.
  Lola told Janie that no friend of hers could be seen with
  someone who dressed as badly as Sasha! When Janie
  refused to end her friendship with Sasha, Lola told
  Janie she would pay for it. Lola started telling everyone
  lies about Janie and even some of her personal secrets.
  Each day when Janie came to school, she would hear a
  new rumor about herself. Lola even told Sasha that
  Janie was saying bad things about her so Sasha would
  no longer be Janie's friend.*

Lola's behavior fits the PIC scheme: It is *purposeful, imbalanced,* and *continual.* Lola is engaging in relational bullying. When Janie would not do as she said, Lola got even by isolating Janie from her peers through telling lies.

Relational bullying has been found to be a common but easily over-looked form of aggression, particularly as it exists among girls. Although as detrimental as other types of bullying to its victims, relational aggression can be invisible to adults. This type of bullying, if ongoing, may eventually lead to a physically aggressive encounter among girls. Teachers may assume that the physical fight is a one-time event, whereas in actuality it is the outcome of continual emotional bullying (Cairns, Cairns, Neckerman, Gest, & Gariepy, 1988).

Introducing Different Types of Bullies to Students: Animal Examples

As we did for different ways of expressing anger (Module 3), we include the following animal examples to convey information about each of the three types of bullies. After you feel comfortable identifying the types of bullies yourself, we encourage you to share these descriptions with your students. Invite them to ask questions about the different types of bullies and talk about their own experiences.

You may wish to introduce the animal stories to your students by saying something like the following:

> Every child in school is affected by bullying, and there are different types of bullies. Children at school are like some of our friends at the zoo. Some of the zoo animals tease and hurt others, just like human bullies. Let's look at some of these animals. After we meet each animal, let's talk about what he or she could do to stop bullying and do things differently.

After sharing each animal story with your class, encourage your students to identify the bullying behavior and suggest ways the animals could improve on their behavior. You can use the following questions to guide your discussion:

- How is the animal bullying his or her friends?

- What could the animal do differently, instead of bullying?

- How could you help the animal do that?

- If the animal stopped bullying, what do you think would happen next?

Burly Bear: An Aggressive Bully

Burly Bear is much bigger and stronger than all the other animals. He always wants things his way and isn't afraid to stomp on the smaller animals to make sure they know he is the king of the animal world. Burly Bear makes sure that all the other animals know he is the strongest, most powerful animal in the land. He chases others, steals their food, and pushes them around just so he can prove he is the most powerful. The other animals get really tired of his hurting others with his big paws and using his loud growl to scare everyone.

Harry Hyena: A Passive Bully

Harry Hyena hangs around with Burly Bear and helps Burly Bear tease and scare the other animals. He copies everything Burly Bear does. If Burly Bear is calling someone names, Harry Hyena will chime in with some names of his own. If Burly Bear tries to take another animal's lunch, Harry Hyena is there to help. Harry Hyena usually doesn't try to hurt the other animals unless Burly Bear is around, but whenever Burly Bear is there, it seems Harry Hyena will do anything to stay friends with him.

The Gossipy Geese: Relational Bullies

The Gossipy Geese feel they are the queens of the lake. They swim gracefully with their long necks poised perfectly. They act so polite and ladylike, but you have to be careful of them. They like to make others feel like they aren't as good as they are—especially poor little Daisy Duck. Daisy tries to play in the lake with the other lake animals, but the Gossipy Geese make fun of her. They say her feathers are a funny color and tease her that they aren't nearly as smooth as their long, elegant feathers. Daisy Duck used to feel good about her feathers and was always so proud to win the swimming contest every year. But now she feels sad and lonely because no one will play with her or even bask in the sun with her. As soon as Daisy Duck finds a new friend to play with, the Gossipy Geese quickly come over and take her new friend away with them. The Gossipy Geese have made sure that no one associates with "Dumb Dopey Duck," their new name for Daisy.

Male versus Female Bullies

Both boys and girls engage in bullying, although the interactions can be quite different. The following discussion points out some of the main differences.

The Male Bully

Male students often exhibit direct, aggressive forms of bullying, which teachers and students alike can usually recognize. They are the most common type of bully, tend to engage in name-calling and aggressive bullying, and bully both male and female classmates.

Research conducted worldwide has demonstrated consistently that there is a higher incidence of bullying among boys as compared with girls (Ahmad & Smith, 1994). Boys engage in four times as much bullying as girls and are victimized twice as often. In the lower grades, boys who are bullies tend to be the oldest members of their peer group (Olweus, 1993).

The Female Bully

Boys who are rough are often called bullies, even if their behaviors do not meet all of the bullying criteria. On the other hand, girls' negative behaviors are more often classified as "mean." Bullying by girls is more difficult to detect because they frequently use less visible and more indirect means of harassment. Whereas males bully both sexes, females usually bully only other females.

In general, girls are relational in nature. This means that girls are commonly socialized to place a great emphasis on interpersonal connections with others. It is through their relationships that girls find meaningful ways to define themselves. Female bullies often attempt to damage the relationships of their victims by spreading rumors, instigating conflicts, and excluding their victims from meaningful social interactions—for example, lunchtime conversation, after-school activities, or special events such as birthday parties. Each of these actions is a form of relational bullying and intentionally targets relationships, leaving victims isolated from their peers.

Many teachers, school personnel, students, and even female bullies themselves have difficulty recognizing the behaviors of the female bully (Eslea & Smith, 1998). Female bullies themselves are frequently not aware that their behavior would be considered bullying and consequently do not see the need for change. Although aggressive bullying is not as common in girls as it is in boys, it is important to point out that girls do also engage in it.

Because female bullying is difficult to detect, it is also difficult to change. Several antibullying programs have documented decreases in male bullying but either found no change or an increase in the amount of female bullying (Farrell & Meyer, 1997). These findings may reflect the fact that the bullying interventions did not effectively target the behaviors of the female bully, or they may suggest that increased awareness of female bullying leads to increased reporting of its occurrence.

BULLY BUSTERS SUPPORT TEAM THINK BLOCK

With your team, discuss the characteristics of aggressive bullies, passive bullies, and relational bullies, as well as the differences between male and female bullying. The following questions may help:

1. Are some forms of bullying easier to recognize than others? Which are easier and which are more challenging?

2. Can you think of examples of female bullying you experienced or witnessed during your own childhood?

3. How would you describe the differences between male and female bullies?

4. Do you respond differently to girls who bully than to boys who bully? If so, how and why?

Module 4: Content Review

The following statements relate to the learning goals of this module. Ask yourself if you feel confident that you can answer yes to each item. If not, please review the material and discuss any difficulties among your Bully Busters Support Team.

1. I understand that children who bully are often victims in other settings and require my special attention and intervention.   Yes ❑ No ❑

2. I understand that children learn bullying from their interactions within a variety of social environments, including the home, school, neighborhood, community, and larger culture.   Yes ❑ No ❑

3. I understand how powerful modeling is in the development of children's behaviors and am aware of my power as a behavioral model for students.   Yes ❑ No ❑

4. I am able to recognize the aggressive bully. He or she tends to enjoy power and control, has not fully developed the ability to empathize with his or her victims, and often uses force.   Yes ❑ No ❑

5. I am able to recognize the passive bully. He or she tends to enjoy the attention and power given to the aggressive bully, desires to be associated with the aggressive bully, but does not tend to initiate aggressive acts against others.   Yes ❑ No ❑

6. I am able to recognize the relational bully. Typically female, she attempts to cause purposeful harm to a peer by spreading rumors, excluding, or manipulating the peer group and causing social disconnection.   Yes ❑ No ❑

7. I understand that, although males and females tend to bully differently, they both can engage in bullying behaviors.   Yes ❑ No ❑

Bully Busters: A Teacher's Manual for Helping Bullies, Victims, and Bystanders (Grades K–5)
© 2003 by Arthur M. Horne, Christi L. Bartolomucci, and Dawn Newman-Carlson.
Champaign, IL: Research Press. (800) 519–2707.

A Reminder . . .

CLASSROOM INTERACTION AND AWARENESS CHART

Use the CIAC to describe any bullying behavior you observe (and that students report to you, if you wish). A copy of the CIAC and a weekly summary sheet appear in Appendix A.

THE BIG QUESTIONS

Honestly appraise your progress by asking yourself the Big Questions. There are no right or wrong answers.

In relation to recognizing bullies and bullying in my school:

1. What is my goal?

2. What am I doing?

3. Is what I am doing helping me achieve my goal?

4. *(If not)* What can I do differently?

PERSONAL GOALS FORM

The Personal Goals Form, on the next page, is designed to help you tailor the content of this module to your own students and situation. Please take a moment to fill out the form now.

Module 4: Personal Goals Form

Goals

- To understand differences between the bully and the well-adapted child
- To learn how bullying behaviors develop and are influenced by child characteristics, family interactions, school environment, community, and culture
- To understand the relationship of learning and behavioral consequences to bullying
- To identify three types of bullies: aggressive, passive, and relational
- To become aware of typical differences between male and female bullying

1. My personal explanation of why children develop bullying behaviors is as follows:

2. I have observed incidents of bullying. *(Please record incidents on the CIAC.)*

    ____ Number of times I intervened   ____ Number of times I chose not to intervene

    Other observations:

3. I will review the classroom activities for this module and select ones appropriate for my class. *(Please list.)*

4. I will accept the challenges associated with the developmental assets. *(Please list the specific assets and describe what you plan to do.)*

5. I will give my students feedback about the bullying incidents I have observed and encourage discussion of bullying and related issues. We will discuss these topics:

6. I will share my experiences in applying the information in this module with other teachers and administrators, as well as with my students' families. *(Please specify who and when.)*

7. I will meet with my Bully Busters Support Team. *(Please specify when and list what issues and questions you will raise.)*

Bully Busters: A Teacher's Manual for Helping Bullies, Victims, and Bystanders (Grades K–5)
© 2003 by Arthur M. Horne, Christi L. Bartolomucci, and Dawn Newman-Carlson.
Champaign, IL: Research Press. (800) 519–2707.

Classroom Activities

ACTIVITY 4.1: THE BULLY BUST (GRADES K–5)

In this activity, students imagine what a bully looks like and does to hurt others, then fill in the details on a page including the outline of a body. They then discuss the ways bullies can hurt others: physically, verbally, through exclusion, and the like. The detail of drawings and level of discussion vary with the age of the students.

ACTIVITY 4.2: BULLY? WHO, ME? (GRADES K–5)

Continuing the process of helping students recognize bullying behaviors, this activity personalizes the experience by encouraging students to examine their own aggressive behavior. A self-reporting worksheet is provided for grades 3–5; students in the earlier grades conduct the activity orally.

ACTIVITY 4.3: BULLIES AT WORK (GRADES 3–5)

In this activity, students receive a handout describing the three types of bullies: aggressive, passive, and relational. Working in pairs or small groups, they then consider a number of scenarios and identify the type of bullying in each.

ACTIVITY 4.4: CAUGHT ON CAMERA (GRADES 3–5)

This activity empowers students to take a first step toward stopping bullying behavior: recording where, when, and what happens when they experience or observe instances of bullying.

The Bully Bust

OBJECTIVES

- To help students recognize the words and actions of a bully
- To increase students' awareness of ways bullies can hurt others

MATERIALS

- Copies of The Bully Bust worksheet
- Crayons, markers, or colored pencils

DIRECTIONS

1. Give each student a copy of The Bully Bust worksheet.

2. Instruct students to close their eyes and imagine a bully. Ask them to consider the actions of the bully. For example, what kinds of things do bullies say to others? What do their faces look like? What do they do with their fists?

3. Ask students to make their worksheet look like the bully they imagined. They can draw the bully's face, write words the bully might say to others, or color the parts of the bully's body the bully uses to hurt others.

4. Encourage students to share their drawings with the class in order to identify as many ways as possible that the bully uses his or her body to hurt others.

5. After several children have shared their pictures of the bully, facilitate a class discussion by asking the following questions.

DISCUSSION QUESTIONS

- What are the most common things bullies do to hurt others?
- How do bullies physically hurt others?
- How do bullies use words to harm others?

- Can bullies hurt people in ways other than hurting their bodies or saying mean words to them?

- Do you think a bully's feelings can get hurt, too?

- Who might hurt a bully's feelings?

The Bully Bust

Bully? Who, Me?

OBJECTIVES

- To help students identify bullying behaviors

- To allow students to look at any of their own behaviors that may be considered bullying

- To encourage students to take responsibility for their own actions

MATERIALS

- Chalkboard or easel pad (grades K–2)

- Pencils or pens (grades 3–5)

- Bully? Who, Me? worksheet (grades 3–5)

DIRECTIONS

1. Tell students that the goal of this activity is for students to recognize their own bullying behaviors, if they have any. You might say, for example:

    Sometimes we act in ways that are hurtful to others. We do this because we feel angry, sad, or embarrassed—or we want to feel like we are really strong. One of the first steps in stopping bullying is to see if and how we ourselves are involved in bullying or other aggressive behaviors.

2. Choose the procedure appropriate for your grade level.

    Grades K–2: Facilitate the activity orally by selecting actions you have seen in the classroom from the worksheet. After reading each one, ask for a show of hands for those who have never done this, sometimes done this, and often or always do this. Tally students' responses on the chalkboard or easel pad.

    Grades 3–5: Give each student a worksheet, and explain its purpose. For example:

    This worksheet shows a list of bullying actions that often make others feel bad and can make us feel bad about ourselves when we do them to others. Put a check mark in the first box if you have never done the action, in the second box if you sometimes do it, or the third box if you often or always do it. As you are answering, please think about yourself—how you behave—and not about the actions of others. You will not get in trouble, and no one will think badly of you for being honest. Our goal is to look at our own behaviors and how they may make us and others feel.

Depending on students' ability, read the scenarios aloud while your students mark their responses, or have students complete the worksheet independently.

3. Encourage students to discuss their responses by asking the following questions.

DISCUSSION QUESTIONS

- How many of you have committed bullying actions? Did you realize that you had been a bully?

- Have you ever had someone do something to bully you? How did you feel in that situation?

- How did you feel when you did something to bully someone else?

- If you find you are bullying others sometimes, often, or always, what help do you think you need to stop?

Bully? Who, Me?

Action	I have never done this to others	Sometimes I do this to others	I often or always do this to others
1. Called someone names			
2. Pushed someone			
3. Left someone out of my group on purpose			
4. Ganged up on another person with a few of my friends			
5. Said bad things about another person			
6. Hit another person			
7. Made someone give me something, like lunch money, food, or crayons			

Activity 4.2

Bully Busters: A Teacher's Manual for Helping Bullies, Victims, and Bystanders (Grades K–5)
© 2003 by Arthur M. Horne, Christi L. Bartolomucci, and Dawn Newman-Carlson.
Champaign, IL: Research Press. (800) 519–2707.

Bullies at Work

OBJECTIVES

- To help students recognize the three different types of bullies
- To encourage students to work together to discuss bullying interactions

MATERIALS

- Copies of the I Know Bullies descriptions
- Copies of the Bullies at Work worksheet
- Pencils or pens

DIRECTIONS

1. Give each student a copy of the I Know Bullies descriptions. Explain this sheet by saying something like the following:

   > When we think of bullies, we often think of kids who push or hurt others much of the time. This is the main type of bully that we recognize in movies and books— and even at school. However, there are really three types of bullies. There are aggressive bullies, passive bullies, and relational bullies.

2. Go over the definitions of the three different types of bullies as a group, answering any questions.

3. Divide the class into groups of two or three students each. Give each group a copy of the Bullies at Work worksheet.

4. Instruct students to work together to read the scenarios and decide what type of bullying is being described.

5. Bring the class together to share the group responses.

6. Process the exercise by asking the discussion questions.

DISCUSSION QUESTIONS

- Can you think of times that you have seen each type of bully at work?

- What type of bullying do you think is most common in our classroom? In our school?

- Can you make up an example of each type of bullying?

- How do the different types of bullies make their victims feel?

- Do you think all types of bullies hurt their victims?

- What type of hurt do aggressive bullies cause their victims?

- What type of hurt do relational bullies cause their victims?

I Know Bullies

Aggressive Bullies

- They push, hit, or toss around other students to get what they want.

- They act very tough and look like they are not afraid of anything.

- They like to have power over other students.

- They never feel bad about hurting their victims.

- They will hurt their victims in front of others.

Carlos

Carlos and his buddies are fourth graders and some of the toughest kids in the school. All of the kids know to watch out for them. Simon particularly tries to avoid them. Every day, Carlos makes fun of Simon in front of everyone in the lunchroom. Carlos purposely looks for Simon to take his lunch, to knock his books off the desk, or to trip him. When Simon becomes upset, Carlos begins laughing and making fun of him even more.

Passive Bullies

- They follow the main bully.

- They may be part of the bullying group.

- They join in the bullying, but they don't bully on their own.

- They think the bully is cool.

- They want to be friends with the bully.

John

John wants to be as tough as Peter. Everyone is scared of Peter. Every time Peter tries to hurt or embarrass one of their classmates, John stands right behind him, making a fist and yelling out names.

Relational Bullies

- They are often girls.

- They try to make students feel bad by excluding them from the group.

- They will spread rumors so other students don't like you.

Mary

Mary is the coolest girl in the class. She is tough and smart. Mary always picks on Becky, saying bad things about her to the other girls and boys in the class. When Mary had a birthday party, she invited everyone except Becky. She told everyone that Becky was the only person not cool enough to come to her house.

Bullies at Work

Type of bullying	*Bullying situation*
1. What type of bully is Gina? ❏ Aggressive ❏ Passive ❏ Relational	Gina was the head of the "Sweeties," the most popular group at school. Bridget was a member of the "Sweeties," too. Gina told all the other "Sweeties" that Bridget was saying bad things about them. All the girls ganged up and kicked Bridget out of the group.
2. What type of bully is Deacon? ❏ Aggressive ❏ Passive ❏ Relational	Deacon loves to pick on people much smaller than himself. He uses his muscles and size to push everyone else in the class around. He has chosen his "special ones" to pick on almost every day.
3. What type of bully is Craig? ❏ Aggressive ❏ Passive ❏ Relational	Jim and Craig are the class bullies. Everyone is afraid of them. Jim always starts pushing people around, and Craig often yells names along with Jim. Craig doesn't look too scary on his own. He can even be nice sometimes. But as soon as he is with Jim, forget it. He tries to act big and tough.
4. What type of bully is Julie? ❏ Aggressive ❏ Passive ❏ Relational	Julie thinks people will like Shari better than they like her. So Julie decides she will ruin Shari's reputation by spreading lies about her.
5. What type of bully is Sam? ❏ Aggressive ❏ Passive ❏ Relational	Everyone listens to Ray. Whatever he tells the other kids, they do. Sam is his right-hand man. Sam always joins in with Ray, but no one thinks he is as cool as Ray.
6. What type of bully is Didi? ❏ Aggressive ❏ Passive ❏ Relational	Didi is everything but nice. She is tough and not afraid of anything. She will do anything to get what she wants, especially from Sara. She pushes Sara around all the time to make herself look tougher.

Bully Busters: A Teacher's Manual for Helping Bullies, Victims, and Bystanders (Grades K–5)
© 2003 by Arthur M. Horne, Christi L. Bartolomucci, and Dawn Newman-Carlson.
Champaign, IL: Research Press. (800) 519–2707.

Activity 4.4

Caught on Camera

Grades 3–5

OBJECTIVES

- To encourage all students to identify the actions that constitute bullying
- To empower students to begin to develop ownership for school safety by identifying where, when, and what bullying is occurring
- To inform all students in the school that the students in your class will watch for bullying behaviors to help make the school a safe, bully-free place

MATERIALS

- Copies of the Caught on Camera page (one per student; cut each page into two forms)
- Pencils or pens
- Chalkboard or easel pad

DIRECTIONS

1. Talk with students about how important they are to the class and the school in identifying bullying behavior. A possible introduction follows:

   > Bullying happens all the time. You are the ones who see and experience bullying. As your teacher, I want to catch bullying, but I am not always present when bullying occurs. I need each of you to join the no-bullying force by noticing when bullying takes place in our school. Talking about the bullying that happens in school is not being a tattletale. We want to talk about bullying together, not get anyone in trouble. We just want bullying to stop. Identifying times and places bullying happens can help us make this school safer for all of us.

2. Give each student a copy of the Caught on Camera form, and explain that students will be using the form whenever they observe

bullying to record what happened, where it happened, and when it happened.

3. As a group, complete a sample form like the following.

Caught on Camera

Date ___1/31/03___

What happened?

_____Randall pushed Josh and locked him in a stall in_

_____the rest room._

Where did it happen?

_____Rest room_

When did it happen?

_____Morning break_

---

4. Encourage students to complete a form every time they witness bullying. Let them know that you will keep extra copies in a central location in your classroom and that they can fill out as many forms as they want, one form per incident.

5. Instruct students to give the forms to you each time they complete one. They should date the forms, but they may choose whether or not to include their names. If they would like you or the school counselor to talk with them privately about what they are witnessing or experiencing, they should include their names.

6. Briefly discuss how students can get help if they or a classmate needs it. (They could talk to you, the school counselor, the principal or another school staff member, other students, and/or their parents.)

7. Each day, take a few minutes to check in with students about what they are seeing, and remind them to continue to fill out the forms.

8. Process the activity by asking the discussion questions.

DISCUSSION QUESTIONS

- Where does bullying occur in our school?

- Does everyone bully, or are there only a few people who bully?

- Do you see certain types of bullying (for instance, pushing, name-calling) more than other types (for example, beating someone up, stealing lunch money)?

- Can you imagine what it is like to be the victim of bullying? How would you feel?

- Have you watched bullying happen? How did you feel? What did you do?

- Do you feel that you would be able to get help if you saw or experienced bullying?

- Have you ever done anything you could get "caught on camera" for? How did you feel when you were bullying? How do you think your victim felt? What did others do or say to you?

Caught on Camera

Date _____

What happened?

_____

_____

Where did it happen?

_____

When did it happen?

_____

Caught on Camera

Date _____

What happened?

_____

_____

Where did it happen?

_____

When did it happen?

_____

Activity 4.4

Bully Busters: A Teacher's Manual for Helping Bullies, Victims, and Bystanders (Grades K–5)
© 2003 by Arthur M. Horne, Christi L. Bartolomucci, and Dawn Newman-Carlson.
Champaign, IL: Research Press. (800) 519–2707.

MODULE

5 Recognizing the Victim

OVERVIEW

The familiar saying "Sticks and stones may break my bones, but names will never hurt me" is commonly used by children, but it is entirely erroneous. Like exclusion and physical aggression, name-calling can inflict harm on a daily basis and create lifelong psychological struggles for its recipients (Besag, 1989). The effects of this and other forms of victimization are far reaching and can extend into adulthood and severely traumatize both boys and girls. This trauma has been linked with depression, feelings of helplessness, and even suicide. In recent years, we have witnessed the link between long-term victimization in the form of school shootings. This is the most extreme form of victim retaliation.

Children who are victimized are often unnoticed or ignored, responses that often perpetuate the problem. Most frequently, it is the bully who receives the attention, whereas the victim is forgotten or even blamed for being the victim. The purpose of this module is to assist you in understanding the victim and the victim's role in the bully-victim interaction.

GOALS

- To define victimization and challenge common myths about victims and victimization

- To recognize the characteristics of victims and the signs of victimization

- To understand the impact of victimization and where victimization takes place

- To identify four types of victims (passive, provocative, relational, and bystander)

- To increase awareness of the victim role and the bully-victim cycle

DEFINING VICTIMIZATION

According to the PIC acronym, described in Module 1, bullying is *purposeful, imbalanced,* and *continual.* It is an interaction involving at least two students in which one student intentionally and repeatedly causes harm to another student who is perceived as less powerful than the bully. The recipients of such treatment are the victims. A victim is any person who is the object of abuse or violence. Victimization includes such behaviors as teasing, ridicule, vandalism, and physical injury (Hoover et al., 1992).

MYTHS ABOUT VICTIMIZATION

Erroneous beliefs about victims and victimization are common. The acceptance of these myths as fact often prevents teachers and students from feeling they can or should help children who are victimized. Instead, these myths promote blaming victims for their role in the interaction and allow bullying to continue. Following are common myths about victimization and their associated facts.

Sometimes kids ask to be bullied by doing things in a way that attracts the bully

It is not uncommon for teachers to think, "If only they did not wear those clothes, glasses, or talk in that manner, they would not be bullied." However, each child is unique, and no child ever asks to be bullied. Each child is also doing the best he or she can and does not deserve to be victimized. Our job is not to blame the victim, but to address the bullying interaction and help the victim learn skills to handle the bullying situation more effectively.

Bullying is just child's play; kids will outgrow bullying and victimization

Although all children can, on occasion, unintentionally cause others emotional or physical harm, victimization is purposeful. It is not normal child's play. Many victims remember their traumatization, and some whose self-concept is severely impaired find themselves unable to engage in meaningful and trusting adult relationships.

Bullying actually helps weaker kids by teaching them to stand up for themselves

Consider the power imbalance in the bully-victim relationship: Bullies typically have more power—in the form of strength, intellectual ability, or social clout—than victims, and the power imbalance is a primary reason bullies select the victims they do. When a child is being victimized, the predominant emotion is fear. Under such circumstances, it is unlikely that the child will learn anything. Children can learn assertiveness skills to stand up to bullies, but those skills are best learned in an encouraging and supportive setting, not in an interaction founded on intimidation.

It is only victimization when kids threaten to harm or harm other kids physically

We generally think of bullying as involving a physical attack. However, name-calling, rumor spreading, and embarrassment are all serious forms of bullying as well. The latter forms, referred to as relational bullying, often lead victims to be isolated or rejected by their peers. The feelings of rejection from peers at school have serious, long-term consequences, such as school dropout, juvenile delinquency, and, possibly, severe adult psychological problems (Asher & Coie, 1990; Boulton, 1997).

Only boys bully, and they only victimize other boys

Both female and male bullies do victimize girls. Although female bullies typically bully other females, male bullies bully both males and females. Male bullies more commonly engage in overt, direct, and physical bullying, making their behavior much easier to identify. Female bullies frequently use indirect tactics, such as excluding peers from social situations, spreading rumors about them, and destroying their friendships by telling lies—all examples of relational victimization.

There just isn't enough time during the school day to address bullying incidents and teach the academic curriculum

This assumption is inaccurate for two reasons: First, victimization can interfere with children's ability to perform academically. The emotional trauma associated with bullying can and will take a toll on both bullies' and victims' ability to attend to their schoolwork. Second, bullying does not disappear if it is ignored; instead, it tends to intensify. By introducing the topic of bullying, creating a forum to discuss issues related to bullying, and teaching problem-solving and conflict resolution skills, you can head off larger problems that will take up more of your time later.

As a teacher, I don't have much power to change the bully-victim interaction

Many teachers feel they do not have the knowledge and skills to intervene in bullying situations and therefore fear that they will do more harm than good. However, if you are committed to implementing this program, you have already taken a major step in increasing your knowledge and skills in this area. You are already an expert at teaching and supporting your students on a daily basis. This position gives you a great deal of influence over bullying.

I hope my students will talk to me, but I don't want them tattling on one another

Initially, you may experience an increase in the number of students coming to you to report problems. This is a good sign because it means that your students trust that you will do something about the bullying. Your entire class can engage in problem-solving discussions to help all students learn the skills to prevent and intervene in bullying. As your students learn new skills, they will feel more confident to handle situations independently. Asking for help and tattling are different. A student tattling is attempting to get another student in trouble and is probably asking for attention; the student who is genuinely requesting help because he or she is being picked on by another student deserves your attention.

Addressing bullying problems is overwhelming—all the change will be on my shoulders

One of the goals of the Bully Busters program is to share the responsibility for bringing about change. A teacher cannot be everywhere all of the time, so one program goal is to have students also take responsibility for producing an aggression-free school and classroom. If you and your colleagues work together as a Bully Busters Support Team, you will find you are not alone and that, with the help of others, you can make positive changes.

Bullying is not a problem in my class or my school

For some teachers and classrooms, this may be the case. However, it is more likely that your students are keeping bullying under wraps so they will not become the bully's next victim. Students of all ages adhere to this "code of silence" out of fear. Introducing the topic of bullying to your class and discussing issues related to bullying can help your students take steps toward ending bullying.

BULLY BUSTERS SUPPORT TEAM THINK BLOCK

Take a few moments to consider what other myths you may have believed or heard about students who are victimized. Discuss the following questions with your team:

1. How many of these myths had you accepted as fact?

2. How does holding these beliefs prevent successful intervention in the bully-victim interaction?

3. Can you remember a time you felt victimized as a student? How would it feel if your teacher did not take you seriously after you alerted him or her to your victimization?

4. Can you think of a time when you have seen others step forward to help a victimized student? How might you encourage your students to take on this role?

RECOGNIZING VICTIMS AND VICTIMIZATION

Overall, victims are children who are commonly overlooked or ignored. This fact is confirmed in the classroom as well as in the literature and research base on bullying. Therefore, we know much less about children in the victim role than we know about children who engage in bullying behavior. Our goal is to increase knowledge about victims in order to give children who are victimized the attention they need and deserve.

We do know that children who are victimized are commonly characterized by anxiety, sensitivity, quietness, and insecurity. They tend to have few friends and are isolated from their peers (Slee & Rigby, 1993), and other students perceive them as physically weak. They may cry frequently, have difficulty handling conflicts independently, and be overprotected by individuals at home and in school. Not all children who exhibit these characteristics are victims. However, it is important for you, the school counselor, or some other person on the school staff to monitor students who exhibit these behaviors, for they may put these children at risk.

IMPACT OF VICTIMIZATION

The effects of victimization may be obvious, as when students show fear or avoidance of particular situations, or the effects may be less clear, as when children manifest changes in their character or customary way of being, when their academic achievement begins to deteriorate, or when they become increasingly explosive with no known reason.

Effects of Victimization

Bullying, as we mentioned earlier, is not child's play. Victims are children who are exposed repeatedly and over time to negative actions on the part of one or more bullies. They are teased, intimidated, threatened, hit, and degraded. The following list includes some of the effects of victimization:

- Illness

- A decrease in school performance

- Absenteeism

- Truancy

- Drop out

- Peer rejection

- Fear and avoidance of social situations

- Feelings of alienation and loneliness

- Stress

- Inability to sleep

- Low morale

- Poor self-confidence and self-esteem

- Bed-wetting

- Depression

- Thoughts of suicide (or completed suicide)

Children do not always talk openly about victimization that occurs in school, and bullies often keep their behaviors hidden from the view of teachers. Therefore, it is important to watch for warning signs of victimization. These *secondary signs of victimization* are the effects of bullying on the victim beyond the immediate bullying situation. If you notice any of the following behaviors in your students, emotional or social difficulties may be present:

- An unusually quiet child becomes increasingly withdrawn.

- A child who is normally restrained becomes aggressive.

- A child skips lunch or is reluctant to be involved in recess or extracurricular group activities.

- A child develops an illness prior to group activities.

- During group activities, no one wants to be paired with this individual.

- A student is absent without a convincing explanation.

- The child's personal property is damaged or missing on a regular basis.

- The child frequently asks to visit the nurse's office.

If you begin to see these signs, make yourself available to the student. You might say, for example, "Sandra, I have noticed that you have become very quiet over the past week and haven't played at recess. It seems as though something may be wrong. Would you like to talk about it? It is safe with me." Explore explanations for the behavioral change. Be active in finding out what is going on and deciding who would be best able to help—sometimes it will be you, but it may be a counselor, social worker, school psychologist, or someone else on the school staff.

> On Monday, before lunch, Destiny told the teacher she had a stomachache and asked if she could go lie down in the nurse's office. Destiny was not typically ill, but her teacher, Ms. Peterson, believed she truly was. Two days later, right before lunch, Destiny again asked to go to the nurse's office—this time because of a headache. Ms. Peterson asked Destiny if she had been feeling sick at home, and Destiny said she felt most sick during the day at school. Ms. Peterson let Destiny go back to the nurse. The following week, Destiny asked Ms. Peterson if she could help her correct papers at lunch instead of going to lunch with her class.

It is easy to attribute symptoms of victimization to other causes. In Destiny's case, for example, the behavior might have been the result of an actual physical ailment. In another case, a child's refusal to participate might be interpreted as oppositionality. It is important that teachers not simply accept children's complaints at face value, but also to consider other possible causes before drawing conclusions. If you see extreme behavioral changes in a child or something just doesn't seem "right" with one of your students, make yourself available. Victims need to know someone believes in them and is willing to help.

BULLY BUSTERS SUPPORT TEAM THINK BLOCK

With your team, discuss the following questions:

1. Were you aware that there are secondary symptoms of victimization, or is this new information for you?

2. Have you noticed significant behavioral changes in any of your students? If so, what are they?

3. Do any of your students get sick often or try to avoid certain activities? Could they be victims of bullying?

4. If you tried to talk to these students, what do you think they would say?

WHERE DOES VICTIMIZATION TAKE PLACE?

Victimization occurs most frequently on the way to and from school and on the playground (Boulton, 1997). However, victimization does not stop there. Generally, victimization occurs throughout the school day and can take place in any location: on the playground, in rest rooms, in the cafeteria, in gym class—and sometimes right in front of teachers. Bullies are skilled and often know how to bully others without getting caught, or they may misbehave in front of educators who are unlikely to take action. Bullies count on the fact that most adults will not be able to detect their manipulation or will perceive their behaviors as benign. However, the victims of bullying often assume that adults do know that they are being hurt but are purposely choosing to overlook that fact.

BULLY BUSTERS SUPPORT TEAM THINK BLOCK

With your team, discuss these questions:

1. What role do you see yourself and other teachers having in stopping bullying in your own classrooms?

2. How much responsibility do teachers in your school have for preventing bullying on the school grounds?

3. Where has bullying commonly taken place in your school? Are there any ways you could protect students in these locations? (For example, you could talk with bus drivers and playground supervisors to create a means for them to report bullying situations to you.)

TYPES OF VICTIMS

Just as there are different types of bullies (aggressive, passive, and relational), there are different types of victims: passive, provocative, relational, and bystander. A description and examples of each type follow.

Passive Victims

Passive victims, also referred to as submissive victims, try to avoid conflict by staying out of harm's way.

Passive victims . . .

- Are the most frequent type of victims (Olweus, 1993).

- Feel abandoned and isolated by others.

- Feel more nervous, anxious, and insecure than their peers (Ross, 1996).

- Are cautious, sensitive, and quiet.

- Often lack physical skills in comparison to bullies.

- Have low self-esteem and may see themselves as unattractive failures.

- Often do not share a solid friendship with a single child in their class.

- Often display emotional outbursts (e.g., crying) in response to fear of being bullied.

- Display behaviors that indicate to others that they are weak and therefore incapable of retaliation when attacked or insulted (Olweus, 1993).

- Demonstrate close, overprotective relationships with parents, especially mothers (Olweus, 1993).

> *Maya is a 10-year-old who looks much younger than most girls in her class. She is quiet and reserved at school and often sits by herself at lunchtime. In her social studies class, she sits next to a boy who taunts and antagonizes her each day. She ignores him when he teases her, hoping that this will make him stop. Maya doesn't tell anyone about her distress and instead tries to keep herself away from the other students. When she thinks about having to face another day of this boy's verbal torture, she often breaks down in tears. The teachers are unaware of her distress, and they mistakenly believe her social isolation is a result of shyness.*

Provocative Victims

These are the children that bullies would say are "asking for it." Bullies often take it upon themselves to put provocative victims in their place through force, to let victims know their behavior is unacceptable (Olweus, 1993, 1994).

Provocative victims . . .

- Are less common than passive victims.

- Set out deliberately to provoke the bully, choosing this behavior over being ignored (Besag, 1989).

- Are more active, assertive, and confident than passive victims (Ross, 1996).

- Are sometimes described as reactive bullies.

- Create management problems within the classroom.

- Engage in distracting behaviors that may provoke irritation and tension, resulting in negative reactions from others (Pellegrini, 1995).

- May engage in this behavior to gain the attention of the rest of the class in an inappropriate attempt at acceptance (Besag, 1989).

- Are at higher risk for negative developmental outcomes (e.g., peer rejection and suicide; Pellegrini, 1995).

- Are unpopular among peers but often do not suffer from low self-esteem.

- May associate with bullies to increase their social status (Smith & Boulton, 1990).

- Often receive positive reinforcement from bullies and peers (i.e., attention).

- May learn aggressive strategies by modeling the bullies' actions and employ these tactics with their more vulnerable victims.

> *Ian is an 8-year-old boy who is easily angered and provoked. Most of the time, however, Ian stirs up trouble by hitting, pushing, and teasing others. Ian is always getting into trouble, but he seems to like playing the role of class clown. He particularly likes to arouse the anger of one particular bully in his class. The bully is much bigger than Ian and hangs around with a big group of friends, but that doesn't stop Ian. Ian tries to trip the bully in the hall or knock his tray over in the lunch line. The bully and the bully's friends often get into name-calling wars with Ian, and they almost always end up punching him until he begins crying or screaming.*

Relational Victims

A third category includes relational victims, who are characterized by being excluded from groups or ignored by peers. Their attempts to establish relationships with peers merely empower the peers to continue and even increase the relational bullying.

Relational victims . . .

- Are frequently female.

- Are usually not physically threatened or abused.

- Are excluded from meaningful peer interactions and peer social activities.

- Are hurt by indirect aggression in the form of social manipulation (Crick & Grotpeter, 1995).

- Are often overlooked because of the indirect nature of bullying.

- Are more common as children age and develop verbal skills (Kaukiainen et al., 1999).

> *Josie was friends with Jana and her group of friends. At least she thought she was. One day when Josie came to school, no one would talk to her. She didn't understand. When Josie went to sit down at the lunch table, Jana and her friends confronted Josie and told her she was not welcome. Jana told Josie that her clothes were a disgrace, her hair was out of control, and they did not associate with people like her. Teary-eyed, Josie left the table and sat by herself. The next day, Jana and the group of girls made up all types of lies about Josie and told others that Josie had said mean things about them. By the end of the week, no one would talk to Josie. Josie had no one to talk to about how her classmates were treating her, no one to play with, and no one to eat with at lunch.*

Bystander Victims

The bully-victim interaction affects numerous children, including those not directly involved in the interaction. These bystander victims may observe bullying on a continual basis and may be deeply affected by the abuse they witness.

Bystander victims . . .

- Witness the act of bullying.

- Tend not to tell an authority figure for fear that they may be the bully's next target.

- Experience fear and apprehension, especially if the bullying goes unpunished.

- Often feel helplessness, sadness, and guilt for witnessing bullying and not doing anything to stop it.

- Experience a "Catch 22": If they stand up for the victim, they may place themselves at risk of becoming the next victim; if they remain silent, they may carry guilt for many years.

- Can develop "learned helplessness," or the sense that they are powerless to have an impact in their own or others' lives (Seligman, 1991, 1995).

> *Evan, a fifth grader, was popular among all of his peers. He excelled in sports as well as academics. Sarah, a girl in Evan's class, was teased by the class bully and many other classmates every day. Several kids even made up a song*

called "Silly, Smelly Sarah" and made sure to sing it to her each day when she came out on the playground. Evan always heard his classmates singing that horrible song to Sarah, but he was afraid that people wouldn't like him anymore if he told them to stop. Even worse, he feared they might make up a song about him, too! So Evan did nothing. Now, 7 years later, Evan is a senior in high school and very successful. Yet he still thinks of Sarah at times and is still angry with himself for not doing anything to help her.

Empathy, the ability to experience the role of the victim, may motivate bystander victims to report or intervene in the bully-victim interaction (Goleman, 1995). However, to overcome the fear associated with involvement, young bystander victims need to know that they have the support of their teachers and peers. As you discuss bullying publicly with your class and welcome students to talk with you privately about the bullying they witness, more bystander victims are likely to come forward or intervene.

BULLY BUSTERS SUPPORT TEAM THINK BLOCK

It is natural to have an emotional response to the preceding victimization scenarios. With your team, discuss your reactions:

1. Which scenarios do you respond to most strongly? Do you know why this is?

2. Do particular scenarios remind you of a victimization experience that you or someone you care about has had?

3. Do you have a difficult time understanding a certain type of victimization and therefore have a hard time feeling empathic toward this type of victim?

Your thoughts and emotions about victimization play an important role in how you perceive and address victimization in your classroom. Becoming more aware of your own emotions and the manner in which you express and manage them will help you intervene effectively in bully-victim situations.

Introducing Types of Victims to Students: Animal Examples

As we did for different ways of expressing anger (Module 3) and types of bullies (Module 4), we include the following animal examples to convey information about each of the four types of victims. After you feel comfortable identifying victim types yourself, we encourage you to share these descriptions with your students. Invite them to ask questions about the different types of victims and talk about their experiences.

You may wish to introduce the animal stories to your students by saying something like the following:

Every child in school is affected by bullying. Some children will be bullied directly, and others will be hurt by watching others being bullied. Children at school are much like some of our friends at the zoo. Our animal friends deal with being bullied, too. Let's look at some of our animal friends who are bullied by zoo bullies. After we meet each animal, let's talk about what that animal must feel like and what he or she can do to get help from the zookeeper and other animals.

After sharing each animal story with your class, encourage your students to identify the feelings of the victims and to describe their own reactions. Doing so will help your students empathize with the different victims and become more comfortable expressing their feelings. You can use the following questions to guide your discussion:

- Who do you think the victim is?

- How do you think the victim feels?

- What would you do if you were in the same situation as the victim?

- Who do you think should help the victims?

- How can you show the victim that you care and want to help?

Amy Ant: A Passive Victim

Amy Ant is a tiny little thing. She is always running here and there. She is just so scared all the time. She is scared of Burly Bear the Bully finding her and squashing her with his big foot. Every day, Burly Bear finds Amy Ant and scares her by trying to step on her. Amy Ant hides, but Burly Bear always finds her. None of the other ants will ask Amy Ant into their homes. They are scared that Burly Bear will squash them, too! Amy Ant feels like everyone hates her. She feels like she is the ugliest of all ants and no one wants to be friends with her. Sometimes Amy Ant is so sad and afraid that she goes to a corner of her anthill and cries until she almost drowns herself in her own tears.

Charlie Chimp: A Provocative Victim

Charlie Chimp is a performer and loves the attention he gets when he causes trouble! But Charlie Chimp never seems to learn his lesson. He is always playing tricks on the zoo animals and bothering them. Charlie Chimp isn't very strong, but that doesn't seem to matter. He will go up to other animals in the zoo, including Burly Bear the Bully, and jump on their toes, throw bananas at them at lunchtime, and call them names. Charlie Chimp knows that Burly Bear and his group of friends are getting mad. Burly Bear and his friends get so angry at Charlie Chimp that they chase after him, hold him down, call him names, and even hit him. This happens almost every week! In the end, Charlie Chimp always gets hurt and starts to cry.

Daisy Duck: A Relational Victim

A large group of geese rule the lake, and they have beautiful feathers and look so graceful. But they sure aren't as nice as they look. The geese do not like Daisy Duck. The geese get in a line so Daisy Duck can't swim freely across the lake. They are also friendly with all the other ducks except for Daisy. They tease Daisy about being a silly duck and make fun of any other ducks who try to be friends with her. No one will be friends with Daisy Duck—no one will spend time with her, swim with her on the lake, or play with her on the banks of the lake. Daisy Duck spends all of her time alone, by herself, and feels very, very sad.

The Birds: Bystander Victims

Bad, bad bullying is happening on the grounds of the zoo. Charlie Chimp has been fighting again with Burly Bear and his friends. Little Amy Ant is so scared of Burly Bear that she ends up hiding from all the other animals and insects. All of the other animals and insects watch this happen every day. Especially the birds: They get the best view of all of the bullying with their "bird's-eye view." All the birds feel sad and upset. They want to help their animal friends, but they are scared. How can they stand up to Burly Bear and his friends? They are so big and mean. What's a little bird to do? Burly Bear will surely come after them, shake their trees, and knock over their nests if they stand up to him, right? The birds keep quiet, but they are very sad that they can't do anything and are very afraid that Burly Bear and his friends may come after them next.

Male and Female Victims

Gender differences are present not only in the ways males and females bully but also in the ways males and females are victimized. Within each of the types of victims, both male and female victims are represented. Victims of aggression appear to be subjected to different types of bullying behavior on the basis of their sex.

Male Victims

- Boys experience physically aggressive bullying more often than girls (Hoover et al., 1992).

- Boys experience violent and threatening behavior more often than girls (Sharp & Smith, 1991; Smith & Sharp, 1994).

- The victimization of males is more clearly observable due to its direct, physical nature.

Female Victims

- Girls experience verbal bullying more often than boys (Hoover et al., 1992).

- Girls experience social bullying more often than boys (e.g., rejection or isolation from peer groups; Sharp & Smith, 1991; Smith & Sharp, 1994).

It is important to note, however, that in recent years, females increasingly have perpetrated and been the victims of physical bullying.

UNDERSTANDING THE VICTIM ROLE

No student would actively choose or want to be in the victim role. Yet thousands and thousands of students every year around the world find themselves the victims of bullying. When working with children who are victimized, we must be cautious not to blame victims for occupying the victim role. Some teachers and students wonder why victims don't just change to escape the victim role. We have all heard comments like "If only she wouldn't wear those clothes!" or "It's hard for the others not to pick on him because he cries so easily!" or "Why doesn't she just stand up for herself? If she doesn't, no one else will!" Each one of these statements is common, and each statement blames the victim for being in the victim role.

Blaming the victim does not facilitate change. Rather, it allows the victim and his or her classmates to continue to accept the bully-victim interaction. What is needed is a shift in perceptions and the language we use to describe victims, both to ourselves and to others. Consider the difference in the following examples.

Blaming: "Carl is such a wuss. If he just wouldn't act so effeminate, then he wouldn't be picked on."

Understanding: "Carl acts very timid around others. He may need to spend some time on assertiveness skills and confidence-building activities."

Blaming: "Suzie looks pretty ridiculous in those clothes she wears. Her mother is about as offbeat as she could be. No wonder Suzie is so weird."

Understanding: "Given her family, Suzie is actually doing pretty well. The class needs to work on helping students accept people as they are and respect individual differences."

BULLY BUSTERS SUPPORT TEAM THINK BLOCK

Take an honest inventory of your thoughts regarding the victimization you observe and how they influence the way you intervene in bullying situations:

1. How do you view victims?

2. What kind of language do you use to describe victims?

3. Do your views or the language you use to describe victims need to change? If so, how?

The Bully-Victim Cycle

Rather than blaming the victim or the bully in a bullying situation, it is more helpful to see the bully and the victim as part of an ongoing cycle of interaction, which both bully and victim perpetuate. The key word here is *interaction*. As noted previously, no child ever seeks to be bullied or asks to be hurt. However, the child in the bully role is interacting with the child in the victim role by continually and purposefully inflicting harm on the victim, and the victim typically reacts in an emotional or helpless manner.

In order to end the bullying, this cycle must be broken. But how do we do this? One or both of the parties involved in the interaction must redefine their role and change their behaviors. It is essential that we realize that the victim is a vital part of the interaction and may be part of the solution as well. By taking the following steps, we can encourage the victim to break this cycle.

Acknowledge the victim

Children who are bullied are often overlooked or ignored by adults and peers and tend not to have extensive social networks or support systems, a situation that leaves them open targets for the bully. Children in the victim role need to know that you, the teacher, are aware of their position and that they are worth your time and effort.

Communicate to the victim that you are interested in lending your help and support

Children need to know that you do not blame them for not defending themselves, but that you do encourage them to consider ways they may contribute to the bully-victim cycle.

Empower the victim

When we address the concerns of victims, we are not giving all the power to the bully in choosing to end or continue bullying. When they learn new skills and attitudes they can use to defend themselves or to manage situations more effectively, victims can gain confidence in themselves and become optimistic that the bullying will end.

Do not give attention only to the bully

Most often, the focus of bullying interactions is on the bully. Although it is absolutely necessary to intervene and create change in the bully, the bully is only half of the equation. Victims of all types, including bystanders, must be armed with skills to end the bullying interaction.

Encouraging Victims to Ask for Help

Victims of bullying can become stuck in their victim role, feeling they do not have the skills, support, understanding, or power to change the situation. They tend not to seek help for the following reasons:

- They are adhering to the "code of silence" or have internalized messages such as "Don't be a tattletale" or "Stand up for yourself."

- They are isolated from their peers and do not have friends that they can turn to for help.

- They are attempting to convince themselves that "names will never hurt you" and choose to withstand their repeated victimization.

- They believe their teachers or other school professionals do not have the skills or knowledge to help them.

- When they know their teachers have observed the bullying and have not intervened, they assume their teachers do not care about them or do not feel it is their position to help them.

Regardless of the reasons children stay in the victim role, victims will likely need help getting out of this position. Without help, victims may feel the only way to effect change is to do something drastic to hurt the bully or themselves. These actions only bring more harm on themselves and their peers. Our goal is to help victims move past the victim role and view themselves as survivors of bullying.

When victims of bullying seek help or choose to share their bullying experiences, they often turn to a family member or teacher. However, because most victims do not seek help, it is up to you to reach out to students in need. By encouraging students to discuss the bully-victim dilemma in your classroom, you can help victims begin to feel more confident in seeking adult support.

Specifically, this type of encouragement includes the following actions:

- Communicating openly about bullying and victimization in your classroom

- Breaking the "code of silence" by encouraging students to report all forms of victimization (by telling you privately or creating a drop box where students can report bullying incidents anonymously)

- Enhancing your relationships with parents in order to create open lines of communication (e.g., by writing a letter encouraging parents to call you if their child reports being victimized or witnessing victimization at school)

- Sharing with students your primary goal of making sure they are safe at school

- Inviting them to work with you in ending bullying and victimization by doing activities such as those described in this manual

Module 5: Content Review

The following statements relate to the learning goals of this module. Ask yourself if you feel confident that you can answer yes to each item. If not, please review the material and discuss any difficulties among your Bully Busters Support Team.

1. I can recognize victims and name common warning signs of victimization.   Yes ❏   No ❏

2. I know how myths about victimization perpetuate bullying.   Yes ❏   No ❏

3. I am aware of the main ways bullying affects victims (both obvious and less obvious effects).   Yes ❏   No ❏

4. I can identify four types of victims: passive, provocative, relational, and bystander.   Yes ❏   No ❏

5. I know what the "code of silence" is among students and how it relates to victimization.   Yes ❏   No ❏

6. I realize that to help victims, I must avoid blaming victims for their victimization and encourage victims to ask for help.   Yes ❏   No ❏

7. I understand how the bully-victim cycle operates and how to interrupt it.   Yes ❏   No ❏

A Reminder . . .

CLASSROOM INTERACTION AND AWARENESS CHART

Use the CIAC to describe any bullying behavior you observe (and that students report to you, if you wish). A copy of the CIAC and a weekly summary sheet appear in Appendix A.

THE BIG QUESTIONS

Honestly appraise your progress by asking yourself the Big Questions. There are no right or wrong answers.

In relation to recognizing victims and victimization in my school:

1. What is my goal?

2. What am I doing?

3. Is what I am doing helping me achieve my goal?

4. *(If not)* What can I do differently?

PERSONAL GOALS FORM

The Personal Goals Form, on the next page, is designed to help you tailor the content of this module to your own students and situation. Please take a moment to fill out the form now.

Module 5: Personal Goals Form

Goals

- To define victimization and challenge common myths about victims and victimization

- To recognize the characteristics of victims and the signs of victimization

- To understand the impact of victimization and where victimization takes place

- To identity four types of victims (passive, provocative, relational, and bystander)

- To increase awareness of the victim role and the bully-victim cycle

1. My personal definition of victimization is as follows:

2. I have observed incidents of bullying. *(Please record incidents on the CIAC.)*

   ____ Number of times I intervened   ____ Number of times I chose not to intervene

   Other observations:

3. I will review the classroom activities for this module and select ones appropriate for my class. *(Please list.)*

4. I will accept the challenges associated with the developmental assets. *(Please list the specific assets and describe what you plan to do.)*

5. I will give my students feedback about the bullying incidents I have observed and encourage discussion of bullying and related issues. We will discuss these topics:

6. I will share my experiences in applying the information in this module with other teachers and administrators, as well as with my students' families. *(Please specify who and when.)*

7. I will meet with my Bully Busters Support Team. *(Please specify when and list what issues and questions you will raise.)*

Bully Busters: A Teacher's Manual for Helping Bullies, Victims, and Bystanders (Grades K–5)
© 2003 by Arthur M. Horne, Christi L. Bartolomucci, and Dawn Newman-Carlson.
Champaign, IL: Research Press. (800) 519–2707.

Classroom Activities

ACTIVITY 5.1: BYE, BYE, BULLY (GRADES K–2)

In this activity, children discuss the different kinds of things bullies do when they victimize other children. To help them consider the perspective and feelings of children who are victims, students draw a picture to show what someone being bullied might look like, then discuss how the victim might feel if students worked together to eliminate bullying.

ACTIVITY 5.2: BULLY, BE GONE! (GRADES K–5)

This activity asks students to become aware of the serious consequences bullying may have for victims. It strengthens students' ability to take the victim's perspective by giving them the opportunity to illustrate how children who are victims feel when they are being bullied and how they might feel once students help end bullying in their school.

ACTIVITY 5.3: WHO IS THE VICTIM? (GRADES 3–5)

Designed for older students, this activity offers an outline describing the characteristics of the four types of victims and gives students the opportunity to work in small groups to discuss and identify the type of victim in several different scenarios.

ACTIVITY 5.4: DOES IT COUNT? (GRADES 3–5)

Many students—and sometimes teachers as well—find it easier to blame the victim for being victimized than to confront the bullying situation. This activity invites students to decide if various situations "count" as bullying, then consider ways they can help support victims.

Bye, Bye, Bully

OBJECTIVES

- To encourage students to recognize what it is like to be the victim of bullying

- To help students understand the seriousness of bullying

- To encourage students to realize that they can help victims of bullying

MATERIALS

- Copies of the Bye, Bye, Bully worksheet

- Crayons, markers, or colored pencils

- Chalkboard or easel pad

DIRECTIONS

1. Introduce the lesson by saying that today the class will be talking about the people who are bullied—the victims. You might say, for example:

   When someone is a bully his or her actions hurt other people. Some kids who are bullied are afraid to come to school, and some kids feel sick every day before they come to school. Other kids may try to skip school and even feel bad about themselves until they are grown-ups.

2. Brainstorm with your class ways bullies hurt their victims. Typical responses include the following:

   Call them mean names, spread rumors about them.

   Kick, punch, or hit them.

   Not invite them to parties.

   Choose them last in games.

3. Discuss with your class what they think it feels like to be a victim of bullying and not to feel like the school or classroom is a safe place to be.

4. Provide students with an example of a bully-victim interaction, asking students how they think the victim feels. For example:

> At recess every day, Jamal and his friends tease Lee, calling him names, chasing him, and pushing him down. Lee has no one to play with because Jamal tells all the other boys he will beat them up if they play with Lee. Yesterday, when Lee was playing pole-tag with some of the girls in the class, Jamal came over and made Lee trip. Everyone started laughing at him.

> In Boone Elementary School, there is a secret club for girls. The three girls who are in charge are bossy and mean. These girls have been spreading rumors and calling Latoya and Aimee mean names. Over the past week, Latoya has missed three school days, and Aimee has visited the nurse's station at recess, complaining of headaches and stomachaches.

5. Distribute the Bye, Bye, Bully worksheets and drawing supplies. Invite students to draw a picture of what they think it feels like to be a victim of bullying. (Depending on their ability, they could also write words or phrases.)

6. Allow students to share their drawings with the class, if they would like.

7. Conduct class discussion by asking the following questions.

DISCUSSION QUESTIONS

- What do you think it is like to be a victim of bullying?

- Do you think it is fair to be a victim of bullying?

- Do you think many students are victims of bullying at our school? Why or why not?

- Do you think you could make a difference in stopping the bullying in our classroom? At our school?

- What do you think we can do in our classroom and at our school to help the victims of bullying feel better and safer?

- How do you think victims would feel if we worked together to stop the bullying?

Bye, Bye, Bully

When a person is bullied, he or she may feel like this . . .

Activity 5.1

Bully Busters: A Teacher's Manual for Helping Bullies, Victims, and Bystanders (Grades K–5)
© 2003 by Arthur M. Horne, Christi L. Bartolomucci, and Dawn Newman-Carlson.
Champaign, IL: Research Press. (800) 519–2707.

Bully, Be Gone!

OBJECTIVES

- To encourage students to understand the negative consequences of bullying for victims
- To help students recognize the seriousness of bullying
- To encourage students to realize that they have the power to help victims of bullying

MATERIALS

- Copies of the Bully, Be Gone! worksheet
- Crayons, markers, or colored pencils

DIRECTIONS

1. Discuss bullying with your students by sharing some of the consequences of bullying. For example, you could say:

   > Did you know that bullying can really hurt your classmates? Some kids are afraid to come to school. Some kids feel sick every day before they come to school. Other kids try to skip school. Some kids feel bad about themselves until they grow up.

   > It isn't fair that so many kids have to feel this way because someone at school is hurting them. School needs to be a place where we can all come, learn, and make friends. But you know what the best thing is? If we all work together, we can make sure our school is safe and none of our students needs to feel this bad. If we make a pact to work together, we can make sure there are no bullies at our school!

2. Give each student a copy of the Bully, Be Gone! worksheet, and distribute the art supplies.

3. Instruct students to draw pictures or symbols (or write words or phrases) on the left-hand side of the worksheet to describe what they think victims feel when they are bullied.

4. After students have finished, allow them to share their work with the class if they wish. Talk with them about how they would like to help the victims of bullying. How can they stick up for the victim or stand up to the bully? What do they think they could do? Whom could they go to for help?

5. Then instruct your students to illustrate, on the right-hand side of the worksheet, how they think victims will feel after everyone works together to get rid of bullying in the school.

6. When they have finished, allow students to share their work once again.

7. Facilitate class discussion by asking the following questions.

DISCUSSION QUESTIONS

- How bad do you think being a victim is?

- Do you think it is fair to be a victim of bullying?

- Do you think many kids are victims of bullying at our school? Why or why not?

- Do you think that if we all join forces we can make a difference in our class and school?

- Do you think each of you has the power to help stop victimization? If not, who can help you gain more power?

Bully, Be Gone!

Victims of bullying feel like this . . .	*When bullying stops, students who used to be bullied can feel like this . . .*

Activity 5.2

Bully Busters: A Teacher's Manual for Helping Bullies, Victims, and Bystanders (Grades K–5)
© 2003 by Arthur M. Horne, Christi L. Bartolomucci, and Dawn Newman-Carlson.
Champaign, IL: Research Press. (800) 519–2707.

Who Is the Victim?

OBJECTIVES

- To increase students' awareness of the effect of bullying on victims
- To help students recognize and understand the four types of victims

MATERIALS

- Copies of the Four Types of Victims handout
- Copies of Victim Scenarios 1–4 (one scenario for each group of three to five students)
- Chalkboard or easel pad

DIRECTIONS

1. Introduce the activity by explaining that today you will be discussing the four types of victims.

2. Give each student a copy of the Four Types of Victims handout. As a group, discuss the general characteristics of the different types of victims.

3. Divide the class into groups of three to five students each.

4. Provide each group with one of the four Victim Scenarios. Have each group identify the type of victim depicted in their scenario and answer the questions that follow it.

5. Bring the groups back together to discuss their answers. *(Answers: Scenario 1, passive; Scenario 2, provocative; Scenario 3, relational; Scenario 4, bystander).*

6. Process the activity by asking the following discussion questions.

DISCUSSION QUESTIONS

- What do you think it feels like to be a victim of bullying?
- Have you ever witnessed someone being bullied? How did that make you feel? What did you do?

- Who do you feel is responsible for helping the victim?

- How can you show victims of bullying that you care about them and want to help them?

- What are some ways you can handle a bullying situation?

Four Types of Victims

Passive victims

- Are the most common type.

- Try to avoid conflict by staying out of harm's way.

- Feel abandoned and isolated at school.

- Are cautious, sensitive, and quiet.

- Show others through how they behave that they are weak and not capable of defending themselves when attacked or insulted.

- Often do not have a solid friendship with a single student in their class.

Provocative victims

- Are less common than passive victims.

- Like bullies, are aggressive.

- Do things that make others irritated and angry.

- Deliberately provoke bullies, preferring a negative reaction to being ignored.

- May be trying to get the attention of the class through inappropriate behavior.

- Unpopular among peers but may not have low self-esteem.

- May be friends with bullies in an attempt to increase their social status.

Relational victims

- Are more often girls than boys.

- Are purposely excluded from groups or ignored by others.

- Harm done is more emotional than physical.

- Feel alone and disliked.

- Have low self-concept and self-esteem.

Bystander victims

- Are students who witness the act of bullying.

- Fear that they might be the bully's next target.

- May feel sad, guilty, and ashamed about what they witness.

- May feel cowardly or weak because they don't know what to do to stop the bullying.

Victim Scenario 1

Johnny is an 8-year-old boy who is much smaller than most of his classmates. He is quiet, and when he does speak, his voice is very soft and almost babylike. Last year, Johnny had his older brother at his school, but his brother moved to the middle school. This year, Johnny doesn't have any family or friends at school. He sits by himself at lunch and usually walks around the playground alone during recess. At lunch, one group of boys always teases him and often will throw their food at him. Johnny tries to ignore them and does nothing. Today when the boys keep throwing food at him, Johnny puts his head down on the table and begins to cry. This only makes the bullies laugh louder at him, and they start yelling to everybody that he is a crybaby and should be at home with his mama.

Questions

1. What kind of bullying is this?

2. Who is the victim, and how do you think the victim feels?

3. What would be your goal if you were the victim in the story?

4. What do you think you would do if you were in the same situation as the victim?

5. Would that be a good way to handle the situation?

Bully Busters: A Teacher's Manual for Helping Bullies, Victims, and Bystanders (Grades K–5)
© 2003 by Arthur M. Horne, Christi L. Bartolomucci, and Dawn Newman-Carlson.
Champaign, IL: Research Press. (800) 519–2707.

Victim Scenario 2

Sammy is in the third grade. He enjoys the attention of his classmates and teacher. However, he tries to get their attention by being "hyper" or silly. Sammy loves to start trouble by hitting, pushing, and teasing others. He particularly likes to stir up conflict with one particular bully in his class. On purpose, Sammy will try to bump into the bully or trip him in the hallway. The bully finally gets fed up and uses force to put Sammy in his place. This sets the stage for ongoing bullying between Sammy and the bully. Now Sammy gets beat up all the time but continues to provoke the bully to get more attention.

Questions

1. What kind of bullying is this?

2. Who is the victim, and how do you think the victim feels?

3. What would be your goal if you were the victim in the story?

4. What do you think you would do if you were in the same situation as the victim?

5. Would that be a good way to handle the situation?

Victim Scenario 3

Marla transferred to the Huckleberry School in the third grade, during the middle of the school year. The other girls had already developed groups of friends and decided they did not want anyone new to join them. Though Marla attempted to make friends with the other girls, they ignored her and constantly left her out of their activities.

Questions

1. What kind of bullying is this?

2. Who is the victim, and how do you think the victim feels?

3. What would be your goal if you were the victim in the story?

4. What do you think you would do if you were in the same situation as the victim?

5. Would that be a good way to handle the situation?

Activity 5.3

Bully Busters: A Teacher's Manual for Helping Bullies, Victims, and Bystanders (Grades K–5)
© 2003 by Arthur M. Horne, Christi L. Bartolomucci, and Dawn Newman-Carlson.
Champaign, IL: Research Press. (800) 519–2707.

Victim Scenario 4

Jared is and always has been very popular among all of his peers. He excelled in sports and in academics. Steve, Jared's classmate, was the target of teasing and pushing on a daily basis. Steve's classmates made a chant about his clothes and funny voice. Every day, the students rehearsed the chant when they saw Steve enter the room. Although Jared is now in college, he is constantly reminded of how the kids treated Steve whenever he meets someone who resembles Steve. Jared now says that he has a permanent wound in his heart, which will never heal.

Questions

1. What kind of bullying is this?

2. Who is the victim, and how do you think the victim feels?

3. What would be your goal if you were the victim in the story?

4. What do you think you would do if you were in the same situation as the victim?

5. Would that be a good way to handle the situation?

Bully Busters: A Teacher's Manual for Helping Bullies, Victims, and Bystanders (Grades K–5)
© 2003 by Arthur M. Horne, Christi L. Bartolomucci, and Dawn Newman-Carlson.
Champaign, IL: Research Press. (800) 519–2707.

Does It Count?

OBJECTIVES

- To encourage students to recognize victimization among their class-mates

- To promote students' awareness of the feelings and behaviors associated with victims of bullying

- To help students learn not to blame the victim for being victimized and offer support instead

MATERIALS

- Copies of the Does It Count? worksheet

- Pencils or pens

DIRECTIONS

1. Introduce the activity by explaining to students that you are going to be talking about the victimization that some students experience and ways everyone can help. You may choose to say something like this:

   > Today we are going to try to identify bullying situations and talk about how they affect victims. Part of what I want us to think about is that no one deserves to be a victim, and so as a class we need to think about what we can do to help the victims in our class and school.

2. Divide the class into groups of three or four students each.

3. Give each group a Does It Count? worksheet. Read the first scenario, and encourage each group to discuss and answer the four questions about that scenario.

4. After a few minutes, allow each group to share answers with the whole class. *(All of the situations "count" as instances of bullying and victimization.)*

5. Facilitate discussion by asking the following questions.

DISCUSSION QUESTIONS

- How did you decide if the student was being victimized?

- Did any of the situations make you mad at the victim? Why or why not?

- Did you ever feel sad or angry toward the bully? Why or why not?

- Would you feel comfortable helping the victim in any of these situations?

- Are there any situations in which you would not want to help? Why?

NOTE

Many students, and some teachers as well, find it easier to blame the victim for being victimized than to confront the situation. If the class begins blaming the victim while discussing the scenarios, refocus the conversation. Ask students if they would feel differently if the person being hurt was a friend, brother or sister, or themselves.

Does It Count?

Misty

All the kids at school make fun of Misty. She is a little clumsier than her classmates, and sometimes she trips over her feet or bangs into her desk. Every time
Misty accidentally hurts herself, Joanne is the first one to point it out to the
whole class. Joanne, very loudly, calls Misty a klutz, stupid, and slow. Joanne also
tells everyone that they shouldn't be friends with Misty because they will become
a klutz, too.

1. Is Misty being victimized?

2. How do you think Misty feels in this situation?

3. How do you feel when you hear about what happens to Misty?

4. What could you do to help Misty?

Buddy

Buddy is much smaller than most of the kids in his class. Although he will probably grow to be very big and strong like his older brother, two boys at school push
him around every day. These boys are twice his size and can be very mean. Some
days they run up behind him, pick him up, and make him drop all his books.
Other days they push him against the wall and won't let him go.

1. Is Buddy being victimized?

2. How do you think Buddy feels in this situation?

3. How do you feel when you hear about what happens to Buddy?

4. What could you do to help Buddy?

Adam

Adam is known as the class clown. He is always doing silly things to make people
laugh at him. Adam really teases Jeff—probably two to three times a week. Jeff
finally decides to put Adam in his place. Jeff and his friends are much bigger and
stronger than Adam, so they push him into a bathroom stall and lock him in there
while he screams and screams.

1. Is Adam being victimized?

2. How do you think Adam feels in this situation?

3. How do you feel when you hear about what happens to Adam?

4. What could you do to help Adam?

Bully Busters: A Teacher's Manual for Helping Bullies, Victims, and Bystanders (Grades K–5)
© 2003 by Arthur M. Horne, Christi L. Bartolomucci, and Dawn Newman-Carlson.
Champaign, IL: Research Press. (800) 519–2707.

MODULE

6 Recommendations and Interventions for Bullying Behavior

OVERVIEW

Now that you have gained an increased awareness of what bullying is and how to recognize bullies and victims, it is time to confront the bullying that may be occurring in your classroom. This module will help you learn specific intervention skills appropriate for all teachers working with bullies. In addition, you will learn new ways to set up for success in an effort to prevent further bullying in your classroom and school (see chapter 1 for related suggestions). The focus is on approaches we have found successful in the classroom and school setting and that are well-suited for your teaching curriculum.

GOALS

- To learn how to use an invitational approach to develop a working relationship with bullies

- To learn the "Four Rs" of bully control

- To understand basic principles of behavior change as they relate to bullying

- To consider the various roles students may assume in the bully-victim interaction

- To learn specific developmental areas that can be addressed in bullies to help them change their behaviors

- To learn the importance of changing bullies' reputations as well as their behaviors

ESTABLISHING A WORKING RELATIONSHIP WITH BULLIES

A positive teacher-child relationship has a far-reaching effect. Children who connect with at least one teacher are more likely to feel they belong in the school environment. Those students who feel that they are valued participants at school are more likely to behave appropriately, feel good about themselves, and excel academically. A positive relationship with a teacher is especially important to children who bully. Bullies are not typically accustomed to adults treating them with respect, support, and care. Bullies often expect negative attention in response to their inappropriate behaviors, and, initially, they may not trust your motives. Therefore, initiating contact and establishing a good relationship with bullies can be challenging. We suggest an "invitational approach," in which you engage bullies in forming a positive relationship with you. That relationship will allow you to address their thoughts, feelings, and behaviors in a meaningful manner. The invitational approach specifically involves inviting bullies to talk, explain their perceptions of problems, discuss and consider additional information, and participate in developing a plan of action. Following are some general guidelines for establishing this kind of relationship.

Understand that bullies' actions often indicate a need for attention, revenge, or power

We all like to be cared for, and a problem most bullies have is that they receive criticism or are ignored more often than they are praised and acknowledged. Most bullies are "walking wounded" in the sense that they have not received the emotional nurturance they crave. Although you may find bullies' behavior intimidating and problematic, these children need your help and attention as much as their victims do.

A frequent goal of bullying behavior is to obtain attention or recognition. Children who act out in the classroom generally escalate the level of their aggression until they obtain the attention they desire. Ignoring may be an appropriate response to some classroom problems, and it is sometimes a very good choice for children who are not hurting others emotionally or physically and who are seeking attention inappropriately. However, it is not a good idea to ignore bullying. If you do, the bully, the victim, and bystanders receive the message that bullying is acceptable.

A second goal bullies often have is to gain revenge when they feel they have been wronged, treated unfairly, or disrespected. It is important that we spend time talking with bullies to get a clear understanding of the reasons they give for behaving as they do. For instance, we have had bullies tell us that they were angry and needed to seek revenge by taunting other students if the teacher seemed to favor them.

Another goal bullies sometimes have is to show that they are powerful or influential. They engage in power struggles with the teacher or with other students to test their ability to influence or intimidate. We have had bullies report to us that they knew what they were doing was wrong, but they thought they had to confront the teacher or another student to prove that they had power in their lives.

Teachers must understand bullies' need for attention, revenge, and power to take steps to help these students meet their needs without having to engage in confrontation or aggression.

Consider your thoughts, feelings, and attitudes toward bullies

When interacting with bullies, the attitude you project often determines whether the experience will be productive or merely a power struggle. If you are feeling angry, cynical, tired, or any of the other emotions natural when you are dealing with a frustrating situation, take a moment to recenter yourself before approaching the bully.

> *As you are entering your classroom after recess, you notice Jack teasing and pushing Denzil in line again. You are so tired of Jack's behavior. You catch yourself feeling furious with Jack, and you know you need to intervene. You decide to ask Jack to have a seat near your desk and to wait for you there.*

Considering your emotions before you take action gives you time to decide the best way to intervene. You may want to take a deep breath and count to five to calm yourself before addressing the bully.

Stay calm

When you become publicly angry with a bully, the bully receives attention, although it is negative attention. Not only does the bully win by having power over the victim, the bully also takes control of you as the teacher by having you lose control. Bullies enjoy placing teachers in a power struggle that is sure to end in an unsuccessful intervention.

Balance support and firmness

Bullying is serious, and it requires a serious approach. Finding a balance between support and firmness is not easy, but it allows the bully to know that you want to work with him or her at the same time you believe the bullying behavior needs to and can change. Be aware of how your emotions might influence your ability to balance your message.

> *You approach Maurice after you observe him and Josh scuffling in the lunch line. You say, "Maurice, I need for us to have a private talk. I can see that something is going on between you and Josh. Neither of you seems happy with how things are going. Pushing Josh cannot continue. You know you will get in trouble for bullying, and Josh will also feel bad. I am responsible for you, for Josh, and for all the students in our class. I understand there is a problem, but I need to help you to find a better way to treat Josh. We need to talk about what you can do differently and how I can help you behave differently.*

During this conversation, you let Josh know that you care and want to work with him, but at the same time you unequivocally assert that bullying behavior is unacceptable. This conversation does not take the place of natural or logical consequences for what Maurice has done; consequences for specific infractions need to be fair and consistently applied. However, conversations before and after consequences have been delivered can be very powerful.

Allow the bully to talk and share his or her perspective

Bullies often feel they are falsely accused and misunderstood. Inviting a bully to tell you his or her side of the story expresses your desire to be fair and your respect for that child's feelings. Discuss with the bully possible explanations for the victim's behaviors. Redirect the bully's energy from defending himself by inviting him to share his thoughts and feelings regarding what he wishes he had done differently. It is important to stay out of power struggles: Rather than focusing on the facts of the situation, focus on strategies for the future.

Teacher: Robert, I like you and think you have lots of great ideas, but I often see you pushing Julio around in class. I need this to stop. I was wondering if you could tell me what is happening between you and Julio.

Robert: He's just such a little punk; he walks funny and snorts when he laughs. I don't like him at all!

Teacher: People have a right to dislike others, but it is important that we find a way for you to develop a plan so that you can have your feelings but you are also careful not to hurt other people in the process. Robert, you have to learn to understand that what you do and say to Julio hurts. None of us wants to be hurt or embarrassed. I sure don't, and my guess is that you don't like to feel hurt either.

Make a commitment to yourself and the bully

When you recognize a child who bullies, make a personal commitment to yourself and to the child that you will work together to find a better way of interacting with others and getting the child what he or she wants. Let the child know that you want the child, the victim, and the other students to feel good about being in your classroom.

> *Intervening with a student who is constantly starting arguments, you say, "Scott, I saw what happened between you and Jared. I am very serious about making this classroom a good place for all of my students. By your actions, it doesn't seem like you are happy with how things are going in this class. I believe that you don't want to be a bully. You don't have to be a bully to get along with others in the class. I am here to help you feel like you're an important part of this class and to help you handle your problems with Jared better."*

Be aware that bullies often believe they are being singled out and treated unfairly

Rather than taking responsibility for their behavior, bullies often see their actions as the inevitable result of their classmates' behavior. Our goal is to help bullies begin to take responsibility for their emotions, behaviors, and the effects of these behaviors on other students.

Teacher: Tierra, I saw you purposely trip Melonie when she was walking to my desk.

Tierra: That's not fair. She is always looking at me funny. You always think I'm the one. She started it first. It just isn't fair how you always defend everyone else.

Teacher: I can see why you feel like I am always singling you out. It does seem like I am on your case a lot, and it is also true that I don't say as much to some of the other students, like Melonie. That is because I often see you doing more things to bring hurt to other students, and I can't let that happen. I want to be fair with you, which means you must also be fair with me and with the other students. I would like to help you get along better with your classmates. I think that you would like to get along better, even with Melonie, but you don't seem to know how to do that. I want you to be happier, and I believe you will be when you learn some new ways to make friends. I want to help you find more positive ways to work with your classmates so you don't feel picked on by me and so Melonie doesn't feel picked on by you.

In this example, the teacher works to help Tierra take responsibility for her feelings as well as her behavior. The teacher makes an effort to understand why Tierra is using this behavior when she states, "I think that you would like to get along better, even with Melonie, but you don't seem to know how to do that." After responding empathically, the teacher would work to help this student find more productive ways of interacting with Melonie.

By empathizing with the student's frustration, you may find that you are able to support the child at the same time you redirect the child's efforts. Your empathy encourages the student to work through his or her emotions, builds your relationship with that student, and sets you up to redirect the student's behavior.

Let the student know he or she is important and deserves your help to learn new skills

Communicate to students that they are worth the time and energy you are putting forth to help them learn new skills. Explain that you are willing to work with them because they are important and strong but are using their strength in an unhealthy or unproductive way. Let them know you believe they have the capability to learn to use their strength more effectively.

Teacher: Fernando, it looks like you might be having some difficulty. I saw that you were having a conflict with Demarkeo. I'm not sure what it was about, but there are several things we need to talk about together. First, you are much bigger than Demarkeo, and although you are strong, you aren't using your strength positively— picking on other kids is not a good way to show how strong you are. That's why we have sports activities and other contests. You can show people how strong you are there. Second, we are clear about not causing hurt or pain to people. You were hurting Demarkeo. Third, I have great confidence in your being able to learn to handle conflicts better than you did today. I want us to explore some other things you can do instead of hurting Demarkeo so that the situation can be addressed differently next time.

THE FOUR Rs OF BULLY CONTROL

The key to successful bully prevention is using what we call the "Four Rs" of bully control:

Recognize that a problem exists, and remember to stay calm.

Remove yourself from the situation if you do not feel you can effectively intervene.

Review the situation.

Respond to the situation.

The Four Rs correspond to the Big Questions, discussed at length in chapter 1 and included in the reminder at the end of each learning module.

Recognize that a bullying problem exists, and remember to stay calm

In earlier modules, you sharpened your awareness of bullying. You are now able to identify bullying, bullies, and the victims in your class.

Question 1: What is my goal? My goal is to recognize that a bullying situation exists and to intervene effectively.

Remove yourself from the situation if you do not feel you can effectively intervene

It is important that you gain confidence about intervening in the bullying situation. However, you want to make sure that you feel ready to intervene to prevent yourself from getting visibly angry or applying inconsistent consequences or unjust punishment. If you do not feel ready to intervene, you can remove yourself and ask for help. You can also talk to the individuals involved separately and refer them for services elsewhere, such as to the school social worker or psychologist.

Question 2: What am I doing? By removing yourself from the situation, you are able to gain a clearer perspective of the bullying situation.

Review the situation

Review the situation you observed. It is important to consider all perspectives. Think about how you would like to respond. Prepare yourself for the reactions the students involved are likely to have when you intervene.

Question 3: Is what I am doing helping me achieve my goal? Asking this question prompts you to review the situation and decide if what you have been doing is helping to resolve the problem. Sometimes even well-planned interventions do not go as we envision. When the outcome is not what you expect, study what is failing. The information you collect from this evaluative process can drive more successful interventions in the future.

Respond to the situation

Your attention to the bullying situation is very important. Your response communicates to students that you are serious about making your class bully-free. Ignoring or withdrawing from the situation may communicate to your students that you do not see bullying as a serious problem.

Question 4: (If not) *What can I do differently?* This question helps guide your current intervention. You may decide to use a different approach this time to obtain different results. If you decide that what you have been doing is ineffective and are unsure how to proceed, you can always discuss alternatives with your Bully Busters Support Team, seek assistance, or refer students to someone else who you believe is better able to handle the problem.

PRINCIPLES OF BEHAVIOR CHANGE

Our intervention goal is to change bullies' negative and intentionally harmful behavior to positive, responsible, and caring behavior. Children who bully need to learn how not to bully, as well as how to interact with others and respond to conflicts appropriately. Throughout this manual, we have emphasized how children learn both negative and positive behaviors through their social interactions. Children can unlearn bullying behaviors, substitute prosocial behaviors, and increase the time they spend engaging in prosocial behaviors.

An understanding of the principles of behavior change is essential in helping all children toward positive interactions and away from the bully-victim struggle. Application of these principles is especially necessary in helping bullies make positive changes. Although our discussion here is focused on changing bullying behavior, these strategies are universally effective in addressing aggressive or acting-out behavior of all kinds.

Modeling

Learning occurs through a variety of avenues, and one of the most powerful is modeling. The advertising industry exemplifies the power of modeling in its assumption that when people observe influential models (e.g., actors, athletes, politicians), others will copy or emulate that behavior and buy products, believe messages, or in other ways be influenced. Children acquire a large portion of their learning experiences by observing others' behaviors. Modeling is likely the most influential aspect of learning available to teachers. Students look to their teachers for leadership and direction on how to behave and treat others. As we said previously, teachers have an inherent power to set standards and guide behaviors in the classroom. If teachers demonstrate respect for others, students are likely to do the same.

Reinforcement

Positive reinforcement

Positive reinforcers are words, actions, or material objects that, when given, increase or maintain a behavior. Reinforcers may take several forms, ranging from points that may be redeemed for tangible items at a later time to tangible items themselves (e.g., stars, stickers, pencils, small toys). Reinforcers may also be social—for example, a student's behavior may be positively influenced by receiving teacher praise or extra time for socializing with classmates. In fact, the most powerful reinforcers are social.

A teacher's social reinforcement might begin as these examples do:

"Brandie, I like it when you . . ."

"Steven, I am proud of you for . . ."

"Rizvi, I noticed how hard you tried . . ."

It is important always to use praise, or social reinforcement, when giving a student any other kind of reinforcer. The effectiveness of the reinforcement is determined by the outcome: Did the student's good behavior increase? Did inappropriate behavior decrease?

Initially, social reinforcement may not bring about behavior change. As noted, children are most likely to respond positively when teachers combine social and other kinds of reinforcers. For example, when a class behaves well for a substitute teacher, the teacher might say, "I am so impressed by your good behavior while I was out yesterday. Hearing about how well you all did made me feel proud. Today I am allowing the class 15 minutes extra at recess." Eventually, students will come to desire the praise, and the words of praise will be sufficient.

Praise versus encouragement

The terms *praise* and *encouragement* are often used together and viewed as interchangeable. However, these things are really quite different. Praise generally comes from the teacher and describes a characteristic that the teacher has noticed and approved. Praise is very powerful in getting students' attention, helping them to identify and recognize appropriate behavior, and encouraging positive behavior. Following are some examples of praise:

"Peter, I really liked how you helped Ryan with moving that desk. Thank you for your help."

"Robin, thank you for including Melissa—I like that a lot."

"Lonny, you really paid attention all during math today. Great job!"

The potential problem with praise is that it is external to the student. The student is inclined to behave in a particular way to get the teacher to notice and give praise, not because the student wants to or feels like behaving in this way. Our goal is to help children learn to be responsible for their own behavior. Although praise helps them initially in recognizing their good behavior and realizing that other people also notice their good behavior, it does not make them take ownership of their behavior.

An alternative to praise is encouragement. With encouragement, the source of the reinforcement switches from external (the teacher) to internal (the student). When the teacher encourages, he or she is helping the student internalize the reinforcing message. When students internalize the importance of behaving well and associate it with feeling good about themselves, they are likely to take ownership of their behavior. For example:

"Jeff, you seemed really happy with how well you did on your school work today. I'll bet that makes you feel good."

"Laura, you were so eager to help Mia get her papers together. You must feel happy to know you are helping someone else."

"Jonas, you really are trying hard on that tough problem. You really seem to be motivated to work through even the hardest problems."

"Karyn and Eric, I know it can be hard to work as partners on this activity, but you two can find a way to work well together and achieve your goals. I'm sure you can do it."

Removing positive reinforcement

If we can assume that a reason for bullies to behave as they do is to get the attention and notice that goes with bullying, one way to reduce the behavior is to reduce the amount of reinforcement—attention—they get for being aggressive. One suggestion for removing the attention reinforcer is to discourage other students from laughing at or provoking students who bully. Other students' attention will only incite bullies to further aggression.

An additional suggestion is to wait until after class to confront the bully. If you do so, you avoid giving the bully class time during which other students watch you direct your attention toward the problem. When a teacher attends to a bully in front of the class, it demonstrates the bully's ability to pull the teacher into the confrontation, thereby giving the bully a sense of control. For a bully, your criticism is better than no attention at all. The bottom line is, do not reinforce the attention-seeking behavior.

Effective reinforcers

A reinforcer should be something desired by the student. If you attempt a program of reinforcement that does not work, then the student did not perceive the consequence as reinforcing, regardless of how effective you thought that consequence would be. In a focused attempt to change behavior, it is helpful to observe the child and consider what is already motivating to him or her. Some children crave public attention and recognition; some enjoy special one-on-one time with the teacher; and others are very happy with items such as pencils, erasers, and stickers.

As an example, we once worked with a disruptive student and established a point system for appropriate behavior. When he accumulated enough points, he received a signed jersey from a famous basketball player, but he seemed disappointed. When asked why, he explained that the jersey was nice, but he did not like basketball. What he really wanted was some one-on-one time with the teacher.

For an item to be reinforcing, it has to be perceived that way by the recipient—the student—not just by the teacher. By getting to know each student individually, you will be better able to choose appropriate reinforcers. Look for activities that excite each student. For instance, you might find that one student is particularly interested in working on the computer, whereas another student enjoys reading. Use information about each child's preferences in determining the reinforcers you use. The more closely the reinforcer matches the child, the more likely you will change the child's behavior.

Tips for using reinforcement

The following guidelines are aimed at helping you to use reinforcement strategies successfully in your classroom.

Reinforce the behavior you observe, not the child. Your goal should be to identify the behaviors you observe as good or bad, not to label the child as good or bad. Children often hear that they are good or bad, and their self-concepts can oscillate depending on the reinforcers they receive. We must communicate that we believe in our students as people, even if we need to address the way they are acting. For example, you might say, "Jamie, I am proud of you for taking time to introduce Sam to the other students." This tells Jamie what you liked and gives him feedback on what to do in the future. The following statement clearly communicates that you are identifying "pushing" as an inappropriate behavior, not labeling the student as bad: "Chad, pushing is not an acceptable behavior in this classroom."

Give reinforcement as quickly and as consistently as possible after the desired behavior. Although adults, and even some students, are used to delayed gratification, bullies generally are not very good at putting off reinforcement. When you decide that you are going to seek opportunities to reinforce these children's positive behaviors, you must reinforce *frequently* and *consistently;* otherwise, they will lose confidence in your efforts.

When a bullying incident occurs, reinforce the nonbullying behavior of bystanders and victims. You want the bully to desire what the others are getting: positive attention and support from you. The bully must understand that the positive attention will not be provided as long as he or she is engaging in aggressive behavior.

Create opportunities for bullies to feel good about themselves. It is important to plan programs or activities bullies can engage in with others in which they will have positive experiences, then receive praise and encouragement for using their new skills and behaviors. Find out what these students excel in, and encourage or provide opportunities for them to engage in these tasks (e.g., being a group leader, organizing a class project). Commenting to the class on the leadership abilities of children who bully may be helpful, although this must be done in a way that does not grant bullies additional status. When commenting on students' strengths publicly, make sure to acknowledge these strengths in the context of good behaviors, and clearly define the good behaviors.

Catching them being good

For all students, but especially for bullies, it is important to take time to "catch them being good." We have had numerous bullies tell us that the only time the teacher ever notices them is when they are messing up, never when they are doing well. Reinforcement is designed to increase the behaviors you want more of, so find opportunities to let bullies know when they are behaving appropriately.

This is very difficult to do! We find that all teachers know they should look for and reinforce positive behavior but do not for several reasons. First, teachers are so busy that there is little time to look for good behavior; good behavior gets taken for granted when it occurs. Teachers are juggling multiple tasks in the classroom. The stress of balancing so many tasks at once can be a tremendous strain. Second, teachers often have such anger or negative feelings about aggressive kids that it is hard for them to think about looking for good behavior. The frustration that comes with working with challenging behavior can present a real obstacle. Third, many students who behave aggressively have fairly negative self-images and don't take being "caught good" very well. In fact, they may escalate their aggressive behavior to see if their teachers will keep looking for the good. Sticking with a new plan can be very difficult when it is met with punishing interactions at first. However, teachers who are able to keep to their plan for a few weeks will begin to see a shift. Students who bully report over and over how important positive feedback from teachers is to them.

When you do catch a bully in positive behavior, consider using some of the following reinforcements:

- Give the student a free pass to the library or water fountain.

- Give the student an important classroom position, such as collector of papers.

- Invite the student to sit in an honorary desk beside yours.

- Draw smiley faces on sticky notes and attach them to the student's desk.

- Create a cozy corner for reading and give the student 10 or 15 minutes to read there.

BULLY BUSTERS SUPPORT TEAM THINK BLOCK

In your Bully Busters Support Team, discuss your use of reinforcement. Ask the following questions:

1. Which reinforcement strategies have worked well for you? Why do you believe they worked?

2. Which strategies have been less successful? Why do you think these strategies did not work?

3. What suggestions for behavior change do you wish you could make better use of in your classroom?

Punishment versus Discipline

How conflicts are resolved, how problems are addressed, and how teachers and students interact in the classroom provide the foundation for social learning. As students experience classroom life, they organize their ideas about how the world works and how they fit into the world.

Children will often model the problem-solving behavior they observe in the classroom. Bodine and Crawford (1999) discuss the differences between punishment and discipline in the classroom and the effects of each on students. Although these terms are often used interchangeably, there are great differences in both approach and behavioral outcomes for the child. At the same time it promotes positive relationships between the child who bullies and other children, discipline fosters the development of personal responsibility and an understanding of natural and logical consequences for behavior. Punishment, on the other hand, can lead to misunderstandings between the bully and other children and result in the bully's blaming others rather than internalizing responsibility. Table 5 helps to show how punishment and discipline differ in the classroom.

BULLY BUSTERS SUPPORT TEAM THINK BLOCK

Discuss the following questions with your team:

1. How do you generally respond to a bully's behaviors?

2. Have you noticed a difference in the bully's reactions based on your response to his or her behavior?

3. What differences have you experienced when you have used punishment versus discipline to address bullying behaviors?

ROLES IN THE BULLY-VICTIM INTERACTION

The behaviors of the bully and the victim, as well as of other students in the class, work together to perpetuate the bullying situation. Christina Salmivalli and her colleagues have defined several roles that

TABLE 5 Punishment versus Discipline

Punishment	Discipline
Authority based: Teacher becomes visibly angry with bully, which may cause pain, embarrassment, and/or a power struggle.	**Logical or natural consequence:** Teacher talks to bully privately about behavior and explains the consequence of bullying. The bully is placed in time-out or refocus room to think about misbehavior and behavior change.
Inconsistent: Usually applied hastily, without full consideration of the situation.	**Consistent:** Continues to address the bullying behavior and assumes teacher and bully are working together to change the behavior.
Teacher imposes punishment on child: Child may not understand reason for punishment, believe treatment is unfair, and consequently not take responsibility for behavior.	**Child and teacher discuss consequence:** Child understands the consequence as a response to behavior and accepts responsibility for behavior.
Case closed: Child is punished, and situation is not discussed further.	**Case remains open:** Teacher and child discuss alternative behaviors to bullying to help the child create new options for future interactions.
Student is bad: "Bad" child is punished, feels bad, thinks teacher and peers see him or her as bad.	**Student is given hope:** Student is respected and feels teacher cares and wants to help him or her be more successful.
Models anger and coercion: Child learns to respond to situation with anger, just as teacher did.	**Models support, caring, and empathy:** Child learns it is OK to talk about a difficult situation with a teacher.
Fast and easy: The situation is addressed quickly, but you must intervene more often.	**Takes time and effort:** Involves taking individual time with the child who bullies to talk about the situation, consequences, and new behavioral alternatives.
Teacher controls behavior: Child learns that teachers and other adults will take responsibility for his or her behavior.	**Child learns to be responsible for own behavior:** Child learns that the teacher is a guide for appropriate behavior but that child is responsible for his or her actions.
Outcome of punishment: Positive change is unlikely because it rests on a child's being told what to do rather than helped to understand the importance of changing the behavior. The child may do as told to avoid a consequence but may not internalize or generalize the lesson.	**Outcome of discipline:** Child learns and understands the importance of being responsible for behavior and can make positive changes.

From *Developing Emotional Intelligence: A Guide to Behavior Management and Conflict Resolution in Schools* (pp. 98–99) by R. J. Bodine and D. K. Crawford, 1999, Champaign, IL: Research Press. Adapted by permission.

children may take that allow the bully-victim interaction to continue (Salmivalli, 1999; Salmivalli, Lagerspetz, Björkqvist, Österman, & Kaukiainen, 1996). They suggest that approximately 87 percent of schoolchildren occupy one of the roles indicated in Table 6. We have added the role of change agent to Salmivalli's schema. The circle that surrounds the various roles represents the school environment, including the feelings, attitudes, behaviors, and level of acceptance of bullying and aggression within the school context.

The ultimate goal of the Bully Busters program is for all children to become active change agents. As distinct from defenders, change agents are children equipped with the knowledge and skills they need to deal with bullying. With the help of school professionals, children can assume this role and exert a positive impact on the school environment.

Figures 6 and 7 show two configurations, the first a diagram that illustrates how these roles interrelate in a way that perpetuates bullying, the second a diagram that illustrates how the various roles might be positioned to help stop bullying. In Figure 6, many children are outsiders, avoiding the bully-victim interaction entirely. Although the victim has two defenders, all the other children reinforce the bully's behavior. In Figure 7, only three of the children are outsiders, and only one is a reinforcer. The rest of the children are either defenders or change agents.

BULLY BUSTERS SUPPORT TEAM THINK BLOCK

With your team take a moment to consider the various roles children can occupy:

1. Can you identify children in your classroom who occupy these roles?

2. Consider your class bully. Who encourages the bully by laughing at him or her? Who joins in?

3. Which children are separate from the entire process? How are these children treated?

4. Which children do you think could take on the change agent's role?

DEVELOPMENTAL SKILLS FOR BULLIES

Bullies may be lacking in their development, and they can usually benefit from specific instruction in a number of areas, including anger and impulse control, empathy, cognitive skills, and social skills.

Anger and Impulse Control Training

Bullies are aggressive, and they also tend to be impulsive. They may tend to feel an emotion strongly and to act immediately without having time to think about the situation, their feelings, or their responses. Many children, including those diagnosed with Attention Deficit/Hyperactivity

TABLE 6 Roles in the Bully-Victim Interaction

Bully

A child who intentionally and continually inflicts harm on another child who is perceived as less powerful than himself or herself

Victim

A child who is the target of the purposeful abuse of the bully

Assistant

A child who follows the bully and engages in bullying behavior *(passive bully)*

Reinforcer

A child who observes the bully-victim interaction and incites the bully through verbal encouragement *(passive bully)*

Defender

A child who sticks up for the victim and attempts to provide support

Outsider

A child who stays far away from the bully-victim interaction and does not engage in the interaction in any manner

Change agent

A child who has learned how to identify bullying and take action to stop it

Disorder, also struggle with impulse control. Learning to control impulses can be beneficial for bullies as well as all other students, for emotional control is a keystone of personal responsibility.

Interventions can be aimed at teaching bullies means other than physical force to control events. One way of doing this is to teach bullies to replace aggressive responses with assertive, constructive ones. A program developed by Goldstein, Glick, and Gibbs (1998) helps students learn to recognize their anger triggers and to apply techniques to reduce their anger. Students are taught the physical cues of anger (e.g., pounding heart, muscle tension, clenched fists) and the thinking processes that lead to aggressive responses.

Anger triggers can be external (e.g., being pushed or shoved, being called a name) or internal (e.g., thinking, "That little jerk is making a fool of me—I'm going to kick his behind"). An external trigger often sets off a series of negative internal messages, the end result being aggression. The key to reducing aggressive acts, then, is to teach bullies how to substitute positive thoughts for negative ones, as well as to recognize the physical cues associated with anger.

FIGURE 6 Roles Configured to Perpetuate Bullying

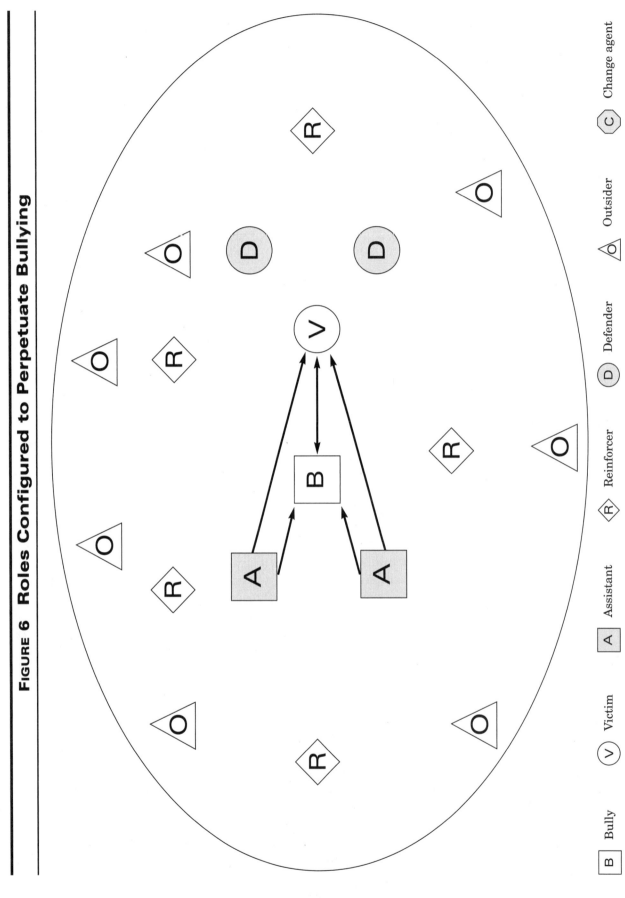

B Bully | V Victim | A Assistant | R Reinforcer | D Defender | O Outsider | C Change agent

FIGURE 7 Roles Configured to Prevent and Reduce Bullying

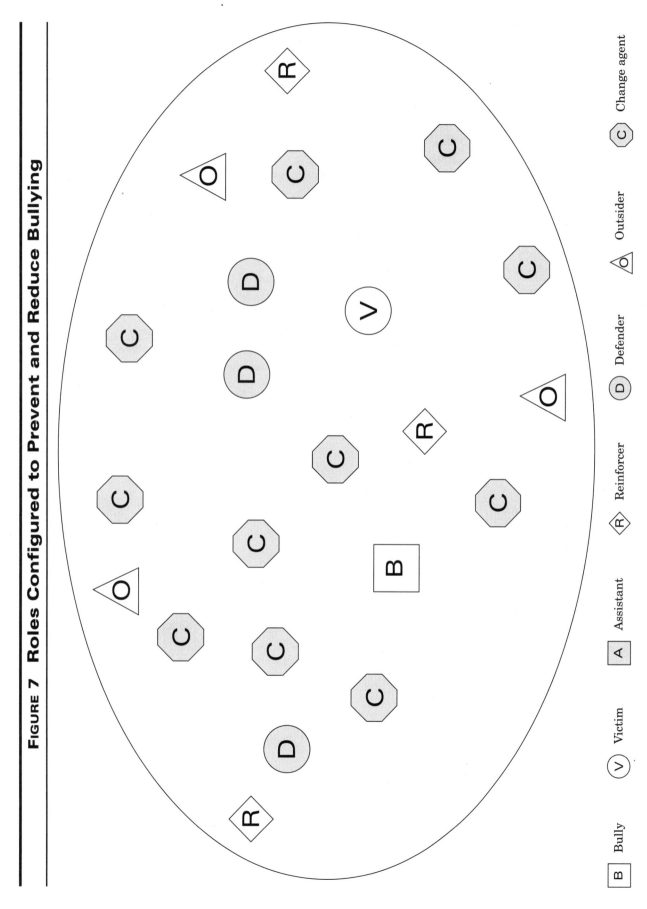

B Bully   V Victim   A Assistant   R̂ Reinforcer   O Outsider   D Defender   C Change agent

Provocative victims as well as bullies often go through the stages of anger development very quickly. Teaching both groups of students to stop before they reach full-blown anger and aggression is, therefore, very important.

Empathy Building

Ideally, students learn through their early social experiences in the family and community to feel empathy toward others and to treat others with respect and dignity. As we all know, however, this learning does not take place for many children. Fortunately, there are a number of ways for students to learn to be more empathic. The most effective ways involve interactions with other students who model appropriate caring behaviors.

Building empathy is crucial for bullies. If bullies are able to understand the pain they induce in their victims, there is less chance they will attempt to inflict harm on others. Although many children naturally empathize with others, children who focus on the benefits they derive from bullying are not concerned with the feelings of others.

Empathy involves taking another person's perspective (i.e., understanding what another person is thinking and feeling) and caring about that person's experience. The ability to be empathic works to prevent aggressive responses in two ways. First, empathy and aggression are incompatible interpersonal responses. This means that becoming more skilled in the former helps diminish the latter (Goldstein, 1999). Second, responding to another individual in an empathic manner decreases or inhibits one's potential for acting aggressively toward the other.

Teaching empathy skills is very important. This can be done in a number of ways, but instruction in empathy needs to be incorporated as a conscious educational activity. It should involve the teacher's modeling empathy for both bullies and victims. Several of the classroom activities at the end of this module suggest ways for students to build their empathy skills. An additional activity that works very well is to read stories to your class and then have your students comment on how different characters thought and felt. Fairy tales and traditional stories provide excellent opportunities for helping children begin to learn about the emotions of others. Role plays and role reversals may be especially useful in helping bullies learn what it feels like to be the victim. In an initial role play, two students act out a bully-victim scenario, expressing the thoughts, words, and feelings of each party. After the students have role-played the scenario, they reverse roles—in other words, the bully takes the part of the victim and vice versa. This procedure requires each role-player to identify with another individual in order to react as that person would and, as a result, helps the bully understand the victim's feelings and perspective.

Cognitive Retraining

Extensive research by Dodge and Coie (1987) and others has demonstrated that nonaggressive children are inclined to attribute an unintentional bump, slight shove, or tactless comment as accidental. Bullies, on the other hand, tend to attribute those activities to malice by others and believe they have both a right and an obligation to retaliate, even when objective observers are clear that the intention was not to harm (Ross, 1996). In brief, cognitive retraining involves teaching bullies to view others' motivations in a more neutral way.

A number of the activities we have developed and include in this manual focus on cognitive retraining. Activities that include taking another's perspective and doing role reversals have as their goal establishing an ability to observe the world from another's perspective or viewpoint. You may also help facilitate this process by "talking out loud." As you talk through your own thought processes in understanding how one student may see a situation one way and another a different way, you can help students develop the skill of looking at both sides of a situation.

Social Skills Training

Ideally, a student observes appropriate social skills at home and in the classroom, recognizes how and why the behaviors are appropriate, and then masters them. However, more often an unskilled student fails to be aware of the behaviors or understand why they are important. Social skills are learned, and some students lack appropriate training (Goldstein & McGinnis, 1997; McGinnis & Goldstein, 1997).

Students can learn new social skills and increase their use of them, given encouragement, support, and the proper learning environment. Briefly, teaching new skills involves the following steps:

1. Identifying the skill to be taught

2. Evaluating the current level of the skill

3. Breaking the skill into a sequence of smaller steps

4. Providing learning models (e.g., peers, television, films, books) that demonstrate the steps

5. Allowing sufficient time and opportunity for practice

6. Providing support and encouragement for use of the new skills

7. Monitoring use of the new skills and providing ongoing encouragement

Although we know teachers do not have time to run social skills groups in their classrooms each day, you may have time at the beginning of each class to share some suggestions. *Group-entry skills* are important for bullies and victims alike. The steps for entering a group may be discussed in class, then printed out on index cards and distributed to students. Whenever a social-entry situation arises, you can refer to these steps:

1. When approaching a group of students, watch and wait before joining in the conversation.

2. Listen and follow the conversation rather than introducing new topics.

3. Ask relevant questions and make comments.

4. Imitate the behavior of the group.

Problem-Solving Training

Problem-solving training can help bullies see alternatives to solving a problem with aggression (see Shure, 1992a, 1992b, 1992c). The steps in the problem-solving process are as follows:

1. Stop and think.

2. Define the problem.

3. Generate alternative solutions.

4. Evaluate consequences of solutions.

5. Select a solution.

6. Implement the solution.

7. Evaluate the solution.

The Big Questions, discussed earlier in this module in relation to the Four Rs of bully control, are a problem-solving process. You can encourage problem solving by using the Big Questions as a whole-class exercise and having all students participate in the process, but you can also apply the questions on a one-on-one basis whenever necessary. The following dialogue illustrates this process.

Teacher: Raymond, what do you want? What is your goal?

Raymond: I don't know what you mean.

Teacher: My goal is for all students to get along, to treat one another with respect, and to learn what I teach. When you are bullying other students, you aren't showing them respect, and you are interfering with their learning as well as yours.

Raymond: But it just keeps happening—they get in my face and really bug me.

Teacher: OK, so you have the goal of getting along, too, right? That's great. Next question: What are you doing? The answer seems to be that you are getting into fights and pushing several of the other students around. When you do this, does that help you achieve your goal?

Raymond: Well, no, but they shouldn't diss me either—they just look at me like I'm stupid or something.

Teacher: You are not stupid, but you do get mad. When you are mad, does that help you achieve your goal of getting along?

Raymond: No, but what else can I do?

Teacher: Great question. What else can you do?

Raymond: I don't know.

Teacher: I've got some ideas about other things you might try. One thing might be to practice ignoring the looks they give you. Another might be to tell them that when they look at you like that, you feel hurt because it seems they don't like you. Let's try these out and see if they will work.

REPUTATION CHANGING

When students begin to change and behave more appropriately, there often is still a problem: Their reputations do not change as fast as their behaviors do. Being violent and aggressive (i.e., acting like a bully) results in a student's being rejected by classmates. Once a child has been labeled by the school as a bully, he or she may be perceived that way long after the behavior has improved. Teachers will need to take an active role in helping other students recognize positive changes and accept the former bully as a peer and fellow student. If students see teachers modeling acceptance and social validation, they will model the teachers' behavior and be more accepting as well.

In addition to modeling more accepting behavior, you can actively incorporate the changed student into various classroom groups. That way, peers can see and evaluate the changes for themselves. Good forums for this are sports and other recreational activities, whole-class projects, and assignments completed in small groups.

Module 6: Content Review

The following statements relate to the learning goals of this module. Ask yourself if you feel confident that you can answer yes to each item. If not, please review the material and discuss any difficulties among your Bully Busters Support Team.

1. I understand the need for an invitational approach when developing a working relationship with bullies.   Yes ❑   No ❑

2. I know the "Four Rs" of bully control and how to apply them in my own classroom situation.   Yes ❑   No ❑

3. I understand the basic principles of behavior change as they relate to bullying and am committed to identifying and reinforcing positive behaviors in my classroom.   Yes ❑   No ❑

4. I am aware of how both positive and negative behaviors are reinforced in my classroom and realize that providing bullies with a great deal of attention can inadvertently reinforce negative behaviors.   Yes ❑   No ❑

5. I understand the difference between punishment and discipline in the classroom and realize that, although providing punishment is easier, discipline more effectively builds positive behaviors and good relationships.   Yes ❑   No ❑

6. I know that bullies can benefit from direct instruction in a number of developmental areas and am able to name these areas.   Yes ❑   No ❑

7. I am aware that bullies often hurt themselves and that they need and deserve my help to change both their behaviors and their reputations with their peers.   Yes ❑   No ❑

Bully Busters: A Teacher's Manual for Helping Bullies, Victims, and Bystanders (Grades K–5)
© 2003 by Arthur M. Horne, Christi L. Bartolomucci, and Dawn Newman-Carlson.
Champaign, IL: Research Press. (800) 519–2707.

A Reminder . . .

CLASSROOM INTERACTION AND AWARENESS CHART

Use the CIAC to describe any bullying behavior you observe (and that students report to you, if you wish). A copy of the CIAC and a weekly summary sheet appear in Appendix A.

THE BIG QUESTIONS

Honestly appraise your progress by asking yourself the Big Questions. There are no right or wrong answers.

In relation to intervening to prevent and reduce bullying behavior in my school:

1. What is my goal?

2. What am I doing?

3. Is what I am doing helping me achieve my goal?

4. *(If not)* What can I do differently?

PERSONAL GOALS FORM

The Personal Goals Form, on the next page, is designed to help you tailor the content of this module to your own students and situation. Please take a moment to fill out the form now.

Module 6: Personal Goals Form

Goals

- To learn how to use an invitational approach to develop a working relationship with bullies

- To learn the "Four Rs" of bully control

- To understand basic principles of behavior change as they relate to bullying

- To consider the various roles students may assume in the bully-victim interaction

- To learn specific developmental areas that can be addressed in bullies to help them change their behaviors

- To learn the importance of changing bullies' reputations as well as their behaviors

1. My role in intervening in bullying incidents and with bullies is as follows:

2. I have observed incidents of bullying. *(Please record incidents on the CIAC.)*

   _____ Number of times I intervened   _____ Number of times I chose not to intervene

   Other observations:

3. I will review the classroom activities for this module and select ones appropriate for my class. *(Please list.)*

4. I will accept the challenges associated with the developmental assets. *(Please list the specific assets and describe what you plan to do.)*

5. I will give my students feedback about the bullying incidents I have observed and encourage discussion of bullying and related issues. We will discuss these topics:

6. I will share my experiences in applying the information in this module with other teachers and administrators, as well as with my students' families. *(Please specify who and when.)*

7. I will meet with my Bully Busters Support Team. *(Please specify when and list what issues and questions you will raise.)*

Bully Busters: A Teacher's Manual for Helping Bullies, Victims, and Bystanders (Grades K–5)
© 2003 by Arthur M. Horne, Christi L. Bartolomucci, and Dawn Newman-Carlson.
Champaign, IL: Research Press. (800) 519–2707.

Classroom Activities

ACTIVITY 6.1: ANGER BUSTERS (GRADES K–2)

Anger is a normal, natural emotion. This activity gives students a chance to identify the types of situations in which they become angry, recognize how they look and feel when they are angry, and brainstorm positive ways of dealing with anger. Three rules for expressing anger are described.

ACTIVITY 6.2: CAUGHT THE FEELING (GRADES K–2)

In this activity, students listen to several scenarios, then identify and discuss the feelings of the characters in them. By doing so, they practice recognizing different types of feelings, identify how others might feel in particular situations, and build their feeling-word vocabulary.

ACTIVITY 6.3: THE TURTLE CLUB (GRADES K–5)

In this activity, students learn the "turtle technique," an anger management strategy for controlling impulses, especially anger. Students have the opportunity to practice this technique and are encouraged to use it in the daily classroom routine.

ACTIVITY 6.4: KNOWING MY ANGER (GRADES 3–5)

In this activity, small groups role-play conflict situations, illustrating first negative, then positive ways of handling conflict. In the larger group, students discuss the feelings that might be associated with and the pros and cons of each approach.

ACTIVITY 6.5: ACT ONE (GRADES 3–5)

This activity includes a worksheet that illustrates the anger process. Students identify anger triggers, how their bodies look and feel when they are angry, how they respond when angry, and consequences of their actions. They also brainstorm positive ways to handle their anger.

Anger Busters

OBJECTIVES

- To help students understand that anger is a normal part of life
- To identify constructive ways of expressing and dealing with anger
- To identify rules for responding to anger

MATERIALS

- None

DIRECTIONS

1. Explain to students that you are going to be talking about feeling angry. As you introduce the topic of anger, explain that anger is a normal, natural feeling that all people experience.

2. Brainstorm what anger is and how students look and feel when they are angry (for instance, getting red in the face, feeling tense or hot, etc.). Depending on the energy level of your class, you can make this activity more interactive by giving students the opportunity to show how they feel and look when angry (act it out, make faces, etc.).

3. Discuss with students the idea that we all have things that make us angry and that it is OK to feel angry; however, what we do with those angry feelings is really important because it can make things better or worse for us.

4. Next introduce the idea that we have certain rules for dealing with our angry feelings. Discuss the following three rules:

   You may not hurt yourself.

   You may not hurt others.

   You may not harm property.

5. Ask whether anyone can briefly describe a situation in which he or she became angry. Choose a situation from the ones that students volunteer, and work through some possible responses and their consequences. For example:

Suppose it's time to line up for lunch, and Julie pushes in front of Tosha. This makes Tosha really mad!

What do you think Tosha should do?

Let's see, Tosha could push Julie back, and what do you think would happen?

Would this make things better or worse?

What if Tosha choose to ignore Julie or tell me or another teacher? What do you think would happen?

Would this make things better or worse?

6. Help students brainstorm positive ways of dealing with anger (for example, taking deep breaths, counting to 10, listening to music, kicking around a soccer ball, asking an adult for help, walking away, etc.).

7. Complete the activity by having the class answer the discussion questions.

DISCUSSION QUESTIONS

- What is something that really bugs you?

- How does your body feel when you are angry?

- What are some ways you express your anger? What happens when you act that way?

- Do these things help or hurt the situation?

- Tell about a time when you handled your anger in a good way.

- What is one good thing you think you might try next time you get angry?

NOTE

Throughout the lesson and as you are processing the activity, as well as on a day-to-day basis, remember that you are a model for your students. It can be very helpful for them to hear and see you handle your anger in appropriate ways.

Caught the Feeling

OBJECTIVES

- To help students recognize and understand different types of feelings

- To expand students' feeling-word vocabulary and promote use of this vocabulary in social situations

- To encourage the development of empathy for others in bullies and other students

MATERIALS

- Chalkboard or easel pad

DIRECTIONS

1. Introduce the activity by telling students that you are going to be talking about feelings.

2. Define the term *feelings* by saying something like this:

   > Our feelings give us information about how we are inside: happy, sad, mad, scared. They let us know when things are fine for us and also when we are hurt or when we may need to ask for help. So knowing our feelings helps us decide how we want to behave.

3. Ask the students to brainstorm as many feeling words as possible. As students give the words, record them on the chalkboard or easel pad.

4. Read each of the words students have generated, after each word asking students to make a face that shows the feeling. (If you like, you can play "Simon Says" as you instruct students to make the feeling faces.)

5. Read each of the following scenarios aloud to the class. After each one, ask students to share how they think each character may be feeling. As students share their perspectives, highlight the differences in their responses as well as the differences in the characters'

suspected feelings. (Possible feelings are given in parentheses following each scenario.)

SCENARIO 1

On Monday, Mr. Smith announces that he is having a drawing contest in his class. The winning picture will be used for a book of stories the class is developing. Eboni loves to draw and spends a lot of time trying to make the perfect picture to turn in for the contest. Eboni works very hard on her picture and likes what she draws. On Thursday, Eboni proudly turns the picture in to Mr. Smith, hoping she will win first place. On Friday, Mr. Smith announces that Ming-Li has won the contest. *(Possible feelings: Eboni—disappointed, upset, sad; Ming-Li—excited, proud, happy)*

SCENARIO 2

Andy is walking out of the rest room when he sees two of the class bullies, Jake and Sam, coming his way. *(Possible feelings: Andy—scared, alone, fearful; Jake and Sam—powerful, sneaky, tough)*

SCENARIO 3

Jonas sits at lunch all by himself. He can hear the boys at the other table calling him names and making fun of his clothes. Once in a while the boys even throw food at him when the teacher isn't looking. None of the other kids wants to sit by him. *(Possible feelings: Jonas—lonely, sad, left out; boys at the other table—happy, silly, powerful)*

SCENARIO 4

Lola and Audra are best friends and always play together. At recess they usually play "Queen of the Castle" on top of the play structure. Lola says that no other girls are allowed to play with them and that they have to play together every day or they are no longer friends. One day at recess, Audra decides she wants to play tag with some of the other students. Lola tells Audra that she is stupid and can't play with her anymore, and then she starts teasing Audra and the group of students playing tag. *(Possible feelings: Lola—mad, betrayed, in control; Audra—frustrated, hurt, trapped)*

SCENARIO 5

Jana is in the first grade and loves coming to school. She has many friends and always tries to help others. Her teacher has been telling Jana's class about bullies and what everyone can do to make school a safer and happier place to be. One day on the bus, Jana sees some of the girls in her class picking on Skylar, a girl in another class, calling her names, sitting in her seat and squeezing her against the window, and saying she smells bad. Jana knows the girls are being bullies and immediately tells the bus driver, who stops the girls and tells their parents. As a result of Jana's actions, she is selected her class's "Student of the Week." *(Possible feelings: Jana—helpful, proud, excited; Skylar—relieved, thankful, happy)*

6. Use the discussion questions to process the activity and to emphasize the importance of recognizing and understanding one's own and others' feelings.

DISCUSSION QUESTIONS

- Why are feelings important? What do they tell us?

- Can we influence how another person might feel? How?

- What are some ways you can tell how you are feeling? How can others tell you are feeling a certain way?

- What are some ways you can tell how others are feeling?

- Have your feelings ever gotten you in trouble? What happened?

- What could you do differently next time?

The Turtle Club

OBJECTIVES

- To teach students a strategy for controlling their impulses, especially anger

- To provide students the opportunity to practice this technique and encourage them to use it in the daily routine

MATERIALS

- *Optional:* A turtle hand puppet or stuffed animal for display, ideally with legs and a head that can be pulled into the shell

DIRECTIONS

1. Introduce the activity by explaining to your students that today students are going to be learning how to control themselves the same way a turtle does.

2. Read the teacher script on page 267 aloud to the class. After you have done so, say something like the following:

   When I read this story, I thought it was so good that I thought we could all learn to do the turtle technique. I have a feeling that we could all use the turtle—I know that I can! What I would like us to do now is to start practicing the turtle so we can all learn to handle our problems and feel as good as Timmy did!

3. Teach the turtle technique, using the following prompts and suggestions as guidelines.

   ### STEP 1: LEARNING THE TURTLE CUE

   The first step of the turtle technique is to help children learn to respond to the "turtle cue." When you say the word *turtle,* children are to respond by closing their eyes, pulling their arms close to their

---

The original concept for this activity is described in "The Turtle Technique: A Method for the Self-Control of Impulsive Behavior," by M. Schneider and A. Robin, in *Counseling Methods,* edited by J. Krumboltz and C. Thoreson, 1976, New York: Holt, Rinehart and Winston.

bodies, putting their heads down, and curling up like a turtle pulling into its shell. Have the children practice doing the turtle. Walk around the room, checking students' turtle positions and helping them if they are having difficulty. Then let the children get up and move about the room for a minute or so. Say *turtle* again, and have students get into the turtle position as quickly as possible. After some practice, children will learn to respond to the turtle cue immediately.

STEP 2: TENSING AND RELAXING

The second step is learning to relax while pulling into the turtle position. Say *turtle,* and have children take the turtle position. Instruct them to tense all of their muscles while in the turtle position. Have them squeeze the muscles in their arms, legs, stomach, and face. Have them hold this tension for several seconds, then instruct them to relax all of their muscles at once. Walk around the room to make sure children are tensed and then relaxed. Ask the children if they are feeling relaxed and if any part of the body still feels tense. If so, ask them to try to relax this part of the body by taking some deep breaths and loosening their muscles. Have the students practice several times.

Ask students to get up and move around a bit, then say *turtle*. Have them assume the turtle position, tense their muscles for a few seconds, and then relax. Practice tensing and relaxing several times.

When the students are good at tensing and relaxing, have them sit up. Tell them that if they breathe deeply and slowly, they can calm themselves down. Tell students that turtles take deep breaths when they go into their shells, then they hold their breath a little, and then they let the breath out as fully as possible. Practice the slow, deep breathing process with the students.

Have students get up and move around, then say *turtle*. Have them tense and relax a few times, then instruct them to take several deep breaths.

STEP 3: ALTERNATE PROBLEM SOLVING

Ask children to identify some situations that are a problem for them. Choose several problems. For each one, discuss different ways to deal with the situation, and decide which alternatives are best. For example, if Segrid makes a writing mistake on her paper, she might consider the following alternatives:

Reach to the floor, pick up the paper, erase the mistake, and continue

Take out another sheet of paper and start the assignment over

Sit there angry and refuse to do the assignment

Start crying and yell out, "It just isn't fair!"

In this third step, when you say *turtle,* children are to assume the turtle position, tense and relax, breathe deeply, then consider a problem situation and how they could handle it best. Have students practice this sequence.

STEP 4: INCORPORATING THE TURTLE TECHNIQUE INTO DAILY ROUTINES

Now that the children know the steps, they need to make the turtle technique a regular part of their day. Practice regularly. You can practice when conflict or energy seems to be running high in the class or when a specific situation is problematic. You can also practice just to help your students get used to using the technique. At any point in the day, you can give the cue *turtle* and walk your students through each step. Encourage your students to use the turtle at home when they are feeling angry or upset. They can tell themselves it is "turtle time," and go through the steps themselves.

4. Process the activity by asking the following questions.

DISCUSSION QUESTIONS

- How do you feel about using the turtle technique?

- Do you think this activity will be easy or hard for you to remember?

- When is a time that you think you might use the turtle technique?

- How do you think the turtle technique will work?

Teacher Script: The Turtle Club

Sometimes at school, I may get mad at you, or one of your fellow students may be angry with you. You may also get mad at other people if they do things you don't like. When this happens, you may think they are picking on you and that they don't understand your side of the story. It feels really unfair. A good thing to remember is how a turtle handles problems like this. Do you know how a turtle behaves when it gets in trouble? Let me tell you about one turtle, named Timmy, who got in trouble lots of times.

Timmy used to do things at school, and sometimes those things were really good, and he, his teachers, and his classmates got along just fine. But sometimes Timmy would do things that hurt his classmates and that made his teacher mad. Often his teacher or classmates would fuss at him and give him a hard time. Timmy would feel so upset that he would get madder and madder. Pretty soon, everyone would be upset, and a fight would break out among Timmy and his turtle classmates. It was really a mess.

One day on the playground, one of Timmy's classmates told Timmy that he was mean, that he didn't know how to share, and that no one really liked him. Timmy got so mad that he called his classmate stupid and pushed him to the ground. He was sick of all the turtles who fussed at him and made him mad. He decided that he was going to leave school and never come back.

As he left the playground, Timmy saw Grand Old Mr. Tortoise. He was the smartest turtle around. Mr. Tortoise asked Timmy why he looked so upset and why he was leaving school. Timmy told Mr. Tortoise what happened and said that it just made him so mad he didn't know what to do. Timmy said that he usually gets so mad that he starts a big fight and gets in lots of trouble. This time he was so mad, he just never wanted to go back.

Mr. Tortoise smiled and said he could definitely understand how Timmy felt because a long time ago, before Mr. Tortoise learned how to use good judgment, he would get so angry at his classmates and teachers that he didn't want to go to school anymore either. He said he would get so mad that he would start fights, blurt out mean things, and pick on his classmates. Timmy was surprised that this smart old turtle would ever have felt like he did. Timmy asked him how he got so smart and learned not to fight or do mean things anymore. Mr. Tortoise said, "Well, Timmy, I just learned to use my natural protection, my shell." Mr. Tortoise went on to say that the way he handled conflicts was to pull his head into his shell, relax, and breathe really deeply—just to calm down a little. Then he would think about the situation he was in and decide how he could handle it. He would come up with four or five ideas and then figure out what would happen if he did each one of those things. Finally, he would choose the best one and do it. That's how he became so wise!

Timmy got really excited because he wanted to be as wise as Mr. Tortoise. So he ran as fast as turtles can go back to school. Timmy saw his teacher and knew she was still very upset and even angrier that Timmy left the school. Timmy went to his teacher and said he was sorry for getting so mad and leaving the school. He told her that he ran into Mr. Tortoise and how Mr. Tortoise told him how to handle his feelings better. He said "Watch!" and pulled into his shell, relaxed, took deep breaths, and came out smiling. Then he apologized to the classmate he picked on.

Timmy kept practicing pulling into his shell, relaxing, taking deep breaths, and considering a plan. He got really good at it. In fact, his teacher thought it was such a good idea that she introduced it to the whole class. Together, the whole class began to practice doing the "turtle technique," just the way Timmy had learned from Mr. Tortoise. They all knew it was a good idea because if it came from Mr. Tortoise, the best and wisest turtle, it had to be good.

Knowing My Anger

OBJECTIVES

- To help students become aware of what makes them angry
- To help students recognize how their bodies look and feel when they are angry
- To allow students to identify how they respond when they are angry
- To encourage students to brainstorm positive ways to handle their anger

MATERIALS

- Copies of the Knowing My Anger worksheet
- Crayons, markers, or colored pencils
- Chalkboard or easel pad

DIRECTIONS

1. Give each student a Knowing My Anger worksheet, and distribute the art supplies.

2. Explain that completing the worksheet will help students recognize what makes them angry and how they respond when they are angry. On the chalkboard or easel pad, work through an example to show the relationship among anger triggers, physiological reactions to anger, and behaviors. For instance:

   What makes me really mad is: I get pushed when I try to get on the bus.

   This is what my body looks and feels like when I am mad: I get red in the face, and my whole body feels stiff.

   When I get mad, this is what I do: I yell at other people.

3. Instruct students to think of a time something made them really mad, either at home or school.

4. Ask them to look at the first column of the worksheet. Instruct them to draw or write words or phrases to illustrate the situation that made them really mad.

5. When students have completed this task, ask them to use the next column to draw or use words to describe how they looked and how their bodies felt when they were mad.

6. When students have finished, ask them to draw or write words or phrases to describe what they did when they got mad. For example, did they yell? Kick? Call someone names?

7. Discuss whether the ways students choose to react in these situations are good ways or bad ways. If students could choose a better way to handle their anger, have them write or illustrate this idea.

8. Ask the discussion questions to process the activity.

DISCUSSION QUESTIONS

- What situations make you really mad?

- Do you feel changes in your body when you get mad? For example, do you make a fist? Feel your heart start to pound? Get red in the face?

- Do you feel you handle your anger well? If not, what are some more positive ways to handle your anger?

- How do others know you are mad?

- Can you tell when your classmates or family members are upset? How so?

Knowing My Anger

What makes me really mad is . . .	This is how my body looks and feels when I am mad . . .	When I am mad, this is what I do . . .	A better way to handle my anger is to . . .

Activity 6.4

Bully Busters: A Teacher's Manual for Helping Bullies, Victims, and Bystanders (Grades K–5)
© 2003 by Arthur M. Horne, Christi L. Bartolomucci, and Dawn Newman-Carlson.
Champaign, IL: Research Press. (800) 519–2707.

Act One

OBJECTIVES

- To provide students with an opportunity to act out their conflict resolution skills

- To encourage students to consider the various consequences of their conflict resolution strategies

MATERIALS

- A copy of the Playwright Scenarios, cut into separate scenarios

- Any props students would like to use from the classroom

DIRECTIONS

1. Divide the class into groups of four or five students each.

2. Give each group one of the Playwright Scenarios. Instruct the groups to read the scenarios and identify (a) the conflict and (b) the characters.

3. Encourage each group to think of three ways they can solve the problem. Tell students first to think of the worst way they know to solve the problem—for example, through violence or bullying. They are to devise a role play no longer than 3 to 5 minutes to illustrate this approach, then select which group members will act out the role play for the class.

4. Next instruct the students to think of the best way they know to solve the conflict, create a 3- to 5-minute role play illustrating their best conflict resolution skills, and choose group members to enact the role play for the class.

5. Bring the groups together. Ask each group to share its role plays with the rest of the class. First, have groups act out the negative way of handling the conflict, then allow them to role-play their positive conflict resolution skills.

6. Process the activity by asking the discussion questions.

DISCUSSION QUESTIONS

- What types of behaviors are common in the bad conflict resolution plays?

- How did the good conflict resolution plays differ from the bad conflict resolution plays?

- Which behaviors were easiest to use when you were trying to solve the problem?

- When you think of how people usually solve problems, what do they most often do?

- How do you think the people involved in the conflict felt in the bad conflict resolution role play?

- How do you think the people involved in the conflict felt in the good conflict resolution role play?

Playwright Scenarios

Scenario 1

Maya and Amber have been good friends all through elementary school. But lately, Maya has become good friends with Jana. Jana says bad things about Amber and calls her names. Jana and Maya start playing together, and they purposely do not invite Amber.

Scenario 2

Travis is walking to lunch. Ed and Al come up behind him and push him. Travis falls to the ground. Ed and Al tell Travis to give them his lunch right away.

Scenario 3

Lisa and Laura never agree. Lisa always wants to play kick ball at lunch, and Laura just wants to hang out by the bench. Every day they get in an argument about what they want to do, and they usually end up calling each other names.

Scenario 4

Robert hears two other boys in class talking about him and telling lies about his family. He doesn't know the boys very well but is very angry about what they are saying.

Scenario 5

In the bathroom, Cara sees two fifth graders picking on a third grader. They are making fun of her shoes and saying her hair is nappy. The fifth graders are blocking the door so the third grader could not leave the bathroom.

Scenario 6

Several class members are playing kick ball at recess. Susan calls John out when he runs past first base. They begin to argue with each other. John says there is no way he was out, and Susan says he was definitely out.

Activity 6.5

Bully Busters: A Teacher's Manual for Helping Bullies, Victims, and Bystanders (Grades K–5)
© 2003 by Arthur M. Horne, Christi L. Bartolomucci, and Dawn Newman-Carlson.
Champaign, IL: Research Press. (800) 519–2707.

Module

7 Recommendations and Interventions for Helping Victims

Overview

We often hear teachers say that helping victims will only make matters worse for them. As discussed previously, this is a myth about the bully-victim interaction. Victims are desperately in need of help, and teachers can help victims in many ways. Addressing the problem of bullying and actively taking steps to prevent bullying in your classroom are ways you are already helping victims. By helping bullies, you are also helping victims indirectly. However, victims also need your direct intervention. Your help openly communicates that you believe in these children and that they are worth your time and energy. Our society has made a commitment to protect children; we value reporting child abuse and neglect. Victimization is another form of childhood trauma that cannot be ignored or overlooked. Learning how to intervene to help victims is the focus of this module.

Goals

- To recognize the importance of teachers' ability to offer victims support

- To learn direct strategies to support victimized children

- To empower children to avoid the victim role through encouragement and social skills training

- To learn about intervention strategies for different types of victims

- To understand various victim responses and their relative effectiveness

VICTIM SUPPORT

Being a victim of bullying is terrifying. Victims absolutely need your support and attention—there are no exceptions. It is sad but true that victims often choose not to seek support because they fear that seeking

275

help will cause the bullying to escalate or because they have witnessed teachers neglecting to help victims in the past.

The work of the Search Institute has suggested that support from parents, teachers, and other adults is necessary to nourish the development of children (Benson, 1997). Giving support communicates that children are worth being cared for. Conversely, even though this is not the intention of teachers, ignoring victimization communicates to children that they are not worth being cared for. Ongoing nourishment of all children's developmental assets is a key to childhood and lifelong success.

Effective Strategies

We suggest the following general ways to create an environment where bullying is not tolerated and where victims feel supported.

Create an "open-door policy"

Establish an open-door policy in your classroom. Let students know that they can seek your support and that you will respond in a caring, nonjudgmental manner. Let your students know your "office hours," times when you are in the classroom and they can talk with you (e.g., 20 minutes before school starts, during lunch, 30 minutes after school).

Take action against all levels of bullying

If teachers are to intervene effectively when bullying incidents occur, then action needs to be taken against all levels of bullying. Students perceive even minor incidents as bullying (e.g., knocking a book bag over, name-calling). If teachers do not take action at a lesser level, then it is likely that they are reinforcing tolerance and acceptance of bullying. In addition, if children receive support for minor incidents from teachers, they will be more likely to seek support for major occurrences.

Intervene immediately with bullies

It is important that teachers intervene rapidly when a bullying incident occurs. They should share their disapproval with the bully right away—the longer the bully goes on believing that he or she will not be corrected, the more entrenched the belief will be that he or she "got away with it." Teachers can encourage the bully to try to understand the victim's view of the problem and punish the bully if necessary, giving a clear explanation of the punishment and why it is being given.

Provide follow-up support

Once a teacher has intervened with the bully, it is important to follow through with the intervention by checking in with the victim. We recommend that the teacher check in with the victim on a daily basis until he or she is confident the victim is no longer being victimized. At this time, the teacher should remind the victim that the teacher's door is always open. For example, the teacher might say, "Martha, feel free to stop by anytime. Anything that you say will be kept between you and me."

Ineffective Strategies

There are a number of responses that educators *don't* want to make when intervening with victims. These following responses are not useful for reducing aggression and violence.

Ignore bullying

Allowing a child to endure bullying by ignoring it is not an effective intervention. In some circumstances, ignoring can be effective—for example, to decrease attention-getting behavior like whining or tattling. However, when bullying behavior is ignored, the bully is likely to increase the aggressive behavior because it is "working." Similarly, if a child being victimized by a bully asks for help and is ignored, he or she will conclude that the teacher is aligning with the bully, that the teacher doesn't care about the needs of victimized children, and that there is no hope of obtaining assistance. Victims cannot afford to have bullying increase in frequency or severity. Just as teachers don't want a little harassment at work, victims do not want a little taunting at school. The trauma and consequences of repeated victimization are too great to allow this to happen.

Help children learn to defend themselves

If children could defend themselves against bullying, they would. Many children who are not victimized have learned skills or have characteristics that buffer them from victimization. Other children need training, skills, and support to stop from being bullied. If children are being victimized at school and you feel you do not have the resources to teach them how to defend themselves, enlist the aid of a school counselor, school psychologist, or administrator with skills in this area to help. Just as we don't want to be left to our own resources on the streets of our communities when a mugger wants to relieve us of our wallets or purses, students in our schools don't want to be left to their own resources to figure out how to manage bullies. They need support and skills training.

Blame victims

It is easy to fall into the trap of blaming victims for being victimized. The assumption is that if children would only dress better, be more assertive, not behave in strange ways, and not express any of a number of other characteristics that make them vulnerable, aggressors wouldn't target them. Although this assumption may be true in some cases, it does not change the fact that children who are victimized do not have the skills or resources other children have, nor does such an assumption justify assigning blame. Victims are victims, not instigators. To take an active role in teaching victims how to deal with their victimization, teachers must understand that they need specific help and guidance, not blame.

Intervene only when bullying becomes a significant problem

The key to successful intervention with victims is to realize that it is better to intervene too early than too late. Victims need to know not only that you are aware of the bullying, but also that you will not tolerate any type of bullying. If you notice a severe bullying problem, the problem has likely existed for a long time. This means that students have been continually victimized without the intervention of a caring adult. Addressing bullying directly and quickly will interrupt the bully-victim cycle and prevent further victimization.

BULLY BUSTERS SUPPORT TEAM THINK BLOCK

With your support team, discuss the following questions:

1. How many of these erroneous beliefs did you hold?

2. Have you ever believed there is nothing you can do or should do to help a bullying victim?

3. What other beliefs or fears do you have about victim intervention? Discuss these with your team in order to gain support and encouragement to overcome these barriers.

EMPOWERING VICTIMS TO TAKE A DIFFERENT ROLE

Bullying is an interaction between bullies and victims. Bullies select victims because they believe these individuals will be easy targets. Just as we teach bullies new skills to substitute positive behaviors for their aggression toward others, we need to teach victims the skills to protect themselves from bullying. Because these skills will allow victims to draw on their own resources to change the bully-victim interaction, they empower victims. As victims learn skills, they no longer see themselves as helpless; rather, they gain confidence in their abilities to change the things they do not like about their lives.

Encouraging Victims to Change

No child is to blame for being a victim, and no child should be subjected to ridicule because of any individual characteristic. However, victims can learn skills and behaviors that will reduce the likelihood that they will be the target of aggressive acts. In the same way, we do not want to strip bullies of their identity and experiences, although we do want to teach them the skills to have more positive interactions and feel better about themselves and their relationships.

When teaching victims ways to reduce their victimization, we do not place the responsibility for change solely on the victims. Rather, we explore possible changes they may be interested in and willing to make. Although victims have no control over certain characteristics (e.g., height or race), they do have control over many of the behaviors and activities that elicit the attention of bullies. At the same time we are working to change the environment to be more accepting and supportive, we offer victims the opportunity to develop skills to help reduce bullying. It is imperative that skill development occur without compromising the integrity of these individuals. There is a difficult balance between allowing victims to express their genuine selves and encouraging the development of new interpersonal skills to handle bullying more effectively.

Teaching Social Skills

Victims as well as bullies often lack the social skills to interact with their peers successfully. Social skills influence the way a person engages in conversation, communicates nonverbally, and deals with conflicts. Fortunately, social skills can be learned, and they have been demonstrated to be effective in helping young people behave in more adaptive ways (see Goldstein & McGinnis, 1997; McGinnis & Goldstein, 1997).

The steps in social skills training, as presented in Module 6, are reiterated here:

1. Identifying the skill to be taught

2. Evaluating the current level of the skill

3. Breaking the skill into a sequence of smaller steps

4. Providing learning models (e.g., peers, television, films, books) that demonstrate the steps

5. Allowing sufficient time and opportunity for practice

6. Providing support and encouragement for use of the new skills

7. Monitoring use of the new skills and providing ongoing encouragement

The following areas are especially important for victims:

• Emotional awareness skills (e.g., identifying one's own and others' feelings)

• Self-presentation skills (e.g., eye contact and body language)

• Friendship-making skills (e.g., starting conversations, joining in)

• Conflict resolution skills (e.g., problem solving, dealing with anger)

• Assertiveness skills (e.g., asking others for help, saying no)

• Interpersonal skills (e.g., teamwork, cooperation)

Social skills training in these areas may be done in a variety of settings and ways. If the teacher has established an atmosphere in the classroom that is supportive and evokes a sense of safety, then whole-class activities may be used. The class can also be divided into small groups (perhaps the ideal way of conducting social skills training). Students with problems that are numerous or severe may need individual instruction by the school counselor or social worker.

Teaching social skills does take time and effort, and often teachers find it more effective to enlist the aid of a school counselor who can run specific social skills training groups or present the information to a whole class. As with many of the techniques and skills we have discussed throughout this manual, it is important to teach skills repeatedly, call attention to them throughout the school day, and give feedback to students consistently when they use their skills.

Using the whole class as a problem-solving, solution-seeking group can provide enormous emotional support and validation for victims. It may also allow other students who have been bystanders when bullying occurred to take a more active role in identifying what stopped them from being helpful. Clear, open, and honest discussion of the problem may be beneficial for all students in the class as they come to grips with the inhumanity of victimization and the importance of having all present be responsible for addressing the problem.

Two areas of social skills training that are especially important for victims concern assertiveness and the ability to ask for help.

Assertiveness Skills

Many children use aggression to get what they want and feel they must act this way to get their needs met. Other children don't know how to speak up for themselves and wind up accepting situations they do not want to accept. Sometimes the latter type of children, especially children who are victimized, keep their feelings inside because they are not able to assert themselves. Consequently, they may "blow" when they cannot take anymore.

All children can benefit from learning to stand up for their rights. When children act assertively, they know and value their personal rights and have the skills to communicate their feelings openly, without force or aggression. Here are some things you can do in the classroom to encourage assertiveness:

- Provide opportunities for all children to express their views. (Typically, there are a few children in the class who will attempt to speak for everyone.)

- Encourage your class to share. If a child wants something from another child, encourage him or her to ask for it, rather than use aggressive measures to take it.

- When talking with children individually, ask them questions. Help them with their responses so they are able to express themselves adequately.

- Encourage children to engage in activities independently to increase their confidence. Provide guided support to children who require help while simultaneously encouraging them to do the task on their own. This is particularly important for children who continually ask for help but who are capable of succeeding, although they may not believe they are.

Asking for Help

Teachers and parents alike often take it for granted that children will ask for help when they need it. Some children have been taught that this behavior is acceptable and that they can ask for help. Others have been taught that they should not ask for help because it is a sign of personal weakness. In addition to modeling and rewarding appropriate help-seeking behavior in the classroom, you can help children master this skill by teaching the following sequence:

1. Decide what the problem is. Who or what is causing the problem? How do you feel when the problem happens?

2. Do you want help with the problem? Sometimes we can solve problems by ourselves. Is this a problem you have been able to solve by yourself in the past, or is this a problem you need help with?

3. Who can help you? Name as many people as you can who would listen and help (e.g., the school counselor, another teacher, a classmate, an older peer).

4. Ask a person if you can talk to him or her about the problem, tell the person the problem, and talk about ways you can solve the problem together. You may decide that you need someone else's help as well.

INTERVENTIONS FOR DIFFERENT TYPES OF VICTIMS

In Module 5, we discussed four types of victims: passive, provocative, relational, and bystander. Passive victims are the most common type. They tend to be very anxious and insecure, and they often react to bullying with fear and frustration. Provocative victims are distinguished from passive victims by the fact that they are, like bullies, aggressive. These youth tend to provoke others deliberately for attention. Relational victims are those who are excluded from or sabotaged in social relationships and activities. Relational victims may blame themselves for their social exclusion and internalize the notion that they are not likeable. Bystander victims are children indirectly affected by bullying. They often feel guilty and weak because they do not stand up to bullies or report bullying incidents. They also tend to live in fear of becoming the next target for bullying.

Passive Victims

The main goals of interventions for passive victims are to provide them with social support and help them become active in changing the bully-victim interaction. Although you cannot always be available, you can inform your students that you are a member of a Bully Busters Support Team and let them know the names of other teachers on the team. One focus of the team should be to help one another's students throughout the school. Tell your students that these teachers are also committed to reducing bullying in the school and will be available for help when students need it. The team can also develop specific interventions to help particular victims. These interventions can be shared with each participating teacher.

Establish a victims anonymous group

A victims anonymous group is a voluntary student-based and teacher-led group that serves as a safe haven in which victims can report bullying incidents and seek support. Some schools have supported the establishment of such a group with the intention of its being both a support group and a group in which students and teachers can improve their problem-solving skills and work to reduce bullying in the school. One or several teachers who are members of the Bully Busters Support Team lead the group. Students of different ages participate so ideas and problems are represented across grade levels and so older group members can serve as role models for younger group members.

Identify the behaviors or characteristics of the victim that elicit the bullying acts, and facilitate changes

As discussed earlier, if they wish, victims may be able to change certain characteristics and behaviors that commonly attract bullies. It may be helpful to engage the parents of victims in efforts of this type. Together, and possibly with the school counselor, you could discuss the targeted behaviors and brainstorm ways to help. For example, if the goal is to help a child become more self-sufficient, it would be important to coordinate the parents' efforts at home and your efforts at school. This is a sensitive issue, and talking about behaviors that have resulted in a victim's being targeted is controversial. Students don't want to be blamed for being victimized, and there is some concern that even if a student changes his or her behavior, the bullying may continue. Care must be taken to follow up; otherwise, we may be leaving the victimized student more vulnerable and less optimistic about the value of the change.

Make sure to inform student and parents that active measures are being taken with the bully as well. Also, remind all involved that change does take time. Let the student and parents know that you need to come up with a plan for protecting the victim and for intervening to manage the problem more effectively, that you will enforce the no-bullying policy, and that you are committed to working with them until the bullying stops.

Help victims build confidence and self-esteem

Bullies are likely to target children who they believe do not have the self-confidence to defend themselves or to tell a teacher. Bullies want to feel powerful and seek victims who will help them achieve this goal. Teachers can help victims gain confidence in themselves by focusing on their strengths and helping them recognize their positive qualities. As discussed previously, victims can be taught specific social skills to address the bullying problem. When victims feel they have support and resources, they are more likely to take a stand against bullying. In doing so, they gain confidence in themselves as well as a sense of personal power.

> *Cassie is in the fourth grade and somewhat of a loner. She is one of those shy, withdrawn, and awkward students. The other students in Cassie's class do not really*

pay much attention to her, except for Jacqueline. Jacqueline repeatedly makes fun of Cassie, calling her names, laughing at her, pulling her hair when she walks by, and so forth. One day, Mrs. Sanchez sees Jacqueline teasing Cassie and decides to intervene. In talking with Cassie, Mrs. Sanchez discovers that this teasing has been going on all year long, unbeknownst to her. Aside from dealing with Jacqueline, she decides to take action to empower Cassie and help her develop a stronger, more positive sense of self. She also enlists the school counselor in her efforts, referring Cassie to an assertiveness skills group.

Provocative Victims

Provocative victims initiate aggressive interactions with others and then, because they are usually smaller or less skilled than the people they provoke, are victimized themselves. Since they are the provocateurs, it is important to help them learn not to instigate the aggression and to understand the role of their behavior in maintaining the bully-victim interaction. Some specific interventions for provocative victims include the following.

Help provocative victims understand how they see the bully and what they hope to gain from their interaction with the bully

For example, they may think they are being funny, like the attention, or express the fact that they are truly upset with the bully.

Help victims recognize the consequences of their actions

Do victims realize that their actions lead to their getting hurt? Work with victims to create a list of the consequences of their behavior, and help them weigh the pros and cons. For example, ask, "When you push the bully back, what happens?"

Explore other ways provocative victims could interact with the bully

You can help victims identify and develop alternate behaviors. For example, if a victim is angry with the bully, explore why, then help the victim and bully settle their differences. If the goal is the bully's attention, discuss why the attention is important and ways the victim can get attention without being hurt.

Help provocative victims recognize their strengths and how they can use their strengths in a more positive way

It is difficult to help provocative victims without making them think they are to blame, which is how they often interpret teachers' suggestions. Help them make changes by assigning them roles in which they can use their skills (e.g., leading a class activity, being team leader).

In addition to these suggestions, you can help provocative victims use the Big Questions to clarify their goals (to get along with others, not to be hurt or victimized by others) and understand their role in the conflict. Clearly, the process is not working to help these victims achieve their goals, so it is important to develop alternative responses. Again, the Big Questions are as follows:

Question 1: What is my goal?

Question 2: What am I doing?

Question 3: Is what I am doing helping me achieve my goal?

Question 4: (If not) What can I do differently?

> *Zach is a third grader who often engages in bully-victim interactions with Jalen. The bullying usually occurs during recess, when Zach and his group of friends are playing basketball. During the basketball game, Jalen runs onto the court and tries to steal the ball, which results in Zach's yelling cruel things at him or tackling him and beating him up. Mr. Jacobson has witnessed this quite often and reprimands Zach and the others involved, but it continues to occur. Recognizing that Jalen is a provocative victim, Mr. Jacobson decides to take a different tactic. He decides to talk with Jalen about his actions and help him work through the Big Questions.*

Mr. Jacobson: Jalen, you just ran out and grabbed the basketball from Zach and the other kids. What's going on? *(Question 2: What am I doing?)*

Jalen: Nothing. They never let me play.

Mr. Jacobson: Is that your goal, to get to play? Is your goal to get along with the others? What is it you want? *(Question 1: What is my goal?)*

Jalen: Yes, that's what I want—I want to play ball, too.

Mr. Jacobson: Is what you are doing working? If you have a goal of playing with the others, is running out and grabbing the ball getting you what you want? *(Question 3: Is what I am doing helping me achieve my goal?)*

Jalen: They don't ever let me play.

Mr. Jacobson: So it isn't working. Running out and grabbing the ball, and the other things you do that irritate the group, those don't get you what you want. What could you do differently? *(Question 4)*

Jalen: I don't know. Nothing. They never let me play.

Mr. Jacobson: Let's talk about some other things you could do. Can you think of some things? *(Question 4: What could I do differently?)*

Jalen: I don't know.

Mr. Jacobson: I can think of some. For example, when the class heads out for recess, you could ask to play with the group. I could help you with that. You also could ask some of the other kids who aren't playing with the group to start another ball game with you. What do you think of those ideas?

Jalen: I want to play on Zach's team.

Mr. Jacobson: Well, if your goal is to play ball with Zach's team, I think we have to come up with a better way of asking to be part of the group. I can teach you a good way to ask. I can also help you figure out some other ways you could be friendly with the group and not get them mad at you.

Relational Victims

Relational victims are the recipients of acts of bullying that include rumor spreading and social exclusion for the purpose of disrupting social relationships. Girls most frequently engage in this type of bullying. Some adults conclude that girls are just mean or "catty," but relational bullying is *not* normal behavior. Girls and women typically define their identity and self-worth through their relationships with others. Therefore, relational bullying is an attack on victims' identity. Some specific interventions for victims of this type of bullying include the following.

Acknowledge that relational bullying is bullying

Because this type of bullying is often overlooked, it is important to acknowledge that these behaviors do indeed constitute bullying. Victims may not feel they will receive assistance and need to know that you recognize the situation as a problem and will help them. They are already being excluded by their peers; if you also ignore them, they can see this as yet another rejection.

Do not tolerate rumor spreading or telling stories

Share with your class that rumor spreading and telling stories about classmates are not acceptable. Storytelling is hurtful and done only to bring attention to the person telling the story. The relational bully wins when other classmates believe the stories and join in the rejection of relational victims. Encourage your students to be "smart cookies" and smarter than the storyteller.

Gain support from other classmates

Relational bullies gain power by watching another child feel alone and isolated. The goal is to gain power while ruining another's social inclusion. If the victimized child has additional social support, the bully's behavior will not be reinforced, and the victim will feel less alone and isolated. Teach your class about relational bullying so they can take an active role in preventing it. If they see it occur, they can invite the relational victim into their group.

Take a stand

Unlike other forms of bullying, no specific characteristics cause one child to be more likely than another to be a relational victim. Often the child is a part of a social group and can even be friends with the relational bully at times. Sometimes the relational bully will cycle through the peer group, differentially alienating specific members. The other members become fearful that they will be the next victim and so choose to stand with rather than oppose the relational bully. Encourage children within their peer groups not to tolerate any form of relational victimization by joining with the victim and refusing to take the lead of the relational bully.

> *Sherika was friends with a group of girls in her class. One of the girls in the group that everyone liked, Jamisella, started to target Sherika. Each day, Jamisella would start rumors about Sherika. She'd say Sherika was saying bad things about the other girls and that she was such a baby she still wet her bed. Jamisella convinced all of the other group members to ignore Sherika— Sherika was mean and dirty. They did not allow her to eat lunch with them anymore and did not invite her over to their houses like they used to. Sherika's teacher noticed the girls' behaviors and talked with Sherika and several different girls in the group individually to assess the situation. It became clear that Jamisella had started rumors to gain more power in the group and that the group members believed Jamisella because everyone liked her. With the teacher's encouragement, Sherika's old friends talked with Sherika about the rumors and realized that none of them was true. Together, Sherika and the rest of the group confronted Jamisella for lying to them. The group welcomed Sherika back and apologized for being so mean.*

Bystander Victims

Children who have observed bullying often receive little attention, but they are also affected by the bully-victim interaction and need attention if they are to make quality future decisions in difficult situations. Bystander victims experience bullying vicariously and fear that they too will become direct victims of bullying. They tend to be very sensitive and empathic, and although they are concerned with the victim of direct bullying, they find it difficult or do not know how to intervene. They often feel guilty because their fear of the bully prevents them from helping.

Hazler (1996) has suggested the following guidelines for intervening effectively with bystander victims.

Help bystanders recognize their feelings of discomfort and give them permission to act on these feelings

Bystanders want the bully-victim interaction to end, and they want to help; however, they are afraid of being physically or emotionally hurt if they intervene. Bystanders need help in recognizing their own feelings. They often do not realize that other observers of bullying feel the same way. Bystanders do not want to admit that they failed to step forward or that they felt fear and intimidation. It is important to discuss these feelings, sometimes referred to as "survivor guilt" or "survivor trauma"—the feelings of guilt one develops for having survived a traumatic situation when others experienced much more pain and suffering.

Encourage bystanders to get off the sidelines and become involved as a group rather than remain in isolation

Allowing bystander victims to talk about their emotional experience and teaching them that their feelings are common can help children feel supported, validated, and encouraged. Normalizing their feelings of guilt and fear at the same time may motivate them to become more active in reducing bullying. By knowing others are with them, students become more willing to take on the injustices they encounter.

Help witnesses join forces to confront the bully and protect the victim

Bystanders can help victims by intervening directly or by giving their personal support. The larger the number of bystanders, the greater the likelihood for successful direct intervention. Bystanders also should find ways outside the immediate conflict to be available, understanding, and supportive of victims. Specific ways to give support include the following:

- Give support consistently.

- Spend time with victims.

- Invite victims to get involved in group activities.

- Encourage victims' efforts and accomplishments.

- Express the desire to find additional ways to help.

- Be a good listener.

> *Most days at lunch, Lauren sits at a table with Ato, Kelly, Lee, Maria, Terrence, Felicia, and Sarah. And on most days, Kelly and Maria make fun of Ato: telling him that he dresses like a girl, making fun of the lunch that his mom packed for him, and sometimes even taking his food. Lauren likes Ato but is afraid of Kelly and Maria, so she never says anything, just watches and wishes she could do something to help Ato. Lauren is also worried to say or do anything because she notices that the other classmates at her table just watch the interactions and sometimes even laugh and join in. Lauren is frustrated*

and asks herself, Why won't Ato just stand up for him-
self? Why won't the others do something to stop it? What
if I tell them to stop and they start to pick on me? After
much thought, Lauren decides to tell her teacher about
what has been happening at lunch. Lauren's teacher
talks with Lauren about what has been happening, vali-
dates Lauren's reactions, and brainstorms with Lauren
some ways that she can support Ato.

Ways Lauren could support Ato include inviting Ato and other bystander victims to sit at a different table during lunch, thus removing them-selves from the situation and ignoring the bullies. She could also seek help from the teacher, who could show interest in Ato and seek opportu-nities to be attentive to other students who are nice to Ato. Finally, she could approach the bullies herself, perhaps saying, "Maria, you teased Ato, but you shouldn't have because we talked in class about treating everyone in a nice way, and teasing isn't nice. I like you and want you to be nice to everyone."

VICTIM RESPONSES TO BULLYING

Victims respond in various ways to bullying, including avoiding or ignoring conflict; nonvictim responses (Hazler, 1996); and counterag-gression, helplessness, and nonchalance (Salmivalli, Karhunen, & Lagerspetz, 1996). In addition, there are gender differences in the effec-tiveness of certain responses.

Avoiding or Ignoring Conflict

In some situations, conflict can be positive and lead to greater under-standing and more effective problem solving. In other situations, it is better to avoid conflict. In order to be victimized, a child must first be a part of the bullying interaction or conflict. Learning how to avoid con-flict can be a useful way to ensure a child's safety. The ability to avoid a conflict hinges on emotional intelligence. It requires that children pay attention to their own feelings and recognize fear or anger, have the ability to recognize the feelings of others (i.e., the rising anger or frus-tration of the bully), know how to manage their feelings, and control how they respond to the conflict.

As we know, when victims engage in conflict, they give the bully more attention and power. Engagement can potentially increase the bully's anger, which in turn may cause the bully to use more force. By avoiding or choosing to ignore the bully-victim conflict, victims deprive the bully of an emotional payoff, reduce the likelihood that the conflict will escalate, and protect themselves from greater harm.

Nonvictim Responses

Another way to empower children who are victimized is to encourage them to make what Richard Hazler (1996) calls "nonvictim responses."

Avoid giving the bully an emotional payoff

The more intensely the victim reacts to the bully, the more likely the bully's behavior will be reinforced and continue. However, when victims can reduce the intensity of their reactions, they become much less desirable targets. When a victim robs a bully of an emotional payoff, this takes the pleasure out of the bully's behaviors and decreases the likelihood that the bullying will persist.

> *Peter has always made fun of Shari; he calls her every name in the book. The teachers think it is cute and that Peter may have a crush on Shari. However, Shari is embarrassed and starts crying. After talking with her teacher, Shari decides that she isn't going to give Peter any attention. Now Shari doesn't mess around; when Peter tries to tease her, Shari just grins and walks away from Peter. Consequently, Peter is left standing alone and looking silly. Since then, Peter has given up trying to harass Shari.*

Be physically and verbally assertive, not aggressive

Bullies seek targets who shy away from standing up for themselves. When victims use assertive words and behaviors, they convey confidence and signal that they will not relinquish their rights. Victims can convey confidence simply by altering their posture (i.e., standing up straight rather than slouching) and making eye contact rather than looking away.

> *Julie is very shy and quiet. Veronica thinks it is funny that Julie hardly ever makes eye contact and ridicules Julie in front of the entire class. Normally, Julie just drops her head in silent embarrassment. Following one of Veronica's taunts, Julie gets fed up and decides to try what she saw another classmate do. When Veronica makes a comment to her in front of the class, Julie looks her straight in the eyes and tells her to get a life! Veronica is shocked into silence and walks back to her desk.*

Do something unexpected

Predictability of victims' responses encourages the bully's continual harassment. Victims can decrease the likelihood of victimization by making their reactions less predictable. When victims can respond in an inconsistent manner or with distracting behaviors (e.g., talking loudly, using assertive responses), this makes them poor candidates for victimization.

> *Every time Ronny bullies Tim, Tim cowers in the corner and trembles with fear. Ronny loves this and feels very powerful. One day, after talking with one of the teachers on the Bully Busters Support Team, Tim tries a different way to respond to Ronny. He decides not to hide in the*

corner, where Ronny could trap him. Instead, Tim looks at Ronny and says, in a sharp voice, "Can I help you with something?" then walks right by Ronny and pretends to throw something in the trash can (located right next to the teacher's desk).

Strengthen existing friendships and make new friends

Victims are often selected because they have few friends or have friends who are unwilling to stand by them in difficult times. Strengthening and developing new friendships are among the best methods for reversing the trend of victim isolation.

Every day, Betsy sits by herself at lunch. She always sits near other groups of kids, but she never joins in the conversation. She just pretends to be a part of the group. She can hear some of the kids snicker at her and say she is a "weirdo." One day, Betsy sees two girls sitting together during lunch and decides to sit with them and join in their conversation. It feels strange to Betsy, but over time as she continues to sit with them, she finds it gets easier and easier. Betsy feels better: She knows she is making good friends.

BULLY BUSTERS SUPPORT TEAM THINK BLOCK

Discuss nonvictim responses with your team:

1. Have you observed children using any of these techniques on a regular basis? Are these children who are typically bullied?

2. What techniques have you observed children who are not bullied using when a peer taunts them?

3. Why do you think some children are not bullied? How do they respond in challenging situations?

Categories of Victim Response

After examining various ways children respond to bullies, Salmivalli, Lagerspetz et al. (1996) identified three categories of response. Let's take a look at these categories and consider how each type of response influences the bully-victim interaction.

Counteraggression

Counteraggression is a tactic most frequently used by male victims of bullying. Counteraggressive responses to bullying include physical retaliation, making fun of the bully, or getting in the bully's face and then running away. Why don't these strategies work? Although victims are standing up to the bully, they are doing so in a manner that creates more tension and conflict in the bully-victim interaction, brings more negative attention to the bully-victim interaction, and causes the bully to increase his or her use of force, consequently increasing the chance that the victim will be harmed. Remember, bullies typically choose victims who are less powerful than themselves, bring attention to themselves, and are easily conquered. In most situations, victims' use of force will not discourage the bully but instead fuel the conflict. In addition, the bully's behaviors are reinforced by the attention he or she is likely to be given during the conflict, whereas victims' behaviors may cause them to be made fun of by or further isolated from peers.

Counteraggression is not an emotionally intelligent means of handling a bully-victim interaction for several reasons. First, victims are likely to be responding to the bully in an impulsive manner, without attending to their own feelings. When children tap into their emotional intelligence, they can identify their feelings, own them, then decide how to manage their feelings and respond most effectively. Children who respond in a counteraggressive fashion are also not considering the social situation or the feelings and goals of the bully. When victims recognize that the bully wants them to fall into a trap, they will know that fighting back will only bring them more harm and embarrassment.

Helplessness

Typically, children in the victim role submit to the bully. For various reasons, these children do not feel able to respond to their victimization. Instead, they cry, pretend to be sick to avoid coming to school, or simply endure the abuse. In these situations, victims do not feel empowered to do anything about their situation and may have come to accept the bully's terms. This is the typical response pattern of passive victims, although all victims may respond in this manner.

Children who feel helpless are likely to experience extreme levels of stress and depression. Often they feel there is no way out of their situation; they are resigned to their victimization as a part of life. Some victims may even begin to internalize the embarrassing, insulting put-downs of the bully and conclude that they are worthless. The consequences of feeling helpless are apparent: Children who feel they do not have power in their lives are unlikely to exercise responsibility for themselves or their behaviors and may become overridden with fear and depression, suffer from low self-esteem, become isolated from peers, and possibly even engage in self-destructive behaviors.

Nonchalance

Both girls and boys can respond to bullies in a nonchalant manner. Children act nonchalant when they ignore the bully, do not reward the bully by responding emotionally or physically, and choose to stay calm. The key word here is *act*; victims still experience emotional discomfort, embarrassment, and possible physical harm, but they act as if the bully does not engage them.

Appearing nonchalant may be an emotionally intelligent means of responding to the bully. These victims are likely to know that the bully is looking for a payoff for his or her bullying efforts. This means the bully wants a show! By refusing to respond to the bully, victims who respond in a nonchalant manner refuse to engage in the bully-victim interaction. They have read the social situation and managed their emotions in a very difficult and trying interaction. Yet inside, these victims still hurt and still need an outlet to identify and express their emotions.

Gender Differences in Response Effectiveness

Salmivalli, Lagerspetz et al. (1996) have not only identified three primary ways that victims typically respond to bullies, they have also observed what methods seem to work for which victims. Interestingly, these researchers found that there are gender differences in the way that male and female victims respond most effectively to bullying.

For girls

Although we do not advocate the use of aggression for boys or girls, Salmavalli, Lagerspetz et al. (1996) found that girls who responded in a counteraggressive manner most effectively ended their victimization. Females are not encouraged to be aggressive; rather, they are more likely to hold their feelings inside. As Salmivalli and her colleagues have suggested, girls often respond in a helpless manner, and this manner is the least effective means to put a stop to bullying. The bully may expect male victims to put up a fight but expect female victims to tolerate the bullying. When victims do what is unexpected, the bullying is more likely to cease. It would appear that when girls are assertive and take action against the bully, they communicate that the bully does not have all the power and that they refuse to engage in the bully-victim interaction.

For boys

Boys are most likely to end their victimization if they respond to the bully in a nonaggressive, nonchalant manner. Boys who engage in counteraggression are most likely to continue being bullied. Furthermore, the peers of male victims who respond in a counteraggressive way see these victims as provoking the bully and have less empathy toward them. When children do not empathize with victims, they are not as motivated to intervene in the bullying interaction.

Unlike girls, boys are typically taught to be aggressive and to fight back if necessary. However, for victims of bullying, this is dangerous advice. As we mentioned, victims are often smaller and less powerful than the bully and often do not have the physical strength to confront the bully. Consequently, male victims who try to fight back are further bullied or resort to extreme force (i.e., weapons) to overcome the bully. Either situation is dangerous and best avoided.

BULLY BUSTERS SUPPORT TEAM THINK BLOCK

With your team members, consider the following questions:

1. Do you think you are more likely to notice the victimization of boys or girls? Why do you think you might tend to notice one type of victim before the other?

2. We have discussed that socialization factors may make it more difficult to notice girls' victimization. What might be done to increase the attention given to girls experiencing relational or overt bullying?

3. Do you feel more prepared to deal with relational or overt bullying? What can you do to feel more effective?

Introducing Victim Responses to Students: Animal Examples

Now that you have learned the different types of responses children can make to bullying, the challenge is to present this information to children in a form that is easy for them to understand. In Module 5, we identified victim types by introducing Amy Ant, Charlie Chimp, Daisy Duck, and the Birds. We introduce responses victims can make in the same way, by sharing various animals' ways of handling victimization. We find that these animal comparisons provide a common language and help children engage in conversation about victimization without feeling vulnerable or threatened. You can refer to the different animals' responses when you read stories, observe interactions in the classroom, or teach related material.

To introduce the "animals' wisdom," you might say something like the following:

> Animals are pretty smart. They have worked out how to handle the bullies in the wild. They all have different ways of dealing with bullies. Let's look at some of the animals and what they have learned.

The Turtle

When the bully comes toward the turtle, the turtle pulls his head into his shell and waits for the bully to finish. But sometimes the turtle gets kicked really hard and tossed around. The turtle feels like he can't do anything else because he is too slow to outrun the bully and isn't able to speak up to tell the bully to get lost, so the turtle pulls inside and waits.

The Rabbit

When the rabbit senses the bully is coming, as quickly and quietly as she can, she hops away and hides from the bully. The rabbit knows that the bully wants to get her and pull on her ears and tail. But the rabbit moves quickly and quietly so the bully won't notice her.

The Pit Bull

The pit bull is a dog that loves a fight. The pit bull goes right for the bully without even thinking that he may also get hurt. He jumps in fighting and clawing, even though he knows the bully is going to fight back. With the pit bull, there is always a fight, he always gets hurt, and he never thinks about other ways he could have handled the situation.

The Owl

The wise old owl is always ready with a plan to handle the bully without ruffling her feathers. The owl knows she is a lot smarter than the bully, and she uses her brain to outwit the bully with her many antibullying skills. The owl knows how to say things like "I don't like to be teased. Please stop" and how to get the teacher's help to solve a problem.

Module 7: Content Review

The following statements relate to the learning goals of this module. Ask yourself if you feel confident that you can answer yes to each item. If not, please review the material and discuss any difficulties among your Bully Busters Support Team.

1. I can identify effective and ineffective strategies for intervening with victims and am committed to making my classroom a safe place for all children.

   Yes ❑ No ❑

2. I know that allowing victims to fend for themselves is ineffective and will lead to increased negative consequences for victims.

   Yes ❑ No ❑

3. I know specific ways that I can support victims, such as creating a supportive classroom environment and conducting social skills training with victims.

   Yes ❑ No ❑

4. I have learned specific skills to intervene with passive, provocative, relational, and bystander victims.

   Yes ❑ No ❑

5. I know that victims can be encouraged to change to the extent that they want to but should not be forced to change or blamed for the victimization.

   Yes ❑ No ❑

6. I can identify different ways victims can respond to bullying.

   Yes ❑ No ❑

7. I understand that different responses to bullying are associated with more or less successful outcomes for victims.

   Yes ❑ No ❑

A Reminder . . .

CLASSROOM INTERACTION AND AWARENESS CHART

Use the CIAC to describe any bullying behavior you observe (and that students report to you, if you wish). A copy of the CIAC and a weekly summary sheet appear in Appendix A.

THE BIG QUESTIONS

Honestly appraise your progress by asking yourself the Big Questions. There are no right or wrong answers.

In relation to helping victims in my school:

1. What is my goal?

2. What am I doing?

3. Is what I am doing helping me achieve my goal?

4. *(If not)* What can I do differently?

PERSONAL GOALS FORM

The Personal Goals Form, on the next page, is designed to help you tailor the content of this module to your own students and situation. Please take a moment to fill out the form now.

Module 7: Personal Goals Form

Goals

- To recognize the importance of teachers' ability to offer victims support

- To learn direct strategies to support victimized children

- To empower children to avoid the victim role through encouragement and social skills training

- To learn about intervention strategies for different types of victims

- To understand various victim responses and their relative effectiveness

1. My role in helping victims is as follows:

2. I have observed incidents of bullying. *(Please record incidents on the CIAC.)*

    _____ Number of times I intervened   _____ Number of times I chose not to intervene

    Other observations:

3. I will review the classroom activities for this module and select ones appropriate for my class. *(Please list.)*

4. I will accept the challenges associated with the developmental assets. *(Please list the specific assets and describe what you plan to do.)*

5. I will give my students feedback about the bullying incidents I have observed and encourage discussion of bullying and related issues. We will discuss these topics:

6. I will share my experiences in applying the information in this module with other teachers and administrators, as well as with my students' families. *(Please specify who and when.)*

7. I will meet with my Bully Busters Support Team. *(Please specify when and list what issues and questions you will raise.)*

Bully Busters: A Teacher's Manual for Helping Bullies, Victims, and Bystanders (Grades K–5)
© 2003 by Arthur M. Horne, Christi L. Bartolomucci, and Dawn Newman-Carlson.
Champaign, IL: Research Press. (800) 519–2707.

Classroom Activities

ACTIVITY 7.1: THE MAGIC BOX (GRADES K–2)

In this activity, students identify situations in which they have become angry, their own and others' feelings in these situations, their responses, and the consequences of those responses. They then brainstorm strategies or "tricks" for dealing effectively with these conflicts.

ACTIVITY 7.2: PEOPLE PUPPETS (GRADES K–2)

This activity gives younger students the chance to identify the individuals to whom they can go to for help in challenging situations. Each student makes a puppet to represent one of these people, then introduces the "people puppet" to the class.

ACTIVITY 7.3: MY BOILING POINT (GRADES K–5)

Anger is a normal emotion, felt by bullies and victims alike. This activity conveys the seriousness of anger in victims of bullying and helps students recognize the effects of holding their anger inside and going over their own "boiling points." Versions are given for grades K–2 and grades 3–5.

ACTIVITY 7.4: HAND TALK (GRADES 3–5)

A variation of Activity 7.2 for older students, in this activity each student has the opportunity to make a "feelings puppet" (expressing the feeling *happy, sad, angry,* or *scared*) and a "people puppet." Students become more aware of the feelings of bullies and victims and identify people who could help in bullying situations.

ACTIVITY 7.5: THE PUPPETS GO TO BROADWAY (GRADES 3–5)

Small groups use the "feelings puppets" and "people puppets" they created in Activity 7.4, "Hand Talk," to act out a bullying situation and show how they could handle it. By using the people puppets, students identify people whom they can trust to help them.

ACTIVITY 7.6: MY TOOLBOX (GRADES 3–5)

This activity encourages students to recognize their own skills and resources ("tools") to cope with bullying situations as well as with their feelings associated with bullying. Students share their ideas and acquire new tools to address conflict.

The Magic Box

OBJECTIVES

- To help students recognize the ways they handle anger
- To allow students to identify new "tricks" to deal with conflict

MATERIALS

- Chalkboard or easel pad
- Large index cards
- Markers
- A "magic box." This could be a large, decorated cardboard box, plastic container, or crate.

DIRECTIONS

1. Tell students that today you are going to be talking about tricks they can use when they are in a tough situation, especially one in which they are angry.

2. Ask students to brainstorm situations in which they have become angry. You may wish to give them an example as a way to start them off. (For example, you might say you felt mad when another driver pulled out in front of you while you were driving to school.)

3. As students share situations, ask them the following questions:

   What happened?

   How did you feel when that happened?

   How do you think the other person was feeling?

   What did you do?

   What happened then?

4. Allow other students to share ideas ("tricks") they may have about how the situation could have been handled or resolved. Write these strategies on the chalkboard or easel pad.

5. Write or, if ability permits, have students write the strategies on index cards. Have the students put the cards in the "magic box" for use in the future when conflict situations come up.

6. Process the activity by asking the discussion questions.

DISCUSSION QUESTIONS

- Have any of you ever seen someone else handle anger or a tough situation in a positive way? What was happening? What did he or she do?

- How do you feel when you are in a tough situation with another student?

- What is something you have found to be helpful when you are in a tough situation?

- What is one of the "tricks" for solving problems that we talked about today?

- What is something you think you will try next time you are having trouble with another person?

NOTE

You may wish to have students draw examples of each strategy for display in your classroom.

People Puppets

OBJECTIVES

- To increase the acceptability of and students' comfort in asking others for help

- To help students recognize times they need to ask for help

- To give students an opportunity to identify the individuals to whom they can go for help in challenging situations

MATERIALS

- Paper lunch bags

- Crayons, markers, or colored pencils

- *Optional:* Construction paper, felt, glitter, yarn, glue, and other items for decoration

DIRECTIONS

1. Give each student a paper lunch bag. Tell students that they are going to make a puppet of a person they feel they can talk to when they are upset or hurt—a friend, teacher, parent, sibling, and so forth.

2. Show students how to make the puppet by putting your hand into the bag: The bottom of the bag becomes the puppet's head, and the crease becomes its mouth. Show students a puppet you made previously to give them an idea of how the puppets might be decorated.

3. Introduce your puppet:

   This is *(name),* he/she is my *(person you talk with),* and I share my feelings with him/her when I am upset or I need help at school.

4. Distribute the art supplies, and encourage students to design their own puppets.

5. After students have completed their puppets, ask for volunteers to share their puppets with the class.

6. Use the following questions to facilitate class discussion.

DISCUSSION QUESTIONS

- Whom do you usually go to for help or to talk about your feelings?

- What does this person usually do to help you?

- Are there others you can go to as well? Whom do you go to at school? At home?

- Are you ever afraid to talk with people about your feelings? If so, when?

- How do you let others know that you need to talk?

My Boiling Point

OBJECTIVES

- To recognize the seriousness of anger in victims of bullying
- To help students recognize their "boiling points"
- To allow students to understand the effects of holding in their anger

MATERIALS

- Copies of the Boiling Point worksheet (Grades K–2, Grades 3–5)
- Crayons, markers, or colored pencils (Grades K–2, Grades 3–5)
- Copies of the Anger Triggers list (Grades 3–5)

DIRECTIONS

1. Introduce the lesson, explaining to your students that you are going to be talking about how bullying makes victims feel. You may choose to say something like this:

   > Today we are going to focus on the victims of bullying. Victims can feel many things about what happens to them, particularly anger and frustration at the bully and the situation. Let's talk about some possible bullying situations and think about how they might make you feel if you were the victim of bullying.

2. Choose the procedure appropriate for your grade level:

   Grades K–2: Give each student a copy of the Boiling Point worksheet.

   Grades 3–5: Give each student a copy of the Anger Triggers list and the Boiling Point worksheet.

3. Distribute the crayons, markers, or colored pencils.

4. One at a time, have students take turns reading an anger trigger. (For grades K–2, read the triggers yourself.)

5. For each new trigger, instruct the students to color the part of the flask that shows how angry they would be if they experienced the

event. Maybe they would experience just a "drop" of anger, but maybe their anger would fill the whole flask. Have students choose a different color for each trigger, and tell them that, if they wish, they can draw their anger coming out the top and over the outline of the flask.

6. Have students raise their hands when their anger is about to overflow the flask. After the majority of students have their hands raised, add one or two more triggers.

7. When all of the students have raised their hands, ask for volunteers to share their drawings.

8. Facilitate a class discussion by asking the following questions.

DISCUSSION QUESTIONS

- What anger trigger made you the angriest? Has this ever happened to you or someone you know?

- Is there anything we did not mention that would have made you really mad?

- How did you feel when you kept hearing anger triggers, even after your flask was overflowing with anger?

- Did you notice any differences in how angry your classmates were? Why do you think this is?

- What would it be like if you were being bullied all of the time? Would your flask overflow more quickly?

- Would anybody know when your anger is about to boil over the top?

- Have you ever gotten in trouble because your anger boiled over? What did you do?

- What would have happened if you could have poured some of your anger out by talking to someone or asking for help?

- Whom can you talk to when you are really mad and don't know what to do?

- How do you know you are angry? What does your body feel like? What does your face look like? Can you show that face?

- What is something you have found useful when you need to find a good way to deal with your anger?

Boiling Point

Activity 7.3

Bully Busters: A Teacher's Manual for Helping Bullies, Victims, and Bystanders (Grades K–5)
© 2003 by Arthur M. Horne, Christi L. Bartolomucci, and Dawn Newman-Carlson.
Champaign, IL: Research Press. (800) 519–2707.

Anger Triggers

1. One of your classmates cuts in front of you in the lunch line.

2. A group of kids in your class make fun of you by calling you names.

3. Your sister or brother takes your favorite video game.

4. You see one of your classmates push another student in your class.

5. You are picked last for the team during gym class or recess.

6. Your teacher ignores you when you have a question.

7. Two other kids tell your friend not to be friends with you anymore.

8. You get a bad grade on a paper.

9. Someone makes fun of you for being too big or too small.

10. Your mom or dad yells at you before you come to school.

11. An older kid at school pushes you into the bathroom and starts hitting you.

12. You get in trouble for something you didn't do.

13. Every day, a kid tries to steal your lunch.

14. You hear someone making up bad things about you.

15. You think your teacher doesn't understand you.

Bully Busters: A Teacher's Manual for Helping Bullies, Victims, and Bystanders (Grades K–5)
© 2003 by Arthur M. Horne, Christi L. Bartolomucci, and Dawn Newman-Carlson.
Champaign, IL: Research Press. (800) 519–2707.

Hand Talk

OBJECTIVES

- To help students become more comfortable identifying, talking about, and expressing their feelings about bullying and victimization

- To give students a chance to decide which people they would go to for help in a bullying situation

MATERIALS

- Paper lunch bags

- Crayons, markers, or colored pencils

- *Optional:* Construction paper, felt, glitter, yarn, glue, and other supplies for decoration

DIRECTIONS

1. Divide the class into four groups. Let students know that they are going to make some puppets.

2. Assign each group a feeling word: *happy, sad, angry,* or *scared.*

3. Distribute the art supplies to each group. Each group member can use the supplies to design his or her own "feelings puppet" to illustrate the group's assigned feeling.

4. Allow the small groups to talk about how they will show the feeling they would like to express in their puppets' faces. What expressions should be included on the puppets' faces so others can tell what the puppets are feeling? Can they make different puppets so that, for example, some look a little mad while others look very angry?

5. When the groups are done creating their feelings puppets, let them know that each student will next work to make his or her own "people puppet." A people puppet is someone to whom students may go for help. Assign each group a "people word," such as *teacher, friend, parent,* or *principal.* You can decide if there are other people puppets you would like to have the students make.

---

6. Encourage students to share their feelings puppets with their class-mates, one group at a time. Have the class talk about the puppets and ask questions about how the puppets are feeling.

7. Have the students introduce their people puppets, one group at a time.

8. To process the activity, ask the discussion questions.

DISCUSSION QUESTIONS

- Why does each puppet feel the way it does?

- What would make a puppet experience the feeling shown on its face?

- Which puppets look like they may be bullies? Why? If none, what would a bully puppet look like?

- Which puppets look like they might be hurt by bullies? Why? If none, what would a victim puppet look like?

- Which people puppets do you think the victims or bullies could go to for help? Why?

- Are there other people puppets you would rather go to for help? Why?

NOTE

This activity not only helps students better understand their feelings about bullying but also reveals students' views regarding help-seeking behavior. If, while they are discussing their people puppet, students voice concerns or discomfort about seeking help, be sure to offer support and assurance in this area. Save the puppets for use in Activity 7.5, "The Puppets Go to Broadway."

The Puppets Go to Broadway

OBJECTIVES

- To assist students in recognizing alternative ways to deal with bullies and the bully-victim interaction
- To encourage recognition that each person has the power to change a bullying situation

MATERIALS

- Feelings and people puppets made during Activity 7.4 ("Hand Talk"). If you have other puppets, you could use these as well.
- Puppet stage. A table or desk will do if a puppet stage is not available.
- A copy of the Puppet Role Plays, cut into separate role plays

DIRECTIONS

1. Introduce the activity by informing your students that today they are going to be doing group role plays, then divide the class into groups of three to five students each.

2. Give a Puppet Role Play to each group, and encourage them to review it.

3. After the groups have reviewed their role plays, allow them to talk about how each character in the play may feel and how they would like the role play to go so no one's feelings get hurt. What could each character do? Are there any people puppets that could help any of the characters? How so?

4. Help each group pick out the puppets for their role play and decide which group members will use which puppets. Each group should first show the bully-victim situation as described in their role play, then show how the puppets could have handled the bullying situation differently.

5. One at a time, allow the groups to act out their role plays.

6. After each role play, ask the discussion questions to process the activity.

DISCUSSION QUESTIONS

- How does the puppet in your role play feel when he or she is getting bullied?

- Why do you think the bully puppet was picking on the other puppet? How did the bully puppet feel?

- What could the bully puppet have done differently to keep the situation from happening?

- Why do you think the victim puppet was getting bullied? Is there anything the victim could do about this?

- What people puppets did you bring in to help out the bully and victim puppets?

- Why did you choose these people puppets?

- Do you think the bully and victim puppets can trust the people puppets to help them? Why or why not?

- Do you think there is a "best way" to handle bullying?

Puppet Role Plays

Erica

Erica is heavier than most of the other girls in her class. Although Erica knows it is OK to be bigger, every day Mary makes fun of her and calls her names in front of the girls and boys in their class. Each day Erica tries to ignore her, but sometimes it hurts her feelings so much that she feels like crying.

Charles

Charles's family just moved to town from a different country. Charles can speak English, but sometimes he has a hard time with some tricky words. Phillip, a class bully, always makes fun of how Charles talks, tells him he is not wanted at the school, and tries to make the other kids stay away from him. Charles really wants to make friends at school, but no one will talk to him.

Dean

Dean is very sensitive, just like his dad, but all the boys make fun of him and call him a sissy. Dean doesn't like to play sports, and the other boys often laugh at him, push him around, and one time even locked him in the school rest room.

Sharita

Sharita is the queen of all the girls at school. She thinks she is the coolest. Sharita has picked Lila as her enemy. Every day, Sharita picks on Lila for what she is wearing, how she walks, how she talks, and even how she does her schoolwork. Sharita has gotten all the other girls to agree not to be friends with Lila.

Terrence

Terrence is the class clown. He tries to make fun of people, tries to push the bullies around, and even does things like make himself trip to get a laugh. Terrence really gets on Jonas's nerves, so each day Jonas has made it his job to shut Terrence up by stealing his books, calling him names, and hitting him in the chest.

Activity 7.5

Bully Busters: A Teacher's Manual for Helping Bullies, Victims, and Bystanders (Grades K–5)
© 2003 by Arthur M. Horne, Christi L. Bartolomucci, and Dawn Newman-Carlson.
Champaign, IL: Research Press. (800) 519–2707.

My Toolbox

OBJECTIVES

- To help students recognize their own skills and resources ("tools") for preventing bullying situations

- To allow students to identify more tools to address conflict

- To help students use their tools to deal with their feelings about bullying

MATERIALS

- Copies of the My Toolbox worksheet

- Crayons, markers, or colored pencils

- Pencils or pens

DIRECTIONS

1. Introduce the lesson by explaining that today students are going to be identifying skills they can use when confronted with a difficult situation like bullying. Share with them that the purpose of the activity is to help them find and use more "tools" to handle these tough situations.

2. Distribute the My Toolbox worksheets and the art supplies.

3. Instruct students to write or draw pictures of what they do when they are in a conflict with someone. Encourage them to think also of how they have seen other people handle tough conflicts. Instruct them to think of as many tools to handle the situation as they possibly can and to put these tools in their toolboxes. For example:

   Talk to the other student.

   Stay calm.

   Ask the teacher for help.

4. Have students split up into groups of three or four students each and share their toolboxes with one another. If they hear new or different ways of handling conflict, students can add these ideas to their own toolboxes.

5. Allow each group to share their tools for handling a bullying conflict with the whole class. Students can add more tools to their boxes if they hear new ones.

6. Process the activity by asking the discussion questions.

DISCUSSION QUESTIONS

- What ways did you think of handling the bully?

- Who can you ask for help with stopping bullying?

- Do you think you would feel comfortable going to this person or persons for help?

- Did you hear of any new tools to handle bullies today?

- Do you feel your "toolbox" will come in handy if you are bullied?

My Toolbox

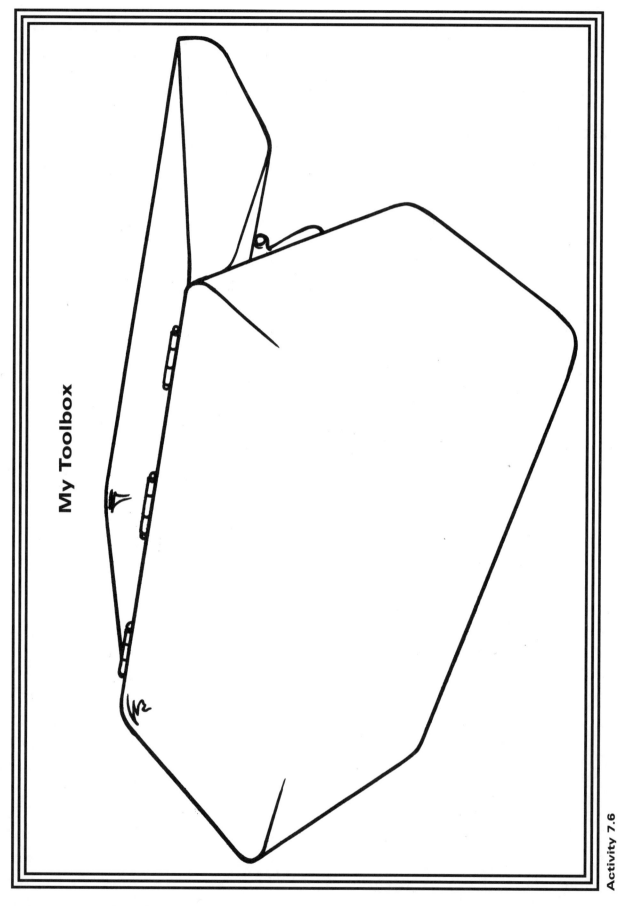

Activity 7.6

Bully Busters: A Teacher's Manual for Helping Bullies, Victims, and Bystanders (Grades K–5)
© 2003 by Arthur M. Horne, Christi L. Bartolomucci, and Dawn Newman-Carlson.
Champaign, IL: Research Press. (800) 519–2707.

Module

8 Relaxation and Coping Skills

Overview

We experience numerous stressors in our lives each day. Stress is an inevitable part of life and an unavoidable component of teaching. How you deal with stress has a profound effect on your ability to teach your students and on whether you are able to avoid teacher burnout. One goal of this module is to help you understand and cope with your stress. The more efficiently you manage your own stress, the more effective you will be in your professional and personal life.

In addition, it is important to remain aware that students also have considerable pressure on them and to provide them with skills to manage conflict and tension. The activities in this module teach students how to relax and cope with everyday stressors. Together, they cover the primary relaxation techniques: imagery, breathing, and muscle relaxation. As the leader, you will want to use a soft and relaxed tone of voice while conducting these activities. This will help to create the proper atmosphere. You can also use these techniques yourself to help reduce stress.

Goals

- To become aware of stress and its effects on well-being

- To understand the role of thoughts, beliefs, and behavior in maintaining or eliminating stress

- To become aware of general stress management skills

- To apply and help students apply specific relaxation techniques to reduce stress on a daily basis

THE IMPORTANCE OF SELF-CARE

You enter the airplane, take your seat, put on your seat belt, and wait. In a few minutes, a flight attendant comes on the speaker and says something like this:

> On behalf of the captain and the entire crew of this flight, we welcome you aboard. At this time we are ready to begin the flight, so I ask that you make certain that

your seat belt is tightened securely, all electronic devices have been turned off, and tray tables and personal belongings are stowed. In case of an emergency, this aircraft is equipped with floor lighting directed toward exits and with oxygen in case there is a loss of cabin pressure. Should they become necessary, oxygen masks will be released. You are to pull the mask to you, place the band on the back of your head, and place the mask over your face. If you are traveling with young children or others who will need assistance, make certain that your own mask is in place before assisting them . . .

Airline personnel know that if you don't take care of yourself in an emergency, you very quickly become unable to care for others as well. The same is true for education. If we are unable to care for ourselves, we soon begin to lose the capacity to care for those we are employed to teach. We believe it is essential that you take care of yourself first; then you will have the strength and ability to care for students and colleagues.

When we meet with teachers who are leaving the field, we almost never hear that these teachers didn't like children, didn't want to teach, or thought they were incompetent in the subject matter. Almost always, the reasons given for leaving education are stress and burnout. The burnout comes from trying harder and harder to be successful with students who are not prepared for school, as exemplified in this teacher comment:

Some students today come to school ill-prepared. This is not often what legislators think about, like not having pencils or books or such. These students are what we call "Not Quite Ready for Sandbox" because they do not know how to share, they do not possess the basic elements of social interactions, they use aggression as their means of interacting, and they have never learned that they are expected to do what an adult tells them to. Am I cynical? Yes. I can teach if given children ready to learn, but I do not know what to do with kids who have never learned the basics of social interaction—in other words, uncivilized kids.

This teacher left teaching at the end of her third year.

We believe that burnout does not occur from working too hard or too long or even from dealing with difficult situations. We have numerous examples of people who work extremely long hours, but, because of their love for their work, they do not burn out. Burnout does not occur from too much work; it occurs when personal needs are not met, as in the following situations:

- When teachers want success in their efforts but do not believe that they are accomplishing their goals

- When teachers' efforts are unappreciated or unrecognized

- When other activities take precedence over teaching, including excessive testing and other responsibilities placed on educators today

- When teachers have the expertise to cover subject matter but students are not prepared or ready to learn at the level necessary for the material

- When disciplinary problems become the focus of teaching rather than the subject matter

And the list goes on. In fact, there are hundreds of reasons that educators become stressed, tired, and hopeless.

STRESS AWARENESS

Stress is cumulative, continually building up until we either erupt or do something about it. Usually, it is not until we are overwhelmed, fatigued, or distraught that we decide to take action. The best way to deal with stress is to become aware of it, then devise a plan for change. Teachers have shared with us that taking the time to identify personal and professional stressors and to make reasonable changes leads to greater satisfaction in both their personal and professional lives. We believe that at least four components are necessary for healthy, less stressful lives: These include having a good diet, getting exercise, practicing stress reduction techniques such as meditation or relaxation, and having a support group. These four components are essential for teachers to have the strength and resources to address the problems of bullies and victims.

In this module, we focus on stress management. We already know a great deal about stress management and what to do with stress. Here are several points that are important to keep in mind.

Attend to emotions and physical reactions

The purpose of an emotion is to motivate us to do something. If we need to change, we should attend to our emotions and determine how we need to be changing. Anger, fear, frustration, depression, and sadness—all are emotions that are directing us to alter an immediate or a long-term situation. However, before we can act on an emotion, we must be aware that we are having it. Learn to listen to your body, and identify what your physical signs of stress are. Does your heart start to beat faster? Does your breathing become shallow? Do you feel shaky? Each of these is a symptom your body may produce under stress.

Learn to listen to your thoughts

Consider for a moment the thoughts that run through your mind when you are feeling stressed. Your mind may begin to race with negative messages that perpetuate or increase your level of stress. Common thoughts teachers express are "What a waste of time," "I wish I didn't have to do this," and "I feel unsafe."

BULLY BUSTERS SUPPORT TEAM THINK BLOCK

Think about the stressors you have been experiencing in your teaching. Turn to page 325 and fill in the boxes with several of the more important stressors that you experience; do not complete the influence column at this time. (Figure 8 shows an example.)

List a number of stressors in the first column. Take time to include different types of stressors—for example, include specific student disciplinary problems or general disciplinary problems in the classroom, relationships between family and school, school scheduling or activities required of you beyond classroom teaching, legislative influence in the educational process, and so on.

Think about when the stressor occurs, and note this in the second column. Is it at a particular time, or does it happen at any time? Maybe it is like the example, an event that goes on all day. It is important to attempt to track timing; some stressors are specifically related to events that happen at a particular time, such as interruptions for morning announcements, whereas others may happen irregularly, such as when a student is called out for a meeting. Knowing when these events occur allows you to begin to track the ABCs: the antecedents, the behaviors or events that are so stressful, and the consequences for you. It may be that by knowing the antecedents, the event can be predicted and planned for in a more effective manner or even eliminated entirely.

Keeping track of the seriousness of the event is also important. At times, we worry about events that may, in fact, not be worth our time and effort. Reviewing stressful events, knowing when they occur, and then identifying their seriousness help us begin targeting our energy and resources to address the stressors.

Next complete the column in indicating the extent to which you have influence over the stressors in your life. You are likely to have little influence over several—salary, legislative action regarding school testing, and the like—but you may have considerable influence over other stressors, such as students' classroom behavior.

With your Bully Busters Support Team, discuss the stressors that you identified in this activity:

1. What stressors are common among the members of your Bully Busters Support Team?

2. Is there a pattern in the stressors for your group? That is, does your group experience a large number of similar stressors, or are your stressors different?

3. How have you seen other teachers handle these stressors? Have you observed both effective and ineffective methods of managing stress? Describe a positive and negative approach you have observed.

4. What feelings do you have when you are in a stressful situation (e.g., depressed, angry, amused)? How do you respond?

5. Do you manage these emotions as effectively as you wish, or do you need to learn additional skills?

		FIGURE 8 My Stressors	
What is the stressor?	**When does it occur?**	**How serious is it?** (1 = not at all; 10 = very serious)	**Influence** (1 = significant; 2 = some; 3 = none)
I have one student who drives me up the wall with his belligerent attitude. He saunters in with a sneer, and all day long he stares as though he's angry.	It starts in the morning, escalates during the day, and usually gets better in the afternoon, after recess.	8	1

APPLYING THE BIG QUESTIONS

In an effort to understand your stressors, you can apply the Big Questions to the topic of stress management:

Question 1: What is my goal? To manage your stress so you are energized and effective in your teaching and classroom management.

Question 2: What am I doing? Consider your stressors and how much control or influence you have over them. Are there similarities among the stressors over which you have little influence or considerable influence? Does a pattern emerge?

Question 3: Is what I am doing helping me achieve my goal? If your stressors are influencing you to be less effective as a teacher and as a human being, it is important to recognize the need for change and take steps to address the problem.

Question 4: (If not) *What can I do differently?* Brainstorm ways to reduce your stress. As discussed previously, your Bully Busters Support Team can be very helpful in solving problems, stress included. Even if some stressors cannot be eliminated—for instance, having a student with a harassing parent—at least the group can provide the emotional and professional support you need to endure the experience.

GENERAL RECOMMENDATIONS FOR MANAGING STRESS

Sometimes a very simple change in the way you live your life can have a profound effect on your level of stress, as well as on that of your students. Some of the recommendations that follow may seem obvious, but we may forget how important they are.

Take Time to Relax

Teachers often tell us they have too much to do to take time for themselves. All day, teachers devote themselves to their students. It is easy to deplete energy and enthusiasm if you do not take time to replenish yourself. Time will not appear miraculously in your daily schedule; on the contrary, you must plan to devote time to yourself. What is something you enjoy doing that you have not done in a long time? Sit quietly and read a book? Go to the coffee shop and a read a magazine? See a movie? Take a long walk in the park? Today is a new day. Take some time to relax.

Students also have worries and stress. Many adults believe children do not experience stress: "It is so nice to be young and carefree with no worries in the world." However, youth today are experiencing increased stress in their families, their communities, and the larger culture. Each child is an individual and brings to the table unique situations with which he or she is attempting to cope. You can serve as a positive role model for coping with stress. You can also give your students permission to relax and do something they love. Have your students write down several activities that they love to do and that make them feel calm and relaxed. Ask them to try to engage in one of these activities at least three times a week. You can create a "Chillin' Chart" in your classroom that includes each child's name and a space to assign stars for engaging in these positive activities. We also encourage you to involve parents in understanding and supporting their children's need for this time.

Take a Daily Dose of Relaxation or Meditation

Numerous resources are available for learning about meditation and the relaxation response; bookstores generally have a number of current books on the topic. In one school, we found that the Bully Busters Support Team members were unfamiliar with these techniques. Several members purchased books to learn about these processes. They then worked together as a team to learn and support one another in using these methods. The group was able to provide ongoing encouragement to incorporate meditation and relaxation into daily experiences.

Take a Daily Dose of Humor

When we are stressed, we lose our sense of humor and our ability to laugh. Next time a situation does not have the outcome you desire, instead of becoming angry and frustrated, try to find humor in the situation—laugh it off. Laughter is an excellent way to release stress and change the level of tension in yourself and in your environment.

Kids need to exercise their humor as well. They need to laugh and have learning be fun. Allow your students to enjoy humor and laughter. If they are able to laugh together in a classroom, maybe they will be less likely to release their stress through aggression. Invite your students to share their sense of humor. Encourage them to tell appropriate funny stories, and share yours with them. Model laughing for your class. If it is OK for you to crack a smile and enjoy what you are doing; your students will follow in your footsteps.

It is also important to teach students appropriate humor. Helping students appreciate that laughing can be a great experience but that it should not be at some one else's expense is essential. Laughing at ourselves or laughing with others is appropriate, but laughing at others is not. It is important to identify examples of inappropriate humor and encourage students to use appropriate humor instead.

Take Time for Exercise and Activity

Exercise has been shown to reduce the chance of heart attacks, strokes, and arteriosclerosis. Incorporating moderate exercise into your daily routine is an effective way to reduce stress. In addition, exercise serves as an outlet for anger and frustration, and it prevents stressors from becoming overwhelming. Exercise can be a time to "blow off steam" or a time to make sense of what is bothering you.

Students also can benefit by incorporating exercise into their daily routine. Youth today watch numerous hours of television, a majority of which model action and violence. In becoming active, students are able to release energy that without release may become negative. In other words, children can use activity to reduce their level of stress without hurting anyone. One teacher led students through exercises inside on days with inclement weather. She reported that taking time to let students move had a positive impact on their behavior.

Don't Take Your Work Home

Teachers share with us that this advice sounds great, but in reality there are just not enough hours in the day to accomplish all of their work. We can relate to this. However, you may not only *deserve* a break, you may *need* a break. If you must work at home, set limits for yourself. For example, you may decide you are most effective from 6:00 to 8:00 P.M. Use this specific time to concentrate on your work. Doing so may reduce feelings of stress or guilt about not completing your work at other times in the evening.

Older elementary students will also benefit from a scheduled time for homework. Homework is inevitable; however, students may perform better if they have a consistent time period to complete their work. Students should be involved in choosing what time they feel they can best complete their work. Some parents prefer their children to complete their homework immediately after school; others, after their chores are complete. In class, you can have your students decide what time best suits them for completing their homework. Have them draw up a contract with a place for three signatures—child, teacher, and parent. Have the children bring home the contract and discuss it with their parents. Having a designated homework time limits the stress of bringing work home and also reduces arguments that may arise about when children should be doing their homework.

Use Your Bully Busters Support Team

Consider two words: *illness* and *wellness*. There are a lot of differences in what the two words imply, but let's examine a simpler difference:

Illness starts with "I," and wellness starts with "We." We often hear teachers who say, "I have so much work to do; I have to do so many things with students; I feel so all alone in the work I'm doing I just don't know what to do." We encourage them to move toward "we-ness" and use the Bully Busters Support Team for help in solving problems, understanding the difficulties of teaching, and taking care of themselves as well as their students.

The support team serves as an ongoing resource to dispel fears, help teachers feel supported, and encourage collaborative problem solving. Sharing and communication are central to the team's purpose and can be very effective in reducing stress. Working together to bring about change in the school is much more effective than working alone: The team can accomplish goals that individuals may be unable to reach. Use your support team.

Encourage your students to create their own support groups to deal with bullying and other stressful situations. Remind them that your door is always open to discuss their stress and their experiences with bullying.

Setting Up for Success: Plan Ahead

In chapter 1, we emphasized how important it is for teachers to set themselves and their students up for success. The same principle applies in managing stress: Develop a plan ahead of time to help yourself cope. If you overwhelm yourself with unrealistic goals, the outcome will likely be negative, so try to keep your goals within reach. Specifically, any goal you set should be observable, achievable within a specified time span, and structured in incremental steps. Ideally, short-term goals should lead to larger long-term goals, and you should reward yourself in a special way for achieving each goal.

My Stressors

What is the stressor?	When does it occur?	How serious is it? (1 = not at all; 10 = very serious)	Influence (1 = significant; 2 = some; 3 = none)

Bully Busters: A Teacher's Manual for Helping Bullies, Victims, and Bystanders (Grades K–5)
© 2003 by Arthur M. Horne, Christi L. Bartolomucci, and Dawn Newman-Carlson.
Champaign, IL: Research Press. (800) 519–2707.

Module 8: Content Review

The following statements relate to the learning goals of this module. Ask yourself if you feel confident that you can answer yes to each item. If not, please review the material and discuss any difficulties among your Bully Busters Support Team.

1. I have taken a close look at all of my stressors and recognize the degree of pressure I am under on a daily basis. Yes ❏ No ❏

2. I know about and will take the time to apply general ways to reduce stress in myself and my students (taking time to relax, exercising, planning ahead, etc.). Yes ❏ No ❏

3. I am using my Bully Busters Support Team for comfort, consultation, and problem solving. Yes ❏ No ❏

4. I have determined to do my best while I am at school and attempt to leave the frustrations of the school day at work. Yes ❏ No ❏

5. When faced with a problem, I will apply the Big Questions to identify it, define my goal, consider my current response, and make appropriate changes. Yes ❏ No ❏

6. I have identified specific relaxation techniques that I will encourage my students to practice and will incorporate into my own daily routine. Yes ❏ No ❏

Bully Busters: A Teacher's Manual for Helping Bullies, Victims, and Bystanders (Grades K–5)
© 2003 by Arthur M. Horne, Christi L. Bartolomucci, and Dawn Newman-Carlson.
Champaign, IL: Research Press. (800) 519–2707.

A Reminder . . .

CLASSROOM INTERACTION AND AWARENESS CHART

Use the CIAC to describe any bullying behavior you observe (and that students report to you, if you wish). A copy of the CIAC and a weekly summary sheet appear in Appendix A.

THE BIG QUESTIONS

Honestly appraise your progress by asking yourself the Big Questions. There are no right or wrong answers.

In relation to increasing awareness of and dealing with stress in myself and my students:

1. What is my goal?

2. What am I doing?

3. Is what I am doing helping me achieve my goal?

4. *(If not)* What can I do differently?

PERSONAL GOALS FORM

The Personal Goals Form, on the next page, is designed to help you tailor the content of this module to your own students and situation. Please take a moment to fill out the form now.

Module 8: Personal Goals Form

Goals

- To become aware of stress and its effects on well-being

- To understand the role of thoughts, beliefs, and behavior in maintaining or eliminating stress

- To become aware of general stress management skills

- To apply and help students apply specific relaxation techniques to reduce stress on a daily basis

1. Reasons it is important to find ways for me and my students to reduce stress are as follows:

2. I have observed incidents of bullying. *(Please record incidents on the CIAC.)*

   ____ Number of times I intervened   ____ Number of times I chose not to intervene

   Other observations:

3. I will review the classroom activities for this module and select ones appropriate for my class. *(Please list.)*

4. I will accept the challenges associated with the developmental assets. *(Please list the specific assets and describe what you plan to do.)*

5. I will give my students feedback about the bullying incidents I have observed and encourage discussion of bullying and related issues. We will discuss these topics:

6. I will share my experiences in applying the information in this module with other teachers and administrators, as well as with my students' families. *(Please specify who and when.)*

7. I will meet with my Bully Busters Support Team. *(Please specify when and list what issues and questions you will raise.)*

Bully Busters: A Teacher's Manual for Helping Bullies, Victims, and Bystanders (Grades K–5)
© 2003 by Arthur M. Horne, Christi L. Bartolomucci, and Dawn Newman-Carlson.
Champaign, IL: Research Press. (800) 519–2707.

Classroom Activities

ACTIVITY 8.1: KEEPING CALM (GRADES K–2)

In this activity, students listen to a story that describes how one girl found a special place that helped her find peace and relaxation after feeling very upset. They then discuss the story and talk about places that could be special for them.

ACTIVITY 8.2: MY MAGIC PLACE (GRADES K–5)

This activity helps students relax through imagery—specifically, by imagining their own special, quiet place they can go to during times of stress.

ACTIVITY 8.3: BALLOON IN MY BELLY (GRADES 3–5)

Students can use the breathing technique students learn in this activity whenever they feel stressed out, either at school or at home.

ACTIVITY 8.4: BODY GAME (GRADES 3–5)

By having students tense and relax separate muscle groups, this activity provides an opportunity for them to recognize and relax tension and tightness in their bodies.

Keeping Calm

OBJECTIVES

- To help younger students identify ways they can calm down and control their feelings

- To provide an example of a calming story to share with your students to help them calm down and relax

MATERIALS

- Chalkboard or easel pad

- *Optional:* Copies of the STOPP poster

DIRECTIONS

1. Invite your students to sit in a circle on the floor. Encourage them to get comfortable, either sitting or lying down.

2. Lead your students in a brief relaxation technique: Ask them to take a deep breath in, then let it all out. Repeat this three or four times.

3. Dim or turn off the lights if possible.

4. Read the Keeping Calm in the Middle of a Storm story (on pages 333–336). At the point in the story where Mr. Dagley talks about different feelings children might have about the storm, solicit and record students' ideas.

5. After you have finished, in a calm and gentle voice, facilitate discussion by asking the following questions.

DISCUSSION QUESTIONS

- What made Lucy so mad?

- How did Lucy find a way to calm herself down?

- Did relaxing help Lucy? How?

- Do you have a special place in your imagination where you could go to feel calm?

- What would it be like for us to play the STOPP game in our class? How many would like to try?

NOTE

After you have conducted this activity, you can post copies of the STOPP poster around the classroom and apply the technique as appropriate in your class.

Keeping Calm in the Middle of a Storm

Lucy was a pretty wonderful girl in many ways. Yes, in many ways, a pretty wonderful girl. She was in elementary school and thought going to school was a really fun thing to do because she got to be with her friends, she always got an interesting lunch, and she liked her teacher a lot. Lucy was pretty wonderful, all right, except for one small thing. When things didn't go the way she wanted, she got as angry as a hornet whose nest has been hit by a baseball, and you know how hornets are when their nest gets hit, don't you? Well, they get really, really mad.

Lucy had a lot of friends in school. Some were from her neighborhood, and they had known each other a long time, for months or even years. Lucy and her friends played nicely and really enjoyed their time together, except when Lucy got one of her temper fits—when she got as mad as a hornet whose nest has been hit—and when that happened, all of Lucy's friends would scatter to their homes. They didn't want to get stung by Lucy's really bad temper! Mostly, though, they got along fine because Lucy got her way. She was the oldest in the group—her birthday was several months before the birthday of any other girl in the neighborhood, and that made her somewhat special.

When Lucy was at school, she was happy and did well because she could learn her lessons quickly and because she was the oldest girl in her class, and the biggest, too, and because the teacher liked her. She was usually a pretty happy person, except when someone made her mad, and then she was just like a hornet whose nest has been hit by a baseball, but that didn't happen very often. But when it did, even the teacher hoped it would be over soon because Lucy could throw one enormous tantrum, and when she did, it was best for everyone to just be somewhere else.

On most days, Lucy would come into the classroom, take her seat, and pull out a library book to read because she really enjoyed reading. She did this most days, and she would be reading her book when the other students came in. She would ignore them mostly until it was time for class to begin, and then she would stand up and smile at everyone and say, "I'm so happy to be here today with my friends and with Ms. Gilmore, my favorite teacher," and the other students would usually laugh because that's what Lucy said every day. Ms. Gilmore would smile and say, "And I'm glad to be with my favorite class and my favorite students. Now let's begin today's lessons." All the students thought that was a fun way to begin the day.

Usually, the day would proceed without much fuss because most of the students liked being there and were interested in learning, though sometimes it did get a bit boring or tiring. On some days, some special event would happen and cause more excitement than usual—like the day they all went to the gym to play ball. On this one day, several kids were playing catch with a big foam-rubber ball, and the ball went flying the wrong way. Lucy was chatting away to a friend and telling how she had been the best student that morning because they had gotten their spelling papers back, and Lucy had a perfect score, which she had expected because she had studied hard, when "Wham!" and "Boom!" The ball hit Lucy right in the back of the head. There was dead silence. The students playing ball knew they had made a mistake, but it was one of those mistakes that once you made it, you couldn't take it back. No matter what you hoped for, Lucy was still hit in the back of the head.

The ball didn't hurt much—it was foam rubber, and it bounced right away. But what was hurt was Lucy's story about how well she had done that day. In fact, the story was over because when Lucy realized she had been hit, she was as mad as a hornet whose nest has been hit by a baseball, and she turned and screamed, "Who did that?" A couple of students who were not involved tittered, laughed a little bit, but Lucy screamed at them, "Do you think this is funny? Do you think it's funny to be hit in the head while talking to a friend? Do you think you can laugh at me, the oldest girl in the class, and get away with it? Do you know what I'll do if you laugh at me?" And then she started stomping her feet and turning red in the face, and some of the students thought she was getting so angry she might just explode. She stormed over to the group of students who had been playing ball and yelled out, "Who threw that ball?" and several of the students pointed to Natalie, who just stood there, kind of frozen. Lucy went running at Natalie with fists clenched, yelling, "I'm going to get you for this—you can't do this to me!" Natalie had tears building up in her eyes and was shaking and then closed her eyes as Lucy stormed toward her, knowing she was about to be hit, when . . .

Lucy was snatched up by the back of her shoulders and held in the air with her feet flying and her fists flailing in the air. She was so mad she was crying because no one was allowed to throw a ball at her. She was as mad as a hornet whose nest had been . . . Well, you understand that by now.

When Lucy looked around she saw she was being held by Mr. Dagley, the school counselor. She yelled, "You let me down! I'm going to get that Natalie . . . ," but Mr. Dagley just held her and said, "No, I don't think so. You see, in our school we solve our problems a different way—we talk about them—but right now you are so angry, I don't think you can talk very well, so let's go to my office while you calm down."

Lucy really yelled then because she didn't want to go to the counselor's office—she wanted to tear into Natalie and teach her a lesson, that's what she wanted to do. But Mr. Dagley guided Lucy by the shoulders and held her hand tightly and walked away from the gym toward his office.

When Mr. Dagley got Lucy to his office, he told her to sit down in a chair that he had there. It was a small chair, just right for children, and it was soft and comfortable, too. He said, "You sit in the chair and calm down, and then we'll talk." After a few minutes, Lucy did begin to calm down, but she was still mad.

"Lucy," Mr. Dagley said, "You can't let this continue. I've heard that you have a temper as mean as a hornet's whose nest has been hit by a baseball and that, when you lose that temper, you get really mad and want to get revenge. We have to work to change that because we can't have students in our school getting as mad as hornets, and certainly we can't have students wanting to hit and hurt other students."

Mr. Dagley said he had some books in his office and that Lucy could sit in the chair and read one of his books if she needed some time before going back to class. She sat for a while just looking around the room, and she was still mad, so she didn't feel like reading anything. But Mr. Dagley had an aquarium in his room, and as she watched the fish swim around, she began to feel calmer, though she was still irritated. Finally, she started looking at the names of some books he had. Then she reached over and picked one up. It was called *Keeping Calm in the Middle of a Storm*.

Mr. Dagley saw that Lucy was looking at the book and said, "That's a good one. It tells how to stay calm even when things around us are not calm. Let's talk about it." Mr. Dagley explained that sometimes our lives are like being in a storm, and there are lots of things happening that we don't have any control over. Although we can't control the storm, we can control how we feel during the storm. Did Lucy know that not everyone feels the same way during a storm? How many different ways might children feel in a storm?

Some are scared because storms can hurt people.

Some worry because animals might be scared and hurt.

Some enjoy seeing how fast the wind can blow and how hard the rain can come down.

Some like storms because they can stay in the house and read books and play games.

Some like storms because they get to be close to their families.

Mr. Dagley explained that one of the reasons children feel different ways about storms is that they tell themselves different stories. For example, if Lucy were to tell herself a story about how storms hurt people, she would be scared. But if she told herself a story about how storms are nice gifts because they bring us rain and a lightning show and we get to be with our families and hold each other tight, then she wouldn't be scared—she would feel good.

Mr. Dagley also said that the same thing was true about getting angry. That some people might have something happen to them, like getting hit on the head with a foam-rubber ball. Some children might tell themselves a story about how mean another person was to hit them, then be really angry. But other children might tell themselves a story about how someone meant to throw the ball straight but it went crooked and accidentally hit someone else. Then that child would understand that an accident had happened and wouldn't be angry.

Mr. Dagley said that what they had to do was practice the STOPP game. He asked Lucy if she knew what the STOPP game was, and she didn't. He said STOPP is a game to play when something happens, particularly if it is something that might not be good. He said STOPP stands for this:

Stop: Stop and settle down. Be calm.

Think: Think about the problem. What is the problem?

Options: Think of options, or things to do. Think of several plans.

Plan: Choose the best plan and do it.

Plan working? Think about whether the plan is working, and, if not, figure out what might work better.

Lucy said she liked the STOPP game but didn't know how to do the first part. So Mr. Dagley said, "I could come to your classroom and teach everyone in the room how to stop and calm down, then everyone would know. But I think I would need an assistant, someone to help me do this. Do you think that if I taught you how to do it, you could help me teach everyone else?"

Well, of course, Lucy thought she could do that. So Mr. Dagley taught Lucy how to calm down and breathe slowly. He said:

> First, close your eyes. Then when your eyes are closed, begin to imagine something you like a lot. Maybe a pretty flower garden. Or maybe being in the woods when it is nice and relaxing. Or maybe at a lake, where you can hear the water lapping against a boat dock. He asked Lucy what to her would be a pretty place, and she said, "I think it would be in my room at home because I like my room a lot."

He told her to imagine she was in her room and a little bit tired, and then to pay attention to her breathing. She was to take deep breaths and hold them a little, then slowly let the breaths out, and as she let them out she was to silently say to herself, "Calm. Be calm. Be relaxed and calm." And Lucy began to breathe slowly and deeply and tell herself to be calm and relaxed. As she did so, she started to feel very good and warm inside.

Mr. Dagley had her open her eyes, and then they talked some more, and he had her practice again, closing her eyes, picturing herself in her room, breathing slowly, and saying "Calm. Be calm. Be relaxed and calm." And she showed him she could do it very well. Mr. Dagley arranged for her to meet him the next day after lunch, and together they would teach the class how to do the STOPP game and practice being calm.

When they got to class, Lucy was a very good helper and demonstrated how to do what Mr. Dagley was telling the class to do. She was so good, in fact, that for the rest of the day she got to keep helping others figure out how to be calm and relaxed. And you know what? From then on she was not mad as a hornet whose nest has been hit by a baseball. Instead, she was calm and happy, a much happier Lucy, and all the other students wanted to be friends with her.

S   *Stop:* Stop and settle down. Be calm.

T   *Think:* Think about the problem. What is the problem?

O   *Options:* Think of options, or things to do. Think of several plans.

P   *Plan:* Choose the best plan and do it.

P   *Plan working?* Think about whether the plan is working, and, if not, figure out what might work better.

Activity 8.1

Bully Busters: A Teacher's Manual for Helping Bullies, Victims, and Bystanders (Grades K–5)
© 2003 by Arthur M. Horne, Christi L. Bartolomucci, and Dawn Newman-Carlson.
Champaign, IL: Research Press. (800) 519–2707.

My Magic Place

OBJECTIVES

- To help students learn to use imagery to promote relaxation
- To encourage students to take this private break at times they are feeling tense

MATERIALS

- None

DIRECTIONS

1. Introduce the activity to the class. You might say something like the following:

   When you are in a difficult situation and you're not sure what to do, do you ever wish you could just go away and get some time to think? Today, we are going to learn how to take a private break for a few minutes of relaxation. You can do this exercise at your desk.

2. Turn out or dim the lights, then instruct students to put their heads on their desks and close their eyes. If students would be more comfortable and space allows, they can also find a place to sit or lie down on the floor.

3. Follow the directions for reading the My Magic Place script aloud (see page 339).

4. Afterwards, encourage discussion.

DISCUSSION QUESTIONS

- Would anyone like to share his or her magic place?
- What did it feel like in your magic place?
- Do you think you can visit this magic place again when you are feeling tense or upset?

My Magic Place

Read each step, slowly and one at a time. (Do not read the numbers at left.) After the third step, allow 20 to 30 seconds between steps to give students time to form a clear mental picture.

1. Take in a deep breath, and count to 5. Now blow your breath the whole way out.

2. Let's breathe deeply again. Breathe in, and count to 5. Then blow all of your breath out.

3. Imagine a perfect place in your mind. This is your favorite place. It can be real, or it can be imaginary.

4. Where are you? Are you in town? Are you far away? Maybe you are by the water. Maybe you are even flying high like a bird.

5. What does your magic place look like? Look around at your magic place. What do you see? Is it light or dark?

6. Is anyone with you? Who would this be? Is it someone you know or somebody new?

7. What are you doing in your magic place? Are you playing? Reading? Just chilling out?

8. Do you have any special abilities or powers? What are they?

9. What do you like most about your magic place? Just think for a moment, and really enjoy this super-special, magic place.

10. Can you take a picture of your place? You will want to carry this picture with you until you can go back and visit it again.

11. I am going to count backwards from 10. When I get to 1, open your eyes. 10 . . . 9 . . . 8 . . . 7 . . . 6 . . . 5 . . . 4 . . . 3 . . . 2 . . . 1. Now open your eyes.

Balloon in My Belly

OBJECTIVES

- To help students learn a breathing technique to promote relaxation
- To encourage students to use this breathing technique to relax when they are upset

MATERIALS

- None

DIRECTIONS

1. Introduce the activity by saying something like the following:

   Today, we are going to learn how to breathe very deeply to allow our minds and bodies to feel very relaxed. When we have a lot of things going on at school and home, it is easy to feel upset, nervous, or stressed out. This new skill we are going to practice is also good to use after you have gotten really mad and you are not sure how to calm yourself down. We will practice this skill together.

2. Turn out or dim the lights in the classroom, and allow students to get comfortable. They can put their heads down on their desks, sit on the floor, or just relax in their seats.

3. Read the Balloon in My Belly script (on page 342), slowly, one step at a time.

4. Afterwards, facilitate class discussion.

DISCUSSION QUESTIONS

- How does your body feel?
- Have you ever felt this way before? When?
- Does this new skill help your body to feel good?
- When would be some good times to do this activity?

• How could we use this activity in our classroom?

NOTE

Sometimes you may sense tension in your students but not know the reason. If so, you can have students practice this activity. Students can also ask you to lead the activity whenever they feel they could benefit from it. As you repeat this activity, students will become more likely to use the technique on their own.

Balloon in My Belly

Pause for 3–5 seconds at the end of each numbered item and elsewhere when pauses are indicated in the script. (Do not read the numbers at left.)

1. Take a moment to get really comfortable.

2. Do you have some thoughts running around your mind? If so, imagine putting those thoughts in a balloon. Tuck them inside a big balloon. *(pause)* Now let the balloon go—let it go way, way up and out of your mind. *(pause)* Do this a few times to help let all the thoughts running around leave your mind.

3. Now *(pause)* let's focus on our breathing. Try to breathe in through your nose and blow out through your mouth. Take a big breath in, and *(pause)* now blow all that air out of your mouth.

4. We are getting good air to all parts of our body *(pause),* making our bodies feel healthy and relaxed.

5. Now *(pause)* take another deep breath in. While you breathe in *(pause)* try to count to 5. Think of taking a really big breath and holding it in for 5 seconds.

6. Imagine a big balloon in your belly. *(pause)* While you are breathing in *(pause),* imagine filling the balloon in your belly full of air. *(pause)* You have a big balloon in your belly full of good air.

7. Now *(pause)* blow out all of the air. Let the air out for 5 seconds. *(pause)* Imagine letting all of the air out of your balloon. You are letting all of the hot and tense air out of your body.

8. Let's try again. Imagine the big balloon in your belly. *(pause)* Are you ready to fill it with air again?

9. Let's take a really big breath. *(pause)* Concentrate on filling up the balloon in your belly with air. You can count to 5 as you take in a really big and slow breath.

10. Now *(pause)* when you are ready *(pause)* empty the balloon in your belly. Try to count to 5 as you let all the air out of your balloon.

Body Game

OBJECTIVES

- To help students learn the technique of muscle relaxation

- To encourage students to recognize when their muscles are tense and to use this technique to reduce tension, especially in anger-provoking situations

MATERIALS

- None

DIRECTIONS

1. Instruct students to find some space in the classroom where they can put their chairs or lie down on the floor. If no space is available, students can do the exercise at their desks.

2. In a calm and relaxed voice, read through each step from the script on page 344.

3. Facilitate class discussion. Discussion should remain relaxed and needs to take place only after the first time you use the activity.

DISCUSSION QUESTIONS

- How did it feel to let go after holding your muscles very tight?

- When your body begins to feel tight or tense, like when you are mad, are you willing to try to do this activity on your own?

- Who thinks they can give this activity a try at home?

NOTE

You can incorporate this activity into your day on a regular basis, especially when students appear restless or agitated. The activity will need to be repeated several times for students to begin to use it independently.

Body Game

Pause for 3–5 seconds at the end of each numbered item and elsewhere when pauses are indicated in the script. (Do not read the numbers at left.) As you read the steps, you may also need to demonstrate the actions.

1. Get as comfortable and relaxed as possible. Close your eyes, and take a deep breath.

2. Wrinkle your forehead. Hold it there. *(pause)* Relax. *(pause)* Wrinkle your forehead again. *(pause)* Relax.

3. Wrinkle your nose. Hold it there. *(pause)* Relax. *(pause)* Wrinkle your nose again. *(pause)* Relax.

4. Clench your teeth. Hold it there. *(pause)* Relax. *(pause)* Clench your teeth again. *(pause)* Relax.

5. Raise your shoulders as high as you can. Hold them there. *(pause)* Relax. *(pause)* Raise your shoulders again. *(pause)* Relax.

6. Make a fist—a very, very tight fist. As tight a fist as you can. Hold it there. *(pause)* Relax your fist. *(pause)* Make a very tight fist again. *(pause)* Relax.

7. Make a muscle in your arm like a bodybuilder. Make the muscle very, very tight. Hold it there. *(pause)* Relax. *(pause)* Make a muscle in your arm again. *(pause)* Relax.

8. Tighten your stomach. Hold it there. *(pause)* Relax. *(pause)* Tighten your stomach again. *(pause)* Relax.

9. Tighten your legs. Hold them there. *(pause)* Relax. *(pause)* Tighten your legs again. *(pause)* Relax.

10. Point your toes. Hold them there. *(pause)* Relax. *(pause)* Point your toes again. *(pause)* Relax.

11. Shake your whole body gently. Make your body feel very loose. *(pause)* Feel the relaxation in your face. *(pause)* Feel how relaxed your arms and shoulders feel. *(pause)* Can you feel the looseness in your stomach and legs? *(pause)* Notice how loose your whole body is.

12. Now, whenever you are ready, slowly open your eyes.

APPENDIX

A Classroom Interaction and Awareness Chart

The Classroom Interaction and Awareness Chart (CIAC) gives you the opportunity to record and track the bullying incidents you observe (and, if you choose, the incidents that students report to you). The chart is helpful in several ways:

- It helps pinpoint where bullying is happening in your classroom and the school.

- It identifies who commits acts of bullying and who is victimized by this type of aggression.

- It provides information about how frequently you address bullying problems.

- It allows you to judge the frequency of different types of bullying.

These data are helpful in informing students, members of your Bully Busters Support Team, other teachers, administrators, parents, and others about the success of the program. If the information on the CIAC reflects no change in students' behaviors, it offers the opportunity for problem solving. In this case, you can use the Big Questions to pinpoint what needs to be changed and how.

Keep a copy of the CIAC at your desk so you can jot down notes about situations as they occur. You can also record incidents at the end of each day if that is more convenient. Complete the form for a week before beginning the Bully Busters program. At the end of the week—and for subsequent weeks—fill out the CIAC Weekly Summary and review the information you have recorded. If necessary, please feel free to adapt the form so it applies more directly to your own situation.

Classroom Interaction and Awareness Chart

Week of _____

Date	Location of bullying	Type of bullying			Child in bullying role	Child in victim role	Did I intervene?	Do I like how I handled the situation?
		Aggressive	Passive	Relational				

Bully Busters: A Teacher's Manual for Helping Bullies, Victims, and Bystanders (Grades K–5)
© 2003 by Arthur M. Horne, Christi L. Bartolomucci, and Dawn Newman-Carlson.
Champaign, IL: Research Press. (800) 519–2707.

347

CIAC Weekly Summary

Week of _____

Students who most frequently bully:

1. _____

2. _____

3. _____

Students most frequently victimized:

1. _____

2. _____

3. _____

_____ Total times I intervened

_____ Total times I did not intervene

Most common locations of bullying:

1. _____

2. _____

3. _____

Total types of bullying interactions:

_____ Incidents of aggressive bullying

_____ Incidents of passive bullying

_____ Incidents of relational bullying

Comments: _____

_____

_____

Bully Busters: A Teacher's Manual for Helping Bullies, Victims, and Bystanders (Grades K–5)
© 2003 by Arthur M. Horne, Christi L. Bartolomucci, and Dawn Newman-Carlson.
Champaign, IL: Research Press. (800) 519–2707.

APPENDIX

B Teacher Inventory of Skills and Knowledge– Elementary

To use the Teacher Inventory of Skills and Knowledge (TISK–E), record your responses for each item on the following Scoring Sheet. Check one box per item. After you finish checking boxes for all the items, total the number of times you indicated "never," "sometimes," "often," or "almost always." Write each total in the box provided at the bottom of each item set.

Your responses can give you an idea of how you are implementing different intervention strategies in the classroom. If you responded that you "never" or "sometimes" use many of the items in one set of questions, then take some time to return to that module to review and take steps to implement these strategies.

Compare your scores each time you take the TISK-E. Doing so provides you with an idea of your retention of information and your general acquisition of prevention and intervention skills in each of the learning modules. If you find that you are responding with "often" and "almost always," good for you! You are on your way toward a safer, more effective classroom and school.

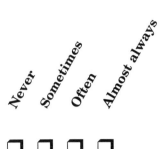

Module 1: Increasing Awareness of Bullying

Intervention

1. Attend to the social and academic development of my students.
2. Recognize that I am a role model and model decision making, respect for others, and a positive attitude.
3. Maintain a record of bullying incidents and interventions.
4. Consult with another teacher for advice.
5. Understand the role of prevention in ending bullying.
6. Understand the PIC criteria for bullying.

TOTAL RESPONSES
Total the responses, then write the number in the box.

Module 2: Preventing Bullying in Your Classroom

Intervention

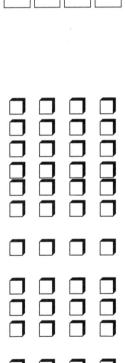

1. Establish a zero-tolerance policy: "No bullying."
2. Create an open-door policy.
3. Establish and implement classroom rules and a code of conduct.
4. Recognize that I am a role model and model decision making, respect for others, and a positive attitude.
5. Believe that I can successfully bring about a desired outcome in my students.
6. Use cooperative learning with bullies and victims (i.e., incorporate group projects/team approach into the curriculum).
7. Understand the role of prevention in ending bullying.
8. Implement classroom activities aimed at preventing bullying.
9. Implement classroom activities to increase awareness of bullying and victimization.
10. Teach collaborative conflict resolution skills to bullies and victims (i.e., teach bullies and victims to become responsible for finding their own solutions through negotiation).
11. Make a disciplinary referral.

TOTAL RESPONSES
Total the responses, then write the number in the box.

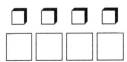

Module 3: Building Personal Power
Intervention

1. Create an atmosphere of kindness and respect in my classroom.
2. Attend to the social and academic development of my students.
3. Teach the basic social skills needed to handle and prevent bullying interactions.
4. Create opportunities for student success.
5. Develop a special relationship with each child.
6. Teach anger management strategies to bullies.
7. Teach bullies and victims verbal and nonverbal communication skills (e.g., sharing opinions, communicating in situations involving conflict, listening to others).
8. Teach collaborative conflict resolution skills to bullies and victims (i.e., teach bullies and victims to become responsible for finding their own solutions through negotiation).

TOTAL RESPONSES
Total the responses, then write the number in the box.

Module 4: Recognizing the Bully
Intervention

1. Differentiate among different forms of bullying (aggressive, passive, relational).
2. Teach students to recognize and identify the different types of bullies according to their characteristics and behaviors.
3. Understand how bullying behaviors develop.
4. Acknowledge the common differences between male and female bullying.

TOTAL RESPONSES
Total the responses, then write the number in the box.

Module 5: Recognizing the Victim
Intervention

1. Recognize the warning signs of victimization.
2. Understand victims and their needs.
3. Understand the "code of silence" that prevents children from reporting bullying incidents.
4. Provide support for victims (e.g., create an open-door policy).
5. Recognize the different types of victims (passive, provocative, relational, and bystander).
6. Teach students to recognize and identify the characteristics and behaviors of different types of victims.

TOTAL RESPONSES
Total the responses, and write the number in the box.

Bully Busters: A Teacher's Manual for Helping Bullies, Victims, and Bystanders (Grades K–5)
© 2003 by Arthur M. Horne, Christi L. Bartolomucci, and Dawn Newman-Carlson.
Champaign, IL: Research Press. (800) 519–2707.

Module 6: Recommendations and Interventions for Bullying Behaviors

Intervention

1. Recognize that I am a role model and model decision making, respect for others, and a positive attitude.

2. Create opportunities for student success.

3. Develop a special relationship with each child.

4. Contact parents regarding student misbehavior via phone call, letter, and/or conference.

5. Teach steps of problem solving and decision making for behavior problems.

6. Refer to counselor.

7. Defuse bullying situation in the classroom immediately and tackle the issue with the bully after class, privately.

8. Use consequences for undesirable acts/misbehavior committed by the bully.

9. Use praise and attention to reinforce good behaviors and accomplishments.

10. Consult with school counselor, school psychologist, and other school staff.

11. Use loss of privileges as consequence for bullies.

12. Contact parents regarding positive behavior of all students.

13. Verbally correct or reprimand bullies individually to avoid reinforcing attention-seeking behavior.

14. Reinforce behavior, not the child (e.g., "Bob, I am proud of you for _____").

15. Use the technique of overcorrection with bullies.

16. Use the four Rs of bully control: Recognize, Remove, Review, and Respond.

17. Reward improvements (successive approximations of desired behavior).

18. Reinforce nonbullying behaviors (e.g., on-task behavior, assertive/nonaggressive behavior, helping behaviors).

19. Encourage bullies to understand the victim's point of view (i.e., help bullies develop an empathic understanding of victims).

20. Teach anger management strategies to bullies.

21. Use an invitational approach (encourage bullies and victims to share their perspectives).

22. Teach collaborative conflict resolution skills to bullies and victims (i.e., teach bully and victim to become responsible for finding their own solutions through negotiation).

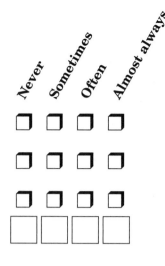

23. Teach bullies nonaggressive and nonbullying behavioral alternatives.

24. Teach bullies a better way of thinking: to shift from aggression-based appraisals to assertion-based ones.

25. Teach bullies new skills for achieving their goals.

TOTAL RESPONSES
Total the responses, then write the number in the box.

Module 7: Recommendations and Interventions for Helping Victims

Intervention

1. Create an open-door policy.

2. Highlight strengths of victims and bullies (i.e., help students become aware of their strengths).

3. Conduct follow-up on bullying incidents.

4. Use teacher-student support teams as a resource for consultation and support for bullying problems.

5. Use an invitational approach (encourage bullies and victims to share their perspectives).

6. Teach students to recognize and identify the characteristics and behaviors of different types of victims.

7. Teach victims physical and verbal assertiveness skills (e.g., assertive words, posture, eye contact).

8. Assist victims of bullying in identifying skills and behaviors they may want to learn.

9. Teach confidence and self-esteem building skills to victims.

10. Teach coping skills to victims.

11. Recognize how each student can actively prevent and intervene in bullying interactions.

12. Teach skills for dealing with bully-victim interactions.

TOTAL RESPONSES
Total the responses, then write the number in the box.

Module 8: Relaxation and Coping Skills

Intervention

1. Recognize the role and impact of stress.

2. Be aware of general stress management skills.

3. Teach stress management skills to my students.

TOTAL RESPONSES
Total the responses, then write the number in the box.

Bully Busters: A Teacher's Manual for Helping Bullies, Victims, and Bystanders (Grades K–5)
© 2003 by Arthur M. Horne, Christi L. Bartolomucci, and Dawn Newman-Carlson.
Champaign, IL: Research Press. (800) 519–2707.

Appendix

C Bully-Victim Measure

The Bully-Victim Measure has been developed to evaluate the extent to which bullying and victimization are occurring in your classroom or school. Part 1 is intended to measure the rate at which students engage in bullying behavior; Part 2 assesses the rate at which they are victims of bullying behavior.

Students should complete this measure three times during the year:

- Have students complete the measure before beginning the Bully Busters program to establish a baseline rate of bullying.

- After you have initiated the program, have students complete the measure again to gauge program impact. Often, rates of reported bullying actually increase at this point. This increase may not reflect an actual increase in bullying but rather may suggest that, as their awareness of what constitutes bullying grows, students are more able to identify bullying.

- Finally, have students fill out the measure at the end of the school year.

Bully-Victim Measure

Part 1

Action	I have never done this to others	Sometimes I do this to others	I often or always do this to others
Called someone names			
Pushed someone			
Left someone out of my group on purpose			
Ganged up on another person with a few of my friends			
Said bad things about another person			
Hit another person			
Made someone give me something, like lunch money, food, or crayons.			

Part 2

Action	I never have this done to me	Sometimes this is done to me	I often or always have this done to me
Be called names			
Get pushed by someone			
Get left out of a group on purpose			
Have others gang up on me			
Have others say bad things about me			
Get hit by another person			
Have someone make me give them something, like lunch money, food, or crayons			

Bully Busters: A Teacher's Manual for Helping Bullies, Victims, and Bystanders (Grades K–5)
© 2003 by Arthur M. Horne, Christi L. Bartolomucci, and Dawn Newman-Carlson.
Champaign, IL: Research Press. (800) 519–2707.

References

Ahmad, Y., & Smith, P. K. (1994). Bullying in schools and the issue of sex differences. In J. Archer (Ed.), *Male violence*. London: Routledge.

Asher, S. R., & Coie, J. D. (Eds.). (1990). *Peer rejection in childhood*. Cambridge, UK: Cambridge University Press.

Bandura, A. (1986). *Social foundations of thought and action: A social cognitive theory*. Englewood Cliffs, NJ: Prentice Hall.

Batsche, G. M., & Knoff, H. M. (1994). Bullies and their victims: Understanding a pervasive problem in the schools. *School Psychology Review, 23,* 165–174.

Benson, P. L. (1997). *All kids are our kids: What communities must do to raise caring and responsible children and adolescents*. San Francisco: Jossey-Bass.

Benson, P. L. (1999). *A fragile foundation: The state of developmental assets among American Youth*. Minneapolis Search Institute.

Besag, V. (1989). *Bullies and victims in schools*. Milton Keynes, Australia: Open University Press.

Bodine, R. J., & Crawford, D. K. (1999). *Developing emotional intelligence: A guide to behavior management and conflict resolution in schools*. Champaign, IL: Research Press.

Boulton, M. J. (1997). Teachers' views on bullying: Definitions, attitudes, and ability to cope. *British Journal of Educational Psychology, 67,* 223–233.

Briggs, D. (1996). Turning conflicts into learning experiences. *Educational Leadership, 54,* 60–63.

Brooks, R. B., & Goldstein, S. (2001). *Raising resilient children*. Chicago: Contemporary Books.

Cairnes, R. B., Cairnes, B. D., Neckerman, H. J., Gest, S. D., & Gariepy, J. L. (1988). Social networks and aggressive behavior: Peer support or peer rejection? *Developmental Psychology, 24,* 815–823.

Carney, J. V. (2000). Bullied to death: Perceptions of peer abuse and suicidal behavior during adolescence. *School Psychology International, 21,* 213–223.

Clarke, E. A., & Kiselica, M. S. (1997). A systematic counseling approach to the problem of bullying. *Elementary School Guidance and Counseling, 31,* 310–325.

Conye, R. K. (1987). *Primary preventive counseling: Empowering people and systems*. Muncie, IN: Accelerated Development.

Crick, N. R. (1996). The role of overt aggression, relation aggression, and prosocial behavior in the prediction of children's future social adjustment. *Child Development, 67,* 2317–2327.

Crick, N. R., & Dodge, K. A. (1994). A review and reformulation of social information processing mechanisms in children's social adjustment. *Psychological Bulletin, 15,* 74–101.

Crick, N. R., & Grotpeter, J. K. (1995). Children's treatment by peers: Victims of relational and overt aggression. *Development and Psychopathology, 8,* 367–380.

Dodge, K. A., & Coie, J. (1987). Social-information-processing factors in reactive and proactive aggression in children's peer groups. *Journal of Personality and Social Psychology, 53,* 1146–1158.

Dodge, K. A., Pettit, G. S., McClaskey, C. L., & Brown, M. M. (1986). Social competence in children. *Monographs of the Society for Research in Child Development, 51*(2, Serial No. 213).

Durlak, J. A., & Wells, A. M. (1997). Primary prevention mental health programs for children and adolescents: A meta-analytic review. *American Journal of Community Psychology, 25,* 115–152.

Eslea, M., & Smith, P. K. (1998). The long-term effectiveness of anti-bullying work in primary schools. *Educational Research, 40,* 203–218.

Espelage, D., & Holt, M. (2001). Bullying and victimization during early adolescence: Peer influences and psychosocial correlates. *Journal of Emotional Abuse, 2,* 123–142.

Farrell, A. D., & Meyer, A. L. (1997). The effectiveness of a school-based curriculum for reducing violence among sixth-grade students. *American Journal of Public Health, 87,* 979–984.

Fleischman, M. J., Horne, A. M., & Arthur, J. L. (1982). *Troubled families: A treatment program.* Champaign, IL: Research Press.

Floyd, N. M. (1985). "Pick on someone your own size": Controlling victimization. *Pointer, 29,* 9–17.

Forehand, R., & Long, N. (1996). *Parenting the strong-willed child.* Chicago: Contemporary Books.

Fried, S., & Fried, P. F. (1996). *Bullies and victims.* New York: Evans.

Geffner, R. A., & Loring, M. (2001). *Bullying behavior: Current issues, research, and interventions.* New York: Haworth.

Gibson, S., & Dembo, M. (1984). Teacher self-efficacy: A construct validation. *Journal of Educational Psychology, 76,* 569–582.

Goldstein, A. P. (1999). *The Prepare Curriculum: Teaching prosocial competencies* (Rev. ed.). Champaign, IL: Research Press.

Goldstein, A. P., Glick, B., & Gibbs, J. C. (1998). *Aggression Control Training: A comprehensive intervention for aggressive youth* (Rev. ed.). Champaign, IL: Research Press.

Goldstein, A. P., & McGinnis, E. (1997). *Skillstreaming the adolescent: New strategies and perspectives for teaching prosocial skills* (Rev. ed.). Champaign, IL: Research Press.

Goleman, D. (1995). *Emotional intelligence.* New York: Bantam.

Gregg, S. (1998). *School-based programs to promote safety and civility* (AEL Policy Briefs). Charleston, WV: Appalachia Educational Laboratory.

Hazler, R. J. (1994). Bullying breeds violence: You can stop it! *Learning, 22,* 38–41.

Hazler, R. J. (1996). *Breaking the cycle of violence: Interventions for bullying and victimization.* Washington, DC: Accelerated Development.

Hazler, R. J., Hoover, J. H., & Oliver, R. (1992). What kids say about bullying. *The Executive Educator, 14,* 20–22.

Hoover, J. H., Oliver, R., & Hazler, R. J. (1992). Bullying: Perceptions of adolescent victims in the Midwestern USA. *School Psychology International, 13,* 5–16.

Horne, A. M. (1990). Social learning family therapy. In A. M. Horne & J. Passmore (Eds.), *Family counseling and therapy* (2nd ed.). Itasca, IL: Peacock.

Horne, A. M., Glaser, B.,& Sayger, T. (1994). *Journal of Counseling and Human Development* (entire issue).

Horne, A. M., & Sayger, T. (1990). *Treatment of Conduct and Oppositional Defiant Disorder in children.* New York: Pergamon.

Horne, A. M., & Orpinas, P. (2003). Primary prevention steps for reducing bullying and victimization of children and adolescents. In M. Bloom (Ed.), *The encyclopedia of primary prevention and health promotion.* New York: Kluwer.

Horne, A. M., & Sayger, T. (1990). *Treatment of conduct and oppositional defiant disorder in children.* New York: Pergamon.

Horne, A. M., & Socherman, R. (1996). Profile of a bully: Who would do such a thing? *Educational Horizons, 74,* 77–83.

Howard, N., Horne, A. M., & Jolliff, D. (2001). Self-efficacy in a new training model for the prevention of bullying in schools. *Journal of Emotional Abuse, 2,* 181–191.

Kaukiainen, A., Björkqvist, K., Lagerspetz, K. M. J., Österman, K., Salmivalli, C., Rothberg, S., & Ahlbom, A. (1999). The relationships between social intelligence, empathy, and three types of aggression. *Aggressive Behaviour, 25,* 81–89.

Kreidler, W. (1984). *Creative conflict resolution: More than 200 activities for keeping peace in the classroom.* Glenview, IL: Scott Foresman.

Lee, F. (1993, April 4). Disrespect rules. *The New York Times Educational Supplement,* p. 16.

Lewis, J. A., & Lewis, M. D. (1983). *Community counseling: A human services approach* (2nd ed.). New York: Wiley.

Lowenstein, J. S. (1978). A comparison of the self-esteem between boys living with single-parent mothers and single-parent fathers. *Journal of Divorce, 2,* 195–208.

Martin, R. P. (1988). *Assessment of personality and behavior problems.* New York: Guilford.

McGinnis, E., & Goldstein, A. P. (1997). *Skillstreaming the elementary school child: New strategies and perspectives for teaching prosocial skills* (Rev. ed.). Champaign, IL: Research Press.

McWhirter, J. J., McWhirter, B. T., McWhirter, A. M., & McWhirter, E. H. (1998). *At-risk youth: A comprehensive response* (2nd ed.). Pacific Grove, CA: Brooks/Cole.

National Center for Injury Prevention and Control. (2001). *Injury fact book: 2001–2001.* Atlanta: Centers for Disease Control and Prevention.

Newman, D. A. (1999). *The effectiveness of a psychoeducational intervention for classroom teachers aimed at reducing bullying behavior in middle school students.* Unpublished doctoral dissertation, University of Georgia, Athens.

Newman, D. A., & Horne, A. M. (in press). Bully Busters: A psychoeducational intervention for reducing bullying behavior in middle school students. *Journal of Counseling and Development.*

Newman, D. A., Horne, A. M., & Bartolomucci, C. L. (2000). *Bully Busters: A teacher's manual for helping bullies, victims, and bystanders (Grades 6–8).* Champaign, IL: Research Press.

Olweus, D. (1978). *Aggression in the schools: Bullies and whipping boys.* Washington, DC: Hemisphere.

Olweus, D. (1991). Bully/victim problems among schoolchildren: Basic facts and effects of a school based intervention program. In D. Pepler & K. H. Rubin (Eds.), *The development and treatment of childhood aggression.* Hillsdale, NJ: Erlbaum.

Olweus, D. (1993). Victimization by peers: Antecedents and long-term outcomes. In K. H. Rubin & J. B. Asendorf (Eds.), *Social withdrawal, inhibition, and shyness.* Hillsdale, NJ: Erlbaum.

Olweus, D. (1994). Annotation—Bullying at school: Basic facts and effects of a school based intervention program. *Journal of Child Psychology and Psychiatry, 35,* 1171–1190.

Olweus, D. (1996). Bully/victim problems at school: Facts and effective interventions—Reclaiming children and youth. *Journal of Emotional and Behavioral Problems, 5,* 15–22.

Patterson, G. R. (1982). *Coercive family process.* Eugene, OR: Castalia.

Patterson, G. R. (1986). Performance models for antisocial boys. *American Psychologist, 41,* 432–444.

Pellegrini, A. D. (1995). *Victims as aggressors.* Unpublished manuscript.

Pellegrini, A. D., & Smith, P. K. (1998). Physical activity play: Consensus and debate. *Child Development, 69,* 609–610.

Pianta, R. C. (1999). *Enhancing relationships.* Washington, DC: American Psychological Association.

Pollack, I., & Sundermann, C. (2001). Creating safe schools: A comprehensive approach. *Juvenile Justice, 8,* 13–20.

Roehlkepartain, J., & Leffert, N. (2000). *What young children need to succeed: Working together to build assets from birth to age 11.* Minneapolis: Free Spirit.

Ross, D. M. (1996). *Childhood bullying and teasing.* Alexandria, VA: American Counseling Association.

Salmivalli, C. (1999). Participant roles approach to school bullying: Implications for interventions. *Journal of Adolescence, 22,* 453–459.

Salmivalli, C., Karhunen, J., & Lagerspetz, K. M. J. (1996). How do the victims respond to bullying? *Aggressive Behaviour, 22,* 99–109.

Salmivalli, C., Lagerspetz, K. M. J., Björkqvist, K., Österman, K., & Kaukiainen, A. (1996). Bullying as a group process: Participant roles and their relations to social status within the class. *Aggressive Behaviour, 22,* 1–15.

Salovey, P., & Mayer, J. (1990). Emotional intelligence. *Imagination, Cognition, and Personality, 9,* 189.

Samples, F., & Aber, L. (1998). Evaluations of school-based violence prevention programs. In D. S. Elliot, B. A. Hamburg, & K. R. Williams (Eds.), *Violence in American schools: A new perspective.* Cambridge, UK: Cambridge University Press.

Schneider, M., & Robin, A. (1976). The turtle technique: A method for the self-control of impulsive behavior. In J. Krumboltz & C. Thoreson (Eds.), *Counseling methods.* New York: Holt, Rinehart and Winston.

Schroeder, K. (2002). Bullying surveyed. *Education Digest, 67*(5), 72–73.

Seligman, M. (1991). *Learned optimism.* New York: Random House.

Seligman, M. (1995). *The optimistic child.* Boston: Houghton Mifflin.

Sharp, S., & Smith, P. K. (1991). Bullying in U.K. schools: The DES Sheffield Bullying Project. *Early Child Development and Care, 77,* 47–55.

Shure, M. B. (1992a). *I Can Problem Solve (ICPS): An interpersonal cognitive problem-solving program for children—Preschool.* Champaign, IL: Research Press.

Shure, M. B. (1992b). *I Can Problem Solve (ICPS): An interpersonal cognitive problem-solving program for children—Kindergarten and primary grades.* Champaign, IL: Research Press.

Shure, M. B. (1992c). *I Can Problem Solve (ICPS): An interpersonal cognitive problem-solving program for children—Intermediate elementary grades.* Champaign, IL: Research Press.

Slaby, R. G., Roedell, W., Arezzo, E., & Hendrix, K. (1995). *Early violence prevention: Tools for teachers of young children.* Washington, DC: National Association for the Education of Young Children.

Slee, P., & Rigby, K. (1993). Australian school children's self-appraisal of interpersonal relations: The bullying experience. *Child Psychiatry and Human Development, 23,* 273–282.

Small, M., & Tetrick, K. D. (2001). School violence: An overview. *Juvenile Justice, 8,* 13–20.

Smith, P. K., & Boulton, M. (1990). Rough and tumble play, aggression, and dominance: Perception and behavior in children's encounters. *Human Development, 33,* 271–282.

Smith P. K., & Sharp, S. (1994). *School bullying: Insights and perspectives.* London: Routledge.

Stephenson, P., & Smith, D. (1987). Anatomy of the playground bully. *Education, 18,* 236–237.

Swearer, S., & Doll, B. (2001). Bullying in schools: An ecological framework. In R. Geffner & M. Loring (Eds.), *Bullying behavior: Current issues, research, and interventions.* New York: Haworth.

Swearer, S., & Song, S. (2001, August). *How can research guide the development of bullying prevention and intervention programs?* Paper presented at the annual convention of the American Psychological Association, San Francisco.

Teglas, H., & Rothman, L. (2001). STORIES: A classroom based program to reduce aggressive behavior. *Journal of School Psychology, 39,* 71–94.

Turpeau, A. M. (1998). *Effectiveness of an anti-bullying classroom curriculum intervention on an American middle school.* Unpublished doctoral dissertation, University of Georgia, Athens.

U.S. Department of Health and Human Services. (2001). *Youth violence: A report of the surgeon general.* Rockville, MD: U.S. Department of Health and Human Services; Centers for Disease Control and Prevention; National Center for Injury Prevention and Control; Substance Abuse and Mental Health Services Administration; Center for Mental Health Services; National Institutes of Health; National Institute of Mental Health.

Voors, W. (2000). *The parent's book about bullying: Changing the course of your child's life.* Center City, MN: Hazelden.

Wilezenski, F. L., Steegman, R., Braun, M., Feeley, F., Griffin, J., Horowitz, T., & Olson, S. (1994, April). *Promoting "fair play": Interventions for children as victims and victimizers.* Paper presented at the annual meeting of the National Association of School Psychologists, Seattle. (ERIC Document Reproduction Service No. ED380744)

Young, G. H. (1994). *Developing students' knowledge, intervention skills, and willingness to participate in decreasing school bullying: A secondary school's use of the curriculum approach.* Unpublished doctoral dissertation, NOVA University. (ERIC Document Reproduction Service No. ED379538)

About the Authors

Arthur M. (Andy) Horne, Ph.D., is Distinguished Research Professor at the University of Georgia in Athens. He received his Ph.D. from Southern Illinois University in 1971 and completed a postdoctoral clinical research internship in 1988. From 1971 until 1989, he taught at Indiana State University, where he served as a member of the faculty and director of training for the counseling psychology program, as well as a member of the marriage and family therapy training program. In 1989, Andy joined the faculty of the University of Georgia as director of training for counseling psychology and head of the Department of Counseling and Human Development Services and as coordinator of a certificate program in marriage and family therapy. He is a fellow of four divisions of the American Psychological Association and former president of the Association for Specialists in Group Work and editor of the *Journal for Specialists in Group Work.* He has coauthored five books, coedited four, and served on the editorial boards of seven journals. Research on violence reduction and bully-victim interventions is a primary focus of his work. Andy has been involved with ACT Early, a program funded by the U.S. Department of Education's Office of At-Risk Children to identify effective teacher interventions for children at risk for emotional and behavioral problems. He is also a principal investigator of GREAT Schools and Families, a multisite violence prevention program funded by the Centers for Disease Control and Prevention to study effective ways to reduce violence in schools, and is the coordinator of the Bully Prevention Project of the College of Education at the University of Georgia.

Christi L. Bartolomucci, Ph.D., received her doctoral degree in counseling psychology and her master's degree in community counseling at the University of Georgia. She completed her clinical internship at the University of Louisville, specializing in child clinical and pediatric psychology. She is currently completing a postdoctoral fellowship in pediatric psychology through Emory University's School of Medicine. Christi has worked with children across various environments, including schools, the juvenile justice system, inpatient and outpatient psychiatric and medical settings, and psychiatric day treatment. For the past 5 years, Christi has been involved with the Bully Prevention Project at the University of Georgia. She has also served as a co-developer of an intervention program designed to address the issues of female juvenile offenders—specifically, to promote their healthy development and prevent further offending. She is the author of several articles and a book chapter regarding children in the juvenile justice system and has a particular interest in consultation and program development.

Dawn Newman-Carlson, Ph.D., is a licensed psychologist. She received her doctoral degree in counseling psychology from the University of Georgia and her master's degree in mental health counseling from the University of Miami. She completed her clinical residency at the Medical College of Georgia, where she specialized in pediatric psychology. In 2000, she joined the University of Florida's Department of Clinical and Health Psychology, where she specializes in pediatric psychology. Dawn is currently the clinical research coordinator of an NIH-funded clinic-based adherence intervention for pediatric patients with diabetes, the HANDling Diabetes Project. She also provides clinical services to patients and families seen at University of Florida/Shands Hospital Pediatric Endocrinology diabetes clinic and supervises doctoral students rotating through the specialty clinic. Dawn is the co-developer and program administrator of the Bully Prevention Project. Since 1993, she has worked with numerous school districts to integrate Bully Busters into elementary and middle schools. As a consultant, Dawn has served school personnel and counselors in the areas of childhood aggression and prevention of bullying. She has conducted teacher education and counselor training in the form of Bully Busters workshops and has been invited to present the program at national conferences. As an individual and group therapist, Dawn has counseled children from local and regional school districts in Georgia and Florida, as well as patients in mental health centers and hospitals. She holds a certificate in marriage and family therapy. Her research and publications concern prevention and early intervention for bullies and victims, health promotion, disease prevention, diabetes, and adherence.